...forta

...ha e ...

...ilare la forta di

...oguizione di che

...uto, però, il te...

...o aveva le cerniere

...uscite in vendita a...

...hicevo, adesso lo sfi...

...ovo. Certamente ...

...leso, l'equilibrio ...

...fei entrare al ...

...tete immaggiuare c...

...tro, si sfilò la ve...

...uu' ...

Dear Alfonso

Cavaliere Alfonso Crolla (1889–1940)

Dear Alfonso

AN ITALIAN FEAST OF LOVE AND LAUGHTER

MARY CONTINI

BIRLINN

First published in 2017 by
Birlinn Limited
West Newington House
10 Newington Road
Edinburgh
EH9 1QS

www.birlinn.co.uk

ISBN 978 178027 480 5

British Library Cataloguing
in Publication Data
A catalogue record for this book is
available from the British Library.

Designed and typeset by Mark Blackadder

Printed and bound by Gutenberg Press, Malta

For Philip,
my personal *consigliere*,
with my love,

and to my dear daughters,
Francesca and Olivia

Contents

Acknowledgements

To my dearest father-in-law, Carlo Contini. In many conversations and during so many feasts of laughter and love together with family in Scotland and in Italy I learned so much about life. Carlo also wrote a manuscript which has so many details in it that he had never told us before, about his younger years, the hardships during the war and the drama of his immigration. He wanted his story to be told, and would have been thrilled we have had this opportunity to publish his letter to Alfonso, the father-in-law he never knew.

My thanks to my editors Helen Bleck and Andrew Simmons who helped with a brilliant edit, and to Professor Emeritus Joseph Farrell. My sincere thanks to Hugh Andrew and all the team at Birlinn, especially Jan Rutherford and all the sales and marketing team. And to Jim Hutcheson for the perfect cover design.

Un ringraziamento di cuore to Zia Rita, Nunzia, Carla and Luigi Silni for the secrets of Annunziata's recipes.

Warm wishes and thanks to all our team, customers, suppliers and family at Valvona & Crolla for sharing the daily drama and deliciousness of the shop.

Eternal love and thanks to the women who led me to my man's heart through his stomach and taught me to cook: my mother, Gertrude Di Ciacca, my paternal grandmother, Marietta Di Ciacca, my mother-in-law, Olivia Contini and the best cook of us all, Annunziata Conturso, Carlo's mother.

Mary Contini, September 2017

Our new friends

Pozzuoli
Carlo's Italian family
Nonna Marianna and Nonno Ernesto (paternal
    grandparents; lived with Luigi and Annunziata)
Nonna Minicuccia and Nonno Vincenzo (maternal
    grandparents; lived beside the port at Pozzuoli)
Luigi 1901–75: Carlo's father
Annunziata 1902–89: Carlo's mother
Carlo Contini, 1925–2008
Ninuccia, 1929–2005
Rosetta, 1930–2009
Annetta, 1932–
Antonietta, 1934–
Vincenzo, 1937–1997
Ernesto, 1939–
Peppino, 1946–
Zi' Alf, Carlo's uncle, the shoemaker
Zi' Antonio, Carlo's uncle and hero

Edinburgh
The Crolla family
Alfonso Crolla, 1889–1940
Maria Crolla, 1888–1964
Domenico, 1913–83

Margaret, 1914–99
Vittorio, 1915–2005
Olivia, 1924–2015
Gloria, 1926–
Phyllis, 1927–78

The Di Ciacca family
Cesidio, 1891–1940
Marietta, 1895–1980
Lena, 1917–2004
Johnny, 1919–95
Anna, 1922–2013
Alex, 1923–2013

Where a birth date only is supplied, date of death is not known.
A dash but no death date means the person is still alive.

Dear Alfonso,

My name is Carlo Contini. I was born at 7.30 a.m. at the 'Istituto Annunziata' in Napoli on 1st May 1925. I grew up in Pozzuoli, an ancient fishing town just north of the city. My family are carpenters.

When I came to Edinburgh to study English in 1952 I fell in love with and married your wonderful daughter, Olivia. When we first met, she was still very broken-hearted that she had lost you, her darling father, in the dreadful tragedy of the sinking of the *Arandora Star*.

She has told me all about you, thought about you every day, and our constant regret is that you were not with us as you should have been on our lives' journey.

Olivia and I are so grateful that fate guided us to be together; our lives have been wonderful, with many blessings, especially our two sons Philip and Victor, and our beautiful grandchildren. Your great-great-grandson is called Alfonso in your honour.

Your loving family welcomed me as a son and brother and I have made it my own. We have had so many happy times, survived so many set-backs and come through it all with our lives still blessed.

With your brilliant and kind-hearted sons, Vittorio and Domenico, I have helped build up the business, Valvona & Crolla, that was your vision.

Together we have brought the sunshine and the flavours of the south of Italy to the Scots.

Caro Alfonso, my only regret is that I did not have the honour of knowing you and asking your permission to marry Olivia. With all humility, I wish to present my story so you can know who I was and who I became. In it you will learn of the challenges and excitement I have lived through. It has been a blessed life; a feast of love and laughter.

If only you could join us now. Lunch is at one.

Un abbraccio, tuo caro genero,

A warm embrace, your loving son-in-law,

Carlo

Part One

Veramente uno scugnizzo
A real Neapolitan street urchin

Chapter One

'Carlo! Carlo! *Aspetta*! Wait for me!'

Ninuccia sounded slightly distressed. Carlo glanced back to see where his little sister was. He caught sight of her far below, the parcel wrapped in newspapers tightly grasped to her chest as she lifted her short legs to climb each step. Her dark curls were dripping with sweat. She called again, louder.

'Carlo!'

He waved to her, frustrated, encouraging her to hurry. 'Ninuccia! *Forza!* Hurry!'

Two women scrubbing clothes at the water fountain watched the scene unfold. They reproached him, laughing. 'Carlo! Wait for her! She's only three. *Poverina*! Poor thing!'

Carlo shrugged his shoulders, flashed an amiable smile and ran barefoot up the steps. Ninuccia would take too long to climb them to get home. She'd arrive when she did. He couldn't wait; he was too hungry. His sister's calls faded into the distance.

Everyone knew Carlo in Rione Terra. He was Luigi and Annunziata's son, a good-looking boy, taller than average for his seven years, fair-skinned with thick blond hair. His large, dark, almond-shaped eyes illuminated his aquiline face; his sweet cherub lips charmed when he smiled.

Everyone knew Carlo because Carlo knew everyone. He never passed without a call of greeting, a quick word of encouragement or a nod of interest. He had the uncanny knack of seeing everyone as a person, an individual: a fortunate talent. The two women at

3

the water fountain had known him since he was born, but it was as if he had known *them* before *they* had been born.

Swinging a brown-paper parcel tied with string, Carlo skipped up the narrow *vicoletto*, counting the 178 steps to reach home. It was almost midday and the shaded alleyway was gratifyingly cool in the summer heat. An occasional shaft of light cut through the gloom and lit the way.

The buildings on either side of the steps were four and five storeys high, jumbled and haphazard, so close together that people leaned out and spoke to each other from balcony to balcony as if in the same room. Washing hung shamelessly between the houses creating a spectacle of underwear, slips and vests, towels, sheets and tablecloths. An endless cascade of children's clothes hung outside narrow balconies in ever-decreasing sizes.

On every doorstep, women huddled together in twos and threes, their aprons pulled up onto their laps, full of vegetables to prepare for the midday meal; long mottled *borlotti* beans, fresh pods of pea-green *piselli* or bunches of leafy green *friarielli*. Their bronzed faces were flushed; to help keep the backs of their necks cool, their dark hair was piled up and tied back with coloured rags. Their dark eyes darted from face to face as they engaged in *una bella chiacchierata* as they podded, topped and tailed the vegetables. They tossed the speckled beans and vibrant leaves into their bowls, discarding the stalks and empty pods casually onto the steps.

Other women were darning clothes or carefully embroidering pieces of lace. Ragged children of all ages ran barefoot up and down the steps shouting and laughing or sitting in huddles, minia-ture imitations of their mothers and aunts.

There was not an inch of space spare, no centimetre unused. Most families lived in one room, a dozen or more people together, with little space for furniture other than a table, some chairs and a bed. There was no such thing as privacy; everyone knew everyone else's business. Windows and doors were thrown open all day so that conversations, confrontations and all manner of canoodling were heard by all.

Life spilled out into the alley, the space and fresh air eagerly enjoyed. The street was each family's living room. Every morning, on every available spot, tables were carried outside and covered with anything to hand, whether a sheet of newspaper or an embroidered tablecloth. A random selection of odd cutlery, plates and glasses were laid, a candle or lamp, a jug of water, a *fiasco* of wine, ready, anticipating the next mealtime. Toothless, ancient great-grandmothers, too old to help, were already perched at tables, keenly observing the goings-on, patiently waiting to eat. Groups of grandfathers sat in sleeveless vests, absorbed in games of *briscola*, their large bellies a sign of comfort and success to their wives and mistresses.

The ancient fortified settlement of Rione Terra perched with authority above the Bay of Pozzuoli, a four-hour walk along the coast north of Naples. For generations past, for as long as anyone could remember, this pile of crumbling, crowded slums had been home to the very poorest of Pozzuoli. The live volcano Solfatara slumbered at the heart of their town and their consciousness. The land they lived on was moving, unstable. The drowned ruins of the ancient Roman market in the harbour had risen back above sea level in living memory. The continuously gasping Vesuvius loomed menacingly over them.

The people of the town had for centuries had an intrinsic ability to survive under occupation by foreign powers. In order to retain their own identity, they had developed their own language, music and a particular sense of humour that ensured laughter was always at hand to boost courage. Living with the daily grind of squalor amidst the glorious Neapolitan sun and sea they had a profound appreciation of life's blessings. They had very little, and expected nothing. They lived intense, immediate lives. Carlo, like all the children around him, had already learned this philosophy; a wise head on young shoulders.

As he climbed the steps, smells of cooking lingered enticingly in the air. Carlo took deep breaths, savouring the flavour of each scent: luscious fresh tomatoes softening into *sugo* with green oil and aromatic basil; creamy onions sweetly sizzling in olive oil; pungent sardines blackening on a grill; a sharp whiff of singed garlic and *peperoncino* which made him salivate. He loitered a moment to indulge in these aromas, hunger gripping his stomach.

'Madonna, *ho fame*. I'm hungry.'

Suddenly he remembered his sister; she had the food. He cupped his hand over his mouth and called down the steps, yelling to her to get a move on, 'Ninuccia! Ninuuccia! *Forza*!'

'I'm coming, Carlo,' she called back.

Jumping over a sleeping tomcat, Carlo swung around some scraggy chickens pecking in the dust. He nodded *'buon giorno'* to Giuseppe *'Faniente'*, the one-legged beggar who always sunned himself in the pool of sunshine at the corner of Carlo's uncle's, Zi' Alf's, cobbler shop.

'Bravo, Giuseppe,' thought Carlo, 'if you need to beg, you may as well beg in the sun.' He admired Giuseppe; he was always at his corner, every day, whatever the weather. 'No matter your job,' observed Carlo to himself, 'you need to put in the hours.'

Spotting Il Professore making his way down from school, burdened with a heavy bundle of jotters, Carlo nipped into a side street. His own book was missing from the pile and he'd rather not have to explain himself right now. He had no time for Il Professore, or for school. In fact, he hated school. He hated the fact that he had to sit in the heat of the day and listen to Il Professore drone on and on about history, science and the virtues of Mussolini.

He detested that after lunch he had to return to school, where Il Professore, now dressed in his *Fascista* uniform, attempted to instruct the class on how to salute, march and handle a rifle. Was the man a teacher or a soldier? Attendance at the Fascist after-school *balilla* was not compulsory but was actively encouraged, especially by his mother. 'Carlo, you get a free pair of boots and a uniform. What's wrong with that?' But Carlo had no time for the *balilla*, Il Professore or even Mussolini himself, for that matter. What was the point of making them all dress up like soldiers, play with guns and pretend to parade? A ruin of an afternoon, that was all it was. He was a lad of the streets, a *scugnizzo*, self-sufficient and street-wise. He was a free spirit and rebelled against constriction and control.

Laughing as he watched Il Professore totter off down the street Carlo congratulated himself, *'Sono una volpe, veramente uno scugnizzo!* I'm a real fox, a real lad of the streets.'

Unexpectedly, he heard his aunt, Zia Francesca, shout from a top-floor window just above him. 'Carlo, *bello*! *Attenzione*! Awwoo!'

Carlo knew what that meant. He looked up towards her through the flapping array of shirts and sheets just in time to see the water, as if in slow motion, falling down, down towards him. He jumped aside niftily and pinning himself against the side of the wall, just managed to avoid it. Not so fortunate, poor Ninuccia. She had just caught up with her brother, proud for an instant after her great effort, when the dirty, cold water drenched her from head to toe.

Carlo burst out laughing. Zia Francesca burst out laughing.

'*Povera* Ninuccia! *Andiam'*. Poor Ninuccia! Come on, let's go!'

Carlo put his arm round his sister and gave her a hug. He took the parcel from her and, holding her hand, led her up the last, steepest steps to their home.

*

Home for Carlo's family was a room with a window on the top floor of a derelict, crumbling tenement, in the area known since Roman times as Rione Terra, 'the Land'. The highest part, where they lived, was simply called *ngopp' 'a terra*, 'the top of the land'. The Continis were a large family: Carlo's parents, Luigi and Annunziata, his paternal grandparents, Nonno Ernesto and Nonna Marianna, his younger sisters, Ninuccia, Rosetta and a new baby girl, Annetta. Zia Francesca, his mother's sister, lived in another room on the landing opposite, with her husband Zio Paolo and their five children.

Their room was dark, with rough, whitewashed walls and a small fireplace in the corner. There was a large bed against the wall and some straw mats beside it. In the summer the heat in the room was suffocating, a magnet for flies and mosquitoes. In the winter, it was damp and smoky from the fire.

At the far end a wide window opened out to a small balcony, bringing welcome light and glorious fresh air into the room. The view from the balcony was unexpectedly rewarding: an enchanting vision of the glorious azure expanse of the Tyrrhenian Sea. On a clear day, the islands of Nisida, Procida and Ischia appeared to float in the bay; in the distance, Capri languished on the horizon. Carlo's mother would look out at the magnificent panorama and feel joyous at her luck, thanking God that heaven itself was right outside her window.

On the way up to their home, on the middle landing, was the *gabinetto* for the whole tenement, nothing more than a rough, filthy hole. The trouble was, it was nearly always *occupato,* and nearly always by signor Bruno Cacasotto, who appeared to spend almost all of his life in the lavatory. Carlo had never seen signor Bruno unless he was waiting to go in or just coming out of the *gabinetto.* Carlo made a point of getting up very early every morning, earlier than signor Bruno. It made sense to get there before him. He was passing anyway; every morning his task was to go down to the well in the top square to fetch fresh water. He filled two flagons full, which he would carry up the steps home, splashing on the stairway as he went. He always enjoyed a deep drink of the ice-cool water with its mineral sulphur taste. The water never tasted so good once he had carried it up the stairs and it had warmed in the stuffy room all day.

In the centre of the family's room was a large wooden table. It had six sturdy chairs with woven straw seats that scratched his legs when he sat on them. A chair at the table couldn't always be guaranteed; there were just too many people. Carlo's ambition was to have a chair of his own at the table, like Papà. Now that his mother had brought another mouth to feed into the family, Carlo was worried. Naturally, his mother would feed the new baby herself for a year or two but at some point, the baby would need a plate of food herself, and then she'd need a chair as well.

Annunziata was the wet nurse of Rione Terra, the *balia*. As far as he could recall in his seven years, Carlo could remember his mother giving birth to babies and feeding babies. Sadly, for one reason or another, a lot of her babies hadn't lived very long. Carlo wasn't sure how many, but he was very aware that some babies she gave birth to went back to the Good Lord very soon. Carlo had had four older siblings, but they had all died quite young as he was growing up, leaving him as the oldest child in the family now.

When his mother lost a new baby she had milk she didn't need, so she would suckle other women's babies instead. She had fed Zia Francesca's baby and Zia Francesca's neighbour's baby. She had fed the neighbours' neighbours' babies. Of course, there were always babies crying in this arrangement, but you just had to accept it. Whatever happened, whether they were his mother's babies or not, hungry or not, they cried and sometimes even they died. As his mother always told him, '*Così la vita*. This is life.'

*

Finally, Ninuccia and Carlo rushed into the house, short of breath having raced each other up the last stairs. They were giggling, as they had just passed signor Bruno going into the *gabinetto* again. Mamma was in her rocking chair in the corner feeding Annetta.

'Put everything on the table.'

With a certain degree of pride, Carlo laid the parcels on the table and carefully untied the string. Ninuccia helped their younger sister Rosetta climb up onto a chair and then onto the table to see what they had brought. His grandmother, Nonna Marianna, came across to help them. They opened the first parcel, saving the string and paper for some later use. A wonderful aroma of crusty warm bread filled the room. The kilo of *pane* was about an eighth of the huge *pagnotta* that the baker had cut through for Carlo and then weighed on the scale before writing on the paper what Annunziata would have to pay him later.

'*Cinquanta centesimi*, Mamma,' Carlo told his mother. She nodded.

The thick dark crust on the outside of the bread was charred and blackened by the wood-fired oven. The fragrance made Ninuccia's mouth water as she reached out to take some of the crumbs that had scattered at the bottom of the package.

'*E l'altro?*' Mamma asked.

Carlo looked sheepish.

'*Apri!* Open it!' Mamma raised her voice, slightly agitated.

Carlo opened the newspaper, slowly, looking at his mother to see her reaction. She stretched her head up to see.

Annunziata was a petite, pretty woman of 32 years, with a

swarthy skin lightened by a bright, animated smile. Her jet-black hair was tied back from her face and wound into a tight, severe bun secured by two ebony combs. One frivolous stray strand of hair fell down over her eye, belying the look of maturity she tried to achieve. She couldn't maintain any severity for very long anyway as she had a spontaneous, infectious laugh that reverberated around the walls and out onto the landing.

'*Apri!*' she shouted again, pulling herself up as high as she could, the baby still attached to her breast. '*Fammi vedere!* Let me see!'

Carlo opened the parcel and lifted it up a bit to show his mother. Inside were five bloodied fish heads: flat, bulging-eyed, tooth-grinning fish heads!

'*Ahhi!*' she cried, bursting out into uproarious laughter. '*Bravo! Stasera si mangia brodo di pesce!* Tonight we'll eat a good fish soup!'

Ninuccia and Rosetta ran around the table clapping their hands. Everyone loved fish soup. When Mamma was happy they were all happy.

From the window, they heard a familiar whistle coming from the bottom at the quayside, where the small fishing boats went out to sea. Ninuccia ran across to the window.

'Papà's coming! Papà's coming!'

'Good,' said Annunziata, handing the baby to her mother.

'*A mangiare!* Let's eat.'

Chapter Two

Carlo had learned very early on that life was short.

More often than not, someone in the household was ill. There were several diseases that kept recurring – malaria, influenza, whooping cough, diphtheria. As he was growing up, when an illness arrived, Carlo was often sent to stay with his paternal grandparents, Nonna Minicuccia and Nonno Vincenzo.

Their house was down at the fishermen's port, on the water's edge, right next to his father's wood yard. It wasn't a house as such, more a cave hacked into the rock, with shelves and furniture built into the stone and a rough floor with straw scattered on top. Pots, jugs and utensils hung on nails hammered into the walls. Garlands of garlic, onions, tomatoes and herbs were suspended at the door drying in the sun – everything Nonna Minicuccia needed for her culinary alchemy.

A fire in the middle of the cave had a chimney that took some of the smoke out, but not all. Two alcoves in the side of the cave had straw mattresses for sleeping on. At the back, she kept a donkey and a few chickens, and even sometimes a pig to fatten to make *salsiccie*, sausages, for the winter. Permanently positioned at the doorway were a wooden table and four chairs: they ate in the open air.

Carlo adored staying with Nonna Minicuccia. There were no babies crying or sisters to look after and, until they died, no sick brothers worrying his poor mother. He enjoyed being near his father and smelling the sawdust and wood as Luigi worked. He loved being by the sea and could already swim. One of his school friends had pushed him from the pier straight into the water. Faced with the choice of whether to drown or swim, he chose the latter as the healthier of the two options. When he was with his grandparents the sea was his playground. After school, if he had no tasks to do, he would spend hours diving from the rocks, scrabbling underwater and fishing for sea urchins and shellfish, which he sucked live from their shells; deliciously juicy, salty and sweet. If an octopus or squid dared to cling onto his arm he learned to bite its head, shocking it to release its hold and sending it scuttling away.

Nonna Minicuccia loved having Carlo with her. She was always cooking his favourite food and trying to fatten him up. All her children were older and earning their own living so there were fewer mouths to feed. He was never as hungry here as at home.

'You're too thin, Carlo. *Vieni, mangia!* Come, eat!'

He would savour the creamy sweetness of her *zuppa di chichierchie*, the thick golden chickpea soup with aromatic rosemary and a hint of garlic drizzled with green olive oil, so appetising he licked the plate, much to his nonna's delight. When she brought an octopus home from one of the stands at the fish market, alive, fat and flabby, squirming in a bag, Carlo was fascinated, watching her bash the bag against the kitchen table, until the squirming stopped. Then, with the broom handle she used for rolling fresh pasta, she would bash it further to tenderise its squelchy flesh before remorselessly taking it by its tentacles and dropping it into the pot of boiling sea water hanging over the fire. Once it was cooked, she'd chop it up and stew the pieces slowly all morning in a thick sauce of tomatoes and wine.

'Ah, Nonna's *polpi in cassuola*.' Carlo salivated just thinking about it.

But, much as he loved his nonna, the real reason Carlo delighted in staying with her was because her youngest son, Zi' Antonio, lived there too. Carlo idolised his uncle, he was a man to look up to. Zi' Antonio was 22, a lot older than Carlo. He wore his long, jet-black hair neatly combed back and smoothed against each side of his head. His soft brown eyes were crowned with heavy brows and his neatly trimmed moustache, fashionably pencil-thin, accentuated his heart-shaped lips. Slim and tall, Zi' Antonio was always immaculately dressed in tight-fitting trousers and crisp white smock. His grooming was completed with an incense and violet cologne which made him, Carlo noticed, very attractive to the girls.

More to the point, Zi' Antonio didn't treat him like a schoolboy or a pretend soldier; he spoke to him man to man.

'Here, Carlo, try a puff of my cigarette! What do you think? *Buono, eh?*'

'Carlo, come with me. We'll stand outside the bar and listen to the football on the radio.'

When Zi' Antonio went out at night Carlo admired his two-tone, cream leather shoes with the ebony black upper, just the right height of heel and a highlight of contrasting stitching. He watched in wonderment as they clip-clipped when his uncle performed his particular little skip and a jump as he strutted along the street, dressed up to go dancing.

'Carlo, when you leave school we can go dancing together. We'll get the girls, Carlo, you and I.'

Carlo's ambition in life, after getting a chair of his own at the table, was to own a pair of shoes like Zi' Antonio's.

Carlo wondered why his father never told him about the fun, and the cigarettes and the girls. Zi' Antonio looked like he was having a wonderful adventure, and Carlo was looking forward to it all when he was 20 years old himself. It looked like things would be a lot better when you could make your own choices. As things stood, life was sometimes a bit confusing; if only adults would tell you what was going on.

The thing was, as far as he could remember, whenever he was taken back home after a visit to Nonna Minicuccia's, one of his older brothers had died. Vincenzo had already gone, and he remembered that only last year Ernesto had had to have a nurse come to take care of him, as he had a big wound in his hip and was in a lot of pain. When Carlo came home that time, Ernesto had gone as well. Carlo was distressed. His mother had been very quiet. She had embraced him and told him the Good Lord had taken his brothers to a better place.

Carlo didn't really understand, but it happened a lot so he had to learn to accept it. As his mother said, it was for the best, you simply had to have faith.

*

Life for Luigi and Annunziata was a constant struggle. They lived hand to mouth, managing with thrift and austerity to survive day to day. There was usually enough to eat, but never anything spare.

Mussolini's new Fascist government kept announcing that if the nation all worked together, life would improve. Maybe it would. '*Speriamo*, let's hope so,' they thought.

Mussolini, Il Duce, said industrialisation would bring prosperity; the trains would run on time; the swamps between Rome and Naples would be drained to defeat the scourge of malaria. Immunisation would reduce infant deaths. More wheat could be planted and harvested. It sounded so optimistic, but so far, little had changed.

'Annunziata, *arrangiarsi per sopravivere*,' Luigi would encourage his wife. 'We'll make do; we'll survive,' consoling her when they had to bury yet another child. When the great Duce announced that the more children a woman had the fewer taxes her family would have to pay Annunziata scoffed. They had never paid any taxes because they had never earned any money. Here in Pozzuoli there was only a barter economy. Luigi made furniture and repaired pieces of woodwork; he built doors and windows to shade the houses from the summer sun. He was never paid with money, only in kind. It wasn't so bad. He'd come home with a bag of ripe tomatoes, a basket of figs, a few eggs. Sometimes, if his customers owed him a lot of money, they would bring a chicken squawking and screeching, tied up in a cotton bag.

Annunziata liked it when he brought home a chicken. She would promptly break its neck, letting its head drop onto its scraggy belly. There was plenty of eating in a chicken: 'Food for three days, not bad.'

Sometimes Luigi would arrive with a brown paper bag dripping with a warm sheep's stomach. Annunziata would tip her head to the side and nod to herself at the thought of the job ahead. Shrugging her shoulders, she would laugh, 'There's nothing wrong with tripe!'

Often in the summer, Luigi would arrive with *melanzane*, aubergines, so ripe they were ready to rot. This never daunted her. Immediately, she would set to work to preserve them in oil. Chopped small, simmered in vinegar then covered with olive oil with some *peperoncino* and a clove of garlic, this would make a tasty meal for the winter. Like her mother and mother-in-law, Annunziata could transform very unassuming ingredients skilfully into tasty dishes. She wasted nothing, not even old crusts of bread.

The great Duce wanted the boys to go to school but Annunziata never saw the benefit of this. From what she could see, Carlo and his fellow students were simply taught how great Mussolini was and encouraged to dress up as soldiers. Why would any man want young children to dress and act as soldiers? Not for anything good, that was sure. In Annunziata's mind Il Duce was a buffoon and, now that he had his free boots and uniform, the best thing for her boy to do was to get a job!

Carlo was more than willing: after his father he was head of the family. It was time for him to contribute. He looked for his first job.

Papà's friend Maestro Ferdinando was a specialist in '*cascia 'e muorte*', making coffins. This was a busy trade as there was always a good market for coffins: after all, Carlo reckoned, everyone needed one eventually.

Maestro Ferdinando already had two other apprentices from the class above Carlo. One of them was the brother of his friend, Pasquale, who said to him one day, 'My brother says Maestro Ferdinando has some extra work. Let's go down this afternoon and we'll see if he'll give us a job.'

Carlo was keen. This could be the opportunity he was looking for.

Maestro Ferdinando's workshop was strategically located near to the Basilica San Procolo, *ngopp' 'a terra*, at the very top of the town. Next door to him signor Polverino carved the stones and marbles to mark the names of the dead on their burial plots. In Pozzuoli all life, short or long, started and finished at the basilica.

The boys were taken on and so, aged seven and three quarters, instead of attending the army drills Carlo and Pasquale went in the afternoons to the workshop and started their training. First, they learned how to build coffins, how to measure the sides and cut the wood. Then they learned how to assemble them, smooth the wood and make a lid that fitted well.

'You need to be accurate, *ragazzi*!' Maestro Ferdinando kept an eye on them. 'We don't want a coffin that the body can't fit into, with its feet sticking out the end!' He laughed uproariously. 'Or one with a lid that can't be closed!'

Ever since he could walk, Carlo had helped his father in his wood yard, fetching wood, holding planks as his father fixed nails, sweeping up sawdust. This new work was familiar, and he was keen to learn. He watched Maestro Ferdinando polishing the coffins and asked if he could help. He enjoyed the rhythm of polishing the caskets, leaving them to dry, then repeating the process two or three times over the following days until they were ready. He found it satisfying as the dull, pale wood became richer, darker and shinier as he polished it.

Maestro Ferdinando saw he could rely on Carlo to do a good job. More to the point, he didn't tell all the gossips in the town who was being buried or how they measured the dead bodies for the coffins. He could trust him. One afternoon when Carlo came to work, Maestro Ferdinando was waiting for him.

'Good, Carlo, here you are. Today we need a coffin finished in a hurry. Come with me. I'll show you how to mix a special polish.' Proceeding to mix the same amount of non-pure alcohol and a shellac called Rapillo, Maestro Ferdinando showed Carlo how to use a sponge to rub it once evenly over the wood. Carlo was amazed as the surface of the wood was instantly transformed into a deep, rich shine after just one application. He felt like a magician. This was so much quicker to do than the laborious polishing of the showroom coffins. As there always is with short-cuts, however, there was a catch. Maestro Ferdinando explained that after only 12 hours the colour would fade away completely, leaving the wood dull and smeared. There was just enough time to get the family to pay their respects, the funeral Mass to be over and the coffin safely dropped into the ground before the stain faded.

Carlo thought about all this and decided it was good value. As long as nobody found out, everybody was happy. Not only that, Maestro Ferdinando was a cash business. No one could pay for a coffin for the dead with a bag of ripe tomatoes. Annunziata was thrilled when Carlo came home with a few *lire* each week, more when he skipped more afternoons at the *balilla*. It was a great way for Carlo to earn some cash, as long as he didn't get caught.

*

On Saturday mornings Carlo liked to go along with Zi' Antonio to hang out with the men lined up outside Don Gennaro's *barbiere*, smoking cigarettes and chatting, waiting for their turn in the barber's leather chair.

Don Gennaro was a very short, very plump man who loved to sing as he worked, which earned him the nickname 'the Barber of Seville'. As often happens with very short, very plump men who are barbers, he was very particular about his appearance. He was aware he could not encourage his clients to invest time and money on their looks if he didn't set an example and inspire just the right level of envy.

He was always impeccably dressed, with a spotless white shirt, sleeves rolled up and secured with a metal band, so his arms and wrists were free to wash his clients' hair without getting them wet. His black trousers, wider than they were long, were hitched round his belly with a long belt, the tail of which hung down long enough for him to sharpen his shaving blade as required.

As they waited for the shop to open, his customers would peer through the frosted window watching as Don Gennaro's freshly shaved reflection peered into the mirror to check his image. They watched enthralled as, with an expert flick of his fingers he would sensuously smooth his tinted jet-black hair at each side of his head. Finally, with a flip of his wrist (not unlike the flip Zia Francesca used when she flipped her special tortellini), he would twist his short fringe into a perfect quiff. Then, with a respectable queue of men congregated, he would pirouette round to open the door, and with wide-open arms welcome his clients in the full voice of an unsuccessful tenor, '*Buon giorno, buon giorno! Vieni, vieni, vieeeeni!*'

Carlo always hung around waiting with Zi' Antonio, who would try to get into Don Gennaro's worn brown leather chair at exactly 12.15 p.m, just enough time for his shave and trim before lunch.

Carlo saw an opportunity and, hoping for the odd free haircut, started helping Don Gennaro, generally making himself useful. He swept the floor (saving the trimmings to sell for mattress fillings), sharpened the shaving knives on the barber's black leather belt and washed the brushes. Before long he had a new Saturday job, with a free weekly haircut almost as smart as Zi' Antonio's.

He enjoyed his Saturdays, especially joining in singing the arias and Neapolitan songs Don Gennaro performed as he worked. He mimicked Don Gennaro's compliments to the customers to make them feel good, volunteering to brush the stray hairs from their collars and hold the mirror to let them admire the cut at the back. This became a lucrative source of tips, which would build up to a tidy sum over the morning.

Before long, Carlo was taking the money at the till and, at the same time, selling as many 'French letters' as he could to get a nice commission. Il Duce had made it illegal to use anything that might impede the birth rate increasing (he needed as many young men as possible to build his army), and though it wasn't illegal to sell birth control, it was actively discouraged. Unfortunately for Carlo this job didn't last long. The next time Monsignor Michele came in for his monthly haircut and realised that young Carlo had a sideline in sales of contraceptives he was not impressed. At his next Confession, he had stern words with the boy and regretfully, the following Saturday Carlo had to tell Don Gennaro that the job was not for him … and had to say 10 Hail Marys as penance into the bargain.

On his way home, Carlo reflected that life was a challenge. In future, he would be more careful about who was watching him. You live and learn. The sun was shining as he wandered home, where his mother was waiting for him. She had heard Carlo was going to have to give up his job; everyone in Rione Terra had heard. She had prepared a very tasty *frittata di spaghetti* for him, two treats rolled into one.

'*Non ti preoccupare,* Carlo. Don't worry. There will be plenty of other jobs.'

Carlo gave her a warm hug and agreed with her.

'You know,' he thought to himself, 'it's not so bad. As long as my mother is making my lunch every day what more do I want? I'll just have to look for another opportunity; there's always something better around the corner!'

Chapter Three

To his mother's amazement, Carlo had learned to read.

Like nearly all the women in Rione Terra, Annunziata had never been to school. She couldn't read or write; had never even learned to add up numbers. If she was required to add a signature to a document, her mark was a simple black 'X'. She kept a small stump of pencil in the drawer in the table especially for that purpose.

On the few occasions when she had to make her mark, usually at the registration of the birth or death of one of her children, she would deliberately trim the end of the pencil with a knife, shaving the wood and sharpening the lead in the hope this would add some authority to her 'X'. She did this even when she made her mark on her own marriage certificate. How could a simple mark mean anything to the authorities? She doubted the authority of it herself. Luigi could be married to any woman in the street who could write an 'X'. What use was that?

Though she would never admit it, she had always been a bit ashamed that she couldn't read or write. She felt at a disadvantage to the men who had authority over her; to Il Professore in the school, to Monsignor Michele in the church, but more acutely she felt at a disadvantage to Il Duce. When Il Duce instructed printed notices to be posted on the walls around the Rione Terra she would stare at them, frustrated she couldn't understand them. She only found out what the notices said when she heard from the *chiacchiere*, the chatterboxes, at the well. The trouble with that was they couldn't read either, so it was mostly by guesswork and gossip that they worked out what the notices decreed.

'For the greatness of the Italian nation all women must bear more children.'

'For the development of their manhood, all boys over the age of four must join the Fascist *Balilla*.'

'In order to be useful to their future husbands, all young girls should learn to sew.'

Once the chatterboxes had repeated the message to each other, passed it by every doorstep, clarified it at every washing line and traded it at every market queue, you couldn't believe a word of it anyway.

Now she had a son who could read she finally felt she had some self-respect. Not only that, Carlo could read better than his father. She couldn't dare let Luigi know, but she had caught him asking Carlo what a word meant or how he could write something. Who would have thought? A son more accomplished than his father!

Though he would never admit it, it slowly dawned on Carlo that going to school had actually reaped rewards. He realised that he now had a skill a lot of the adults around him needed.

Now he had an advantage over most of the women in his life: over his mother, his nonna, his aunts, even over his sisters who had just started school but attended even less frequently than him. Frankly, he had an advantage over nearly all the women in the town, and to be honest, a lot of the men as well. Unless they had been in the army, most of the men older than Carlo had never conquered the skill of reading either.

He noticed he had become more popular. People respected him.

When the women came to Annunziata to nurse their babies, they would ask if they could talk with Carlo. He would sit with them and read through a document or letter for them, explain what it meant as best he could and show them, if needed, where to make their mark.

Sometimes they would ask him to write a letter for them, and then they would place their mark on that. Perhaps they would want to send a letter to an ageing relative, making sure they were kept in their thoughts, and their will, until they died. Sometimes they asked him to compose a letter to an estranged lover, wishing things could be different. On occasion, he would prepare a letter to a landlord to complain the rent was too high.

Of course, this became a great source of interesting information. Carlo always knew who was quarrelling with whom, who was trying to make love to whom and who would soon be needing to borrow money.

It was lucrative as well. The women would thank him with small gifts, sometimes an embroidered handkerchief or neck scarf or even a few *centesimi*.

At his work, Maestro Ferdinando also noticed how well he was progressing.

'Carlo, I hear you can read now. And count? How are your numbers?'

'Not bad, maestro. Sometimes I get all the right answers.'

Carlo thought it prudent not to point out that his counting was not his best skill at all and that although he 'sometimes' did get all the right answers, more often than not he didn't.

'Good. I am going to teach you how to make up the formula for French polishing; I need a careful job for a special client.'

'Well I never,' thought Carlo as he measured out the recipe for the French polish to start work on a fancy sideboard. 'Who'd have thought school would have been so useful?'

He had better stop playing truant. He might miss something.

*

One day, Il Professore called him to the front of the class.

'Carlo, you have to go home. Something has happened.'

At first, he was not worried. Mamma often needed him to fetch things for her, or maybe the maestro needed him to polish a coffin in a hurry. But making his way home he noticed something was odd. Even though it was warm and humid the shutters were tightly shut over all the windows of the houses. When he passed the women at the well they fell quiet as he approached. Instead of their usual smile or banter, they lowered their eyes and greeted him quietly.

He started to worry as he made his way up the path and began to move faster, taking the steps two at a time. As he approached the door of his tenement he heard crying coming all the way down the stairs. Something terrible must have happened.

As he reached the top, on the landing, a group of men stood huddled, hats in their hands, ashen-faced and murmuring in low voices. They stepped aside when they saw him, patting him on the back as he passed through into his home.

The room was full. He could just see his mother and father, all four grandparents, uncles, aunts, the lady across the street. Even signor Cacasotto was standing quietly at the side of the wall.

Sitting at the table, with drained cups of coffee in front of them and a half-empty bottle of Anisetta, he noticed the priest, Monsignor Michele, the doctor, dottor Artiaco, and his boss, the coffin-maker, Maestro Ferdinando.

'*Oddio!*' thought Carlo, 'I've put the wrong polish on a coffin! I've put the one with the Rapillo that fades quickly on the wrong coffin and the mourners will have seen the polish and shine fade in front of their eyes at the altar. I'm finished!'

He looked at his mother. She was crying.

'Mamma? *Cosa è successo?* What's wrong?'

His mother nodded her head to him. She couldn't answer.

He looked at his father. He was talking quietly to Nonno.

Why would no one talk to him? Carlo looked round to find an ally. He looked for his favourite, Zi' Antonio: he would tell him what was going on. But there were so many people; he could hardly see who was in the room.

He looked down; he'd check for Zi' Antonio's shoes and find him that way. He manoeuvred round the adult legs, searching for Zi' Antonio's beautiful cream and black shoes.

No luck, he couldn't see them anywhere.

Not wanting to draw attention to himself, and as the adults all looked preoccupied, he called gently, 'Zi' Antonio! Zi' Antoooonio?'

He felt a strong hand on his shoulder. At last, there he was. He looked up, 'Zio …?'

Carlo was disappointed. It wasn't his uncle. It was Nonno Vincenzo.

'Carlo?' Carlo looked up into his eyes. They looked strange, as if he had been crying. 'Carlo,' Nonno Vincenzo sat down and pulled the boy towards him, putting his arms around his grandson's narrow shoulders, 'Carlo, *carissimo*, I'm sorry. Your Zi' Antonio *è morto. Non c'è più.* He is no more.'

It took Carlo a while to realise what his *nonno* was saying and then a long time after that to stop crying himself. He tried to be brave and he tried to control his weeping, but he couldn't understand. How could it be that Zi' Antonio, his favourite uncle, the person he wanted to be like when he grew up, had died? He knew babies and young people died all the time, and old people. They died when they were worn out. He understood that.

But Zi' Antonio?

Zi' Antonio, with his lovely face and neat moustache and successful life with so many girlfriends and so much dancing, had gone. Just like that. *Finito. Non c'è più.*

How could that be?

It was not until much later that Carlo found out what had happened. Zi' Antonio had gone out dancing as usual. He had been sweating a lot. On the way home, he had caught a chill and before he knew it, it had developed into bronchial pneumonia. He was taken to the hospital. Try as they might, the doctors couldn't help. Even praying to the Madonna and Holy Mass couldn't help him.

Within a week Zi' Antonio had died.

Carlo was shocked. His favourite uncle in the prime of his life had been taken away from him. For the first time in his life Carlo realised what '*non c'è più*' really meant and suffered the grief accordingly.

*

Carlo had polished a lot of coffins, but Zi' Antonio's coffin was made of glass. He had been at a lot of burials, but Zi' Antonio's was an incomparable funeral, a funeral fit for a prince.

Antonio's body was prepared by Maestro Ferdinando and dressed carefully in his best dancing suit. Don Gennaro came personally and washed and waxed Zi' Antonio's hair, then trimmed and combed his black moustache to perfection. The young man was laid in the coffin with his hands crossed over a picture of the Madonna and a rosary draped over his fingers. A spray of white lilies framed his face. He lay in the polished glass cabinet for three days so that all could pass by and put their hands on the glass, bless themselves, press their hands to their mouths in a gesture of regret and mourn their loss.

On the day of the funeral all the men in the family lifted the glass cabinet and laid it gently onto an ebony and gold carriage. The carriage was drawn by six magnificent black horses, each with a black plume arranged on its head, just like the *carabinieri* when they were riding with the king. As they pulled the carriage away the horses lifted their forelegs together, slowly and just high enough to show that even they understood the terrible loss and expressed their regret.

Walking directly behind the carriage, Maestro Ferdinando, dressed in a black suit with long starched tails at the back of the jacket and the highest black hat Carlo had ever seen, whipped the air slowly with a long black polished cane, beating the time of the funeral march. The town band followed, dressed in black with as many medals and sashes as they could find adorning their jackets as a sign of respect. The music was solemn, loud and majestic. Even Verdi's *Requiem* was not a challenge for them; the slow, drawn-out notes pulled the agony from the souls of the mourners.

The church bells tolled in time, the shops all closed their doors, and houses closed their shutters, the town stopped. The procession made its way, the horses straining to pull the carriage up the narrow, single road, *ngopp' 'a terra*, towards the Basilica di San Procolo, to the burial grounds at the town walls.

The neighbours, friends and family, Il Professore and the schoolchildren, the mothers with their babies in their arms, Giuseppe Faniente, the fishermen from the seaside, the butcher, the baker, the man who sold the salami, the man who sold the wine, the old woman who swept the streets ... everybody was standing in their usual place, quiet, eyes lowered, heads bowed. As the coffin passed the men removed their hats and the ladies lifted their black lace shawls respectfully over their heads.

The nuns, usually isolated in the convent, the ones who made the delicious *amaretti* and delectable *pasta frolla*, were there too, eyes lowered to the ground. Acolytes and the three priests from all the churches processed in front of Monsignor Michele, who followed the last altar boy, tripping over his white, lace cassock, swaying the censer, creating a waft of fragrance and fumes dark and mysterious enough to match the vapours from Vesuvius itself.

Carlo walked behind, between his grandparents and followed by his family, the fragrance of incense reminding him of his *zio*.

Monsignor Michele led the rosary.

'*Madre di Dio, prega per noi peccatori.* Mother of God, pray for us sinners.'

The procession chanted the reply.

As the coffin passed, the people threw white sugared almonds onto it.

This, thought Carlo, was a great waste. Sugared almonds were distributed at weddings, baptisms and communions, but very scarce at any other time. To see them being thrown onto the chariot and drop to the ground was an extravagance he found hard to justify. He looked up at Nonno to see if he was aware of this extravagance.

'Maybe I could just pick one up?' he thought. It would be very comforting just to suck the sugar from one of the almonds, round and round in his mouth until, sooner than expected, not long enough to prevent you wanting another, the sweet, nutty flavour of the brown almond would rub against the top of your mouth.

Carlo glanced behind him. He knew it! His friends from school at the back of the procession kept dipping down to the ground, as if to adjust the laces in their shoes or to take a stone from their bare foot. They were picking up the discarded sugared almonds and popping them in their mouths.

*

That evening, at Nonna Minicuccia's house by the sea, there was the funeral feast.

It was a different feast from normal. This time, Nonna didn't cook at all. She sat in her chair at the table at the mouth of the cave. All the women who came brought a plate of food. Some brought *fagioli*, some *scarola*, some brought *pasta*, some only an orange. Mamma brought some ricotta-filled *sciadun* and Papà brought a half-empty bottle of Anisetta.

Everyone kissed Nonno and Nonna and then kissed each other, both cheeks, again and again.

'*Condoglianze.*'

'*Che bravo ragazzo.*'

'*Condoglianze.*'

'*Che bel ragazzo.*'

The queue at the door was as long as Carlo could imagine. His friends came with their parents, lined up, kissed and repeated their condolences then settled in a corner and ate the food.

As the evening wore on a second bottle of Anisetta appeared and the talking started to get louder. As soon as Monsignor Michele left, tripping up the steps with his sweeping black soutane and his wide-brimmed hat, they started to talk even louder.

The women were congregated all around the table now; the men had all spilled out across the road, neckties finally loosened, cigarettes finally lit.

'*Che peccato!* What a pity!'

'What a pity.'

'A good lad.'

'The best.'

'Did you see the horses? We could have told Maestro Ferdinando the horses wouldn't get up *ngopp' 'a terra.*'

'Did you see it coming? Everyone knows the street gets narrower and narrower as you go up. You'd think they would have realised!'

'It gets steeper and steeper.'

'*Mannaggia!* Damn! The horses could never have turned at the top, not with that big long carriage.'

'Did you see? They had to come back down backwards, all the way back down the road, *Oddio!*'

Once the funeral procession had reached the top of the town and the coffin had been gently lowered into the ground, the mourners had all turned to make their way back down the hill. They hadn't realised that the fancy carriage which had been ordered all the way from Naples was too big to turn at the top of the cemetery and, with a lot of embarrassment and not a few red faces, they had to walk the horses and the carriage backwards all the way down the hill.

'Young Antonio had the horses dancing at his funeral!'

'Trust Antonio; having the last laugh from the other side.'

By the end of the night all the men were laughing and slapping each other's backs, still sorry Antonio had gone, but more relieved that they were still alive.

Carlo didn't see what was funny. Nothing was funny. His uncle was dead and the funeral had been a disaster.

Not a single piece of *pizza scarola* was left on the table. Not a single drop of Anisetta left in the bottle. Not even a single white almond left in any corner of the street! He had even spotted Monsignor Michele as he stooped to retrieve the last of the stray almonds from the corner of the steps.

And to top it all, he had just seen Tommaso, Zi' Antonio's younger cousin, clip-clipping along the road, proudly wearing Zi' Antonio's cream and black shoes.

Chapter Four

In a rare moment of peace, Annunziata, lost in thought, stared into the distance. The sea was becalmed, sapphire and glittering. A breath of jasmine perfume wafted towards her.

The scrapings of a scratched recording drifted in the air; the familiar harmony of a mandolin and a tender voice, '*Che bella cosa,* what a wonderful thing …'

Tired already, Procida shimmered lethargically beyond the small islands of the bay. Oar in hand, balanced at the bow of his boat, a lone fisherman pushed himself slowly away from the shoreline hopeful of a catch; silver *acciughe*, ivory *calamari*, fleshy *branzini.*

Delighting in the splendour around her, enjoying the gentle warmth of the September sun at her back, she inhaled the cool sea air. Using the moment, she whispered her perpetual prayer of gratitude.

'*Che Gioia! Grazie a Dio. Pausilypon, Posillipo.* A pause from care. Our forebears named this place well.'

In the distance was a three-masted sailing ship, sailors suspended from ropes, unfurling the masts, to capture any whiff of breeze to nudge her forwards, southwards, past the lemon groves of Amalfi, carrying marble from Carrara to the ancient shores of Sicily.

A small regatta of yachts nipped quickly past with handsome men, bronzed and taut. Scantily clad women, their hair tied back with red and white spotted kerchiefs flirted, their laughter carrying towards her in the breeze, as if to tempt her to a different life of money and leisure.

Annunziata glanced round at her small balcony high above the port. She looked again at the yachts and the women.

'The burden of wealth,' she thought. 'With nothing, I have more than I need.'

Now alert, she scrutinised the slow-moving traffic of the sea. Grey, sullen tankers, low in the water, loaded with naphtha heading for the storage tanks in the hills behind Pozzuoli. A sinister container ship, loaded with cargo, heading for Mussolini's Libyan war, slyly slinking past a charming blue and white-liveried cruise ship, a white star on its bow, taking sated holidaymakers back from the warmth of Sicily.

The moment passed. The deep boom of the Ischia ferry sounding its horn broke her reverie.

'*Forza! Forza!*' The ferryman called impatiently as the last passengers piled onto the ship. Running around the corner, as usual, another load of passengers came tumbling towards the quayside loaded with supplies and much-needed items to take across to the islands. Wicker baskets full of flour and corn, a cart with flagons of water piled high, a barrow loaded with pans and pots and cylinders of gas.

The horn sounded again.

'*Forza!* Why don't you people arrive on time? *Mannaggia!* Madonna, you know the boat leaves every day! Do you think the sea waits for you?'

He ushered the last family on board: mothers, children, grand-parents, aunts and lovers. He looked to double-check everyone was safe before signalling to *il capitano* to raise the gangplank.

'*Aspetti!* Wait!'

A shrill, agitated call echoed through the air.

Huffing and puffing, Monsignor Michele tripped towards the quayside, holding his skirts up high with one hand, stopping his black biretta flying off in the wind with the other.

'*Mannaggia!*' thought the ferryman. 'That's just my luck! I'll have to wait for him. It's the devil's curse. He'll not let me out of Confession without a penance if I don't wait.'

The church bells started to peal.

'It's nearly time for lunch!' thought Annunziata. 'I'd better hurry.'

At the final stroke of eleven the ship's horn sounded again, long and definite. The tide waits for no one, not even a man of the cloth! The familiar clunking and scraping heralded the start of the anchor being pulled up across the jetty. The ship's landing platform started to slowly but surely rise, creaking and groaning.

The monsignor, now red and puffed, raised an arm and shouted a word men of the cloth should not be heard to shout. The passengers and crew, children and grandmothers crowded high up on the deck and strained to watch the drama.

It was particularly delicious to witness a clergyman at a disadvantage.

'*Aspetta!*'

With a final effort, as if San Gennaro himself had lifted the distressed monsignor with a host of angels, his skirts flying in the breeze, he found time to bless himself and jumped on board.

*

Laughing, Annunziata lifted her parcel of vegetables and fish and turned to go back to the house.

She called to her daughters, 'Rosetta, Annetta! *Venite!*'

Barefoot they ran laughing and skipping up the steps ahead of her. Annunziata laid her hand on her belly. She was expecting again. She had almost lost count of the number of babies she had lost; lost at childbirth, lost to diphtheria, whooping cough, pneumonia. It was better not to count.

Sometimes she thought of what might have been. But who was she to doubt God's will? She thanked God she was able to care for the children she did have. She thought of all the mothers whose babies she had fed; she had long since lost count of them as well.

Life was beautiful if you had the resilience to accept it.

She thought of the women who couldn't look after their own offspring. Those who had to give their babies away; who left them in *la ruota dei bambini abbandonati,* the foundling wheel at the Basilica Annunziata in Naples. To lose a child to God was a burden she bore. To lose a child to an orphanage and know it walked on this Earth without its mother would be insufferable.

She wondered why her happy thoughts of the morning had become clouded and saddened. It was the evil eye. Something was going to happen. She shivered and shook her shoulders, trying to shake off her change of mood. She spat vehemently on the earth, angry at herself for giving in to such thoughts.

Back in her kitchen, she set about preparing the meal. Carlo and Ninuccia would be back from school soon. Nonna Marianna was sitting at the table holding the new baby, Antonietta, who was just about six months old and thriving. She had already rolled out some dough of flour and eggs this morning. The pasta was drying on the table.

Annunziata had soaked the old bread with water and now she rubbed it with a slice of garlic, crushed some *peperoncino* over it and sprinkled it with some salt. She reached for the bunch of wild oregano hanging at the window and pinched some to sprinkle over the plate. As she rubbed it between her fingers the aroma filled the room: Carlo's favourite. Her mood lifted again as she smacked her lips, smiling.

The water was already boiling in the pot suspended over the fire in the hearth. She rinsed a handful of ripe plum tomatoes and squashed the soft, plump flesh through her fingers. They fell into her battered black frying pan already drizzled with some dark green olive oil and some slivers of garlic. She set them to warm in the heat.

Annunziata gave a crust of bread dipped in the tomato to the baby to keep her settled.

Looking down to see if Carlo was coming she noticed Luigi, just coming into view. As usual he looked up to see if she was at the window.

'Whee, whee!' he whistled his greeting, raising his hand to attract her attention. The girls ran to the window.

'Papà!' they screeched in delight. He whistled back. In the labyrinth of vennels and passageways, whistling was a time-honoured and effective method of attracting attention and alerting others to danger.

At the door, Carlo and Ninuccia arrived. They kissed their mother.

32

Luigi arrived and put a bag of mozzarella and a small basket of figs on the table.

Nonno Ernesto arrived behind him, slightly short of breath after climbing the steps.

It was nothing to Luigi when more family arrived at meal times; his door was always open. They had four girls now as well as Carlo, and by the look of his wife's swollen belly, another mouth to feed soon.

As the thought crossed his mind, more mouths arrived in the shape of his own mother, Nonna Minicuccia and his ageing father. With a nod to them both he scooped the air to invite them in.

'Welcome,' he said to his mother. 'Come on in, Mamma, *siediti.*'

They all ate together. Annunziata placed all the food in front of Luigi. Like Jesus with the loaves and fishes he tore the bread apart and handed it out, sharing what was meant for nine mouths among eleven. He shrugged to himself. What did it matter? There was always enough. The older ones hardly ate a thing, they came for the company.

He tore the *mozzarella di bufala* into pieces and sprinkled it with green olive oil and a grinding of black pepper. Pulling the long soft curds between his rough, calloused hands he shared it around them all, savouring the last piece as he sucked the salty milk from his fingers.

Annunziata put the pasta in the water just till it rose to the surface then, draining it, she added it to the tomato and oil and tossed it round. The aroma of the sweet *pomodoro* and garlic filled the room. She lifted the pan with both hands and laid it in front of Luigi.

She nipped some aromatic basil leaves from a plant that was growing in a crevice of the window ledge and tore them onto the pasta.

Luigi nodded in approval.

He looked at his son at his side.

'Carlo,' he winked, '*il vino.*'

After they had eaten, Luigi loosened his belt. His sleeveless vest, dusty and marked from working in the yard, had risen from his waist revealing his bronzed, bare belly in all its glory.

Putting his arm round his wife and pulling her towards him

he laughed, 'Look, Mamma, we've both got swollen bellies!'

He moved to the chair by the window, lit a cigarette and wedged it into the corner of his mouth. He closed his eyes and sighed, the racket in the room fading into a happy blur. This moment was always the success of his day. His family were all together, fed and safe.

After his *mezz'oretta*, Luigi woke. His cigarette had gone out, the ash scattered on his vest. The coffee had dripped through the Napoletana coffee pot, filling the room with its invigorating aroma. Annunziata poured the coffee into a small cup and added a teaspoon of sugar. She put down a bottle of Anisetta beside it on the table. It always worked to move Luigi back from the soft chair.

He stirred his coffee using the tiny silver spoon with a dark coffee bean attached at the end, reflecting how they had been given a set of six of these by Annunziata's mother on their wedding day, 15 years ago. Over the years they'd lost five until they had just this one spoon and – glancing across at Nonna Marianna – his mother-in-law!

'*Così la vita!*'

Luigi was resigned. He looked across the room. Carlo was still hanging around; that was unusual. He had been very quiet when they were eating.

Carlo had been working for his cobbler uncle for the last few months. His uncle was very strict and Carlo had found the work of cutting leather, sewing and nailing shoes very tedious. Most of the customers were old and fussy and so was Zi' Alf. Carlo was bored. He would prefer to just play football.

'*Figlio mio*, Carlo,' Luigi said. 'Are you not going to work? Zi' Alf will be looking for you.'

Carlo fidgeted a bit. Nonna Minicuccia looked over. She was washing some plates in the corner.

'Why is she still here?' Luigi thought suspiciously. Things were not normal; something must have happened.

'Mamma? Why have you got your clean apron on? It's not Sunday.'

Ninuccia came across and tucked herself under her father's arm, trying to distract him. She looked across at Carlo.

What were they all up to? Luigi smelled a rat.

'Out with it! Come on! Carlo! What's going on?'

Annunziata was looking out of the window, trying to look uninterested. She was listening to every word.

'Oh Madonna!' she mumbled under her breath. 'I just knew something was going to happen today!'

Luigi knew Annunziata too well. When she mumbled under her breath things were going to take a turn for the worse.

'Sant' Antonio!'

Carlo shouted with fright as he jumped up and backed off to stand beside the wall, eyes startled, staring at the door.

Everyone else turned towards the door.

Filling the doorway, puffed up with his jaw pushed out, was a thunderous, angry Zi' Alf.

Carlo felt his knees buckle. '*Oddio!*' he panicked. 'Madonna mia! *Aiutami!* Help!'

It was his sister who came to his rescue. 'Papà! Good news. Signora Carmelina has offered Carlo a job at the *farmacia*.'

Everyone stopped looking at Zi' Alf and Carlo, and focused on Ninuccia. She was almost five now and since she had started school she had gained confidence. She was skinny, with dark skin blackened by the sun, the whites of her round dark eyes and her sparkling teeth shone in her face. Her thick black hair tumbled right down her back in curls and her infectious giggling and laughing reminded Luigi of Annunziata.

'You see, on the way to school this morning, signora Carmelina asked Carlo if he would like to come and work in the pharmacy now that he is no longer working with Zi' Alf!'

As she spoke her voice trailed off. Oops. She shouldn't have said that.

She caught Carlo's eye. He gave her a thunderous look. He didn't have a new job, signora Carmelina had just mentioned she might have one. This was getting worse than ever.

'That's it. I'm lost.'

Ninuccia kept talking, mumbling, elaborating on her fib, trying to keep the attention away from her brother.

'You see, Papà, when Zi' Alf left to go to Napoli today to buy the leather in the Spaccanapoli he left Carlo in charge of the new shop. The displays of shiny shoes, and the bone shoe horns and horsehair brushes and polish looked lovely; I saw them on the way to school. Carlo knew he wasn't to let any customers in but just tell them to come back tomorrow ...'

She stopped to draw a breath.

'And ...?'

Her father was getting impatient and he was also concerned that Zi'Alf was now even redder.

'Will somebody just tell me what is going on?' He looked at Carlo, challenging him to answer.

'Papà, I've never wanted to be a shoemaker's apprentice and I've never managed to be interested in cutting leather and sewing shoes. I'm not very good at banging nails and ...'

'And ...?' Luigi stood up from his chair. He was getting angry now as well.

Carlo moved towards the door. He was now in direct line of Zi' Alf's left fist.

'And,' Ninuccia thought she would help, '... and Carlo thought he might be a good carpenter so decided to unscrew the new window off Zi' Alf's lovely new shop to see how it was made.'

She looked at her father. He looked confused. He had helped his brother-in-law build the new shop front. It had taken a lot of work and they were pleased with the job. He already had more work because of it. Ninuccia saw her uncle start to speak and blurted out the truth before he could.

'And Carlo dropped the window and it is now all smashed on the ground!'

'*Mannaggia!* Aaaaghhh!' Zi' Alf couldn't contain his temper anymore.

He took a massive swing at Carlo. Carlo ducked and jumped out of the door practically under Zi' Alf's legs, Luigi stood up and ran towards him. He was the father. It was his privilege to smack him first.

As Luigi ran towards the door, Zi' Alf moved to grab Carlo. They both banged into each other and got stuck. By the time they untangled from each other Carlo was gone.

Annunziata, the grandmothers, Ninuccia and Rosetta all clambered to the window to see if he was all right. Far down below, in the fresh air and glorious afternoon sunshine they caught sight of Carlo running like the wind, running towards the quayside.

Carlo had let his inquisitive mind get the better of him and in his boredom and mischievousness had managed to smash up his uncle's new shop.

'That's it,' he thought, 'The only thing for it is to tie a stone round my neck and jump into the sea.'

There was only one way out of this mess. He'd go to see signora Carmelina and take the other job if it was really available. He had abandoned his career as a coffin polisher, he'd never make it as a hairdresser and he had obviously ruined his chances as a bootmaker: there was nothing for it but to turn to drugs!

*

Carlo was outside the *farmacia* the next day at 3.45 p.m. He was nearly ten years old, after all, so he had to make an effort. He had responsibilities. He was still in big trouble with Papà and Zi' Alf so he wanted to do all he could to redeem himself. The only thing for it was to go on a charm offensive and make himself useful.

His new boss, signora Carmelina, was the owner of the *farmacia*. She was a widow, living alone, and her only son's wife was expecting a baby. She was distracted. She deeply regretted employing the girl; the first thing she did was marry her son and now she was having a child.

'What is it with women?' Carlo thought to himself. 'They're always having babies.'

Carlo saw an opportunity and made sure he became indispensable. He worked every evening after school, and was soon measuring potions and mixing prescriptions. He really enjoyed this work. He was learning something new every day.

With signora Carmelina's supervision he wrapped powders in *ostie*, thin rice papers, just like the host in Communion which he took every Sunday at Mass. He prepared concoctions of aspirin powders and learned about the benefits of *camomilla* to help sleep and settle anxiety in the stomach.

He made pastes of basil leaves, black pepper and saffron strands to cure fever and typhoid. He learned to grind marsh mallow roots and mix the juices with sugar and egg whites to make a meringue. Once it was dried it could be broken into pastilles to make throat lozenges.

Things didn't go well for signora Carmelina. Her daughter-in-law had twins, Vera and Vanda! Her son was distracted and her daughter-in-law was worn out. Signora Carmelina started to rely on Carlo even more.

'Carlo, when dottor Artiaco or the wealthy customers from the villas at the seafront come in, remember not to talk to them in *Puteolano* dialect. They won't understand you. Speak to them in Italian.'

So, with this advice, young Carlo gained another life skill: the skill of speaking in tongues! He realised if he used the same accent that the person talking to him used he immediately gained rapport and he could easily recommend another product and sell a bit extra.

Signora Carmelina was impressed.

'Carlo, you have the natural gift of a salesman.'

Carlo got his first-ever wage rise. At last things were looking up!

On Sunday, he went to the *pasticciere* in the *caffè* outside the church and with his wages bought two trays of *rum babà*.

Proudly he made his way home, the parcels of *babà* wrapped in shiny paper tied with pink ribbon. He stopped at Zi' Alf's house and handed him one of the trays.

'Zi' Alf, a gift for you,' Carlo apologised.

Zi' Alf took the shiny parcel, encouraged that the boy had made amends, and watched him with some admiration as he climbed the rest of the steps home.

After lunch in his own house he brought out the other tray.

'I took a tray to Zi' Alf to apologise.'

His *papà* looked at him. 'Bravo, Carlo. You're a true Napoletano!'

This was the best compliment he could ever have hoped for. He looked at his mother, who smiled as she bit into one of the juicy, sweet sponges dripping with delicious alcoholic syrup.

'Bravo, Carlo,' she said, smacking her lips with pleasure. 'I was right. You just need to have faith. You never know what is ahead of you and if one thing fails, another opportunity will come along where you least expect it. Work hard and you'll reap the benefits. You'll see.'

Carlo winked at Ninuccia who was sharing a *babà* with Rosetta and Annetta. His life was back on track.

Chapter Five

Carlo was not to know it yet, but far away in Scotland, two Italian families that were to have a lasting impact on his life were also working hard to make a new and more prosperous future for themselves.

Walking towards Cockenzie harbour, Cesidio Di Ciacca felt refreshed. On a morning like this he didn't have a care in the world. His thinning, dark hair was swept back off his forehead; his sleepy brown eyes had a permanent quizzical look. A tall, thoughtful man, he was cautious by nature and was content to work steadily, avoiding any risks. At 45 he was looking forward to a quiet life. Running his café and fish-and-chip shop in this small fishing village outside Edinburgh was all he could wish for. He knew he was fortunate with his wife. Marietta was the boss in his house and, though he would never admit it, he liked it that way. Their four children worked with them: Lena, Johnny, Anna and young Alex. Alex had left school this summer and even although he was not yet 13, he was doing very well selling ice cream from his cart as he cycled up and down the village.

Cesidio was looking forward to a visit from his friend Alfonso Crolla. Although Alfonso was just a couple of years older than him, he had recently taken on another business and gone into the grocery trade. The majority of the Italians who had emigrated to the east of Scotland were from the province of Frosinone, and though most of them had been shepherds or farmers, now they were either ice cream sellers or had fish-and-chip shops. Cesidio couldn't understand why Alfonso, who had a very successful ice cream shop in Edinburgh himself, had decided to take such a risk at this stage in his life. According to Marietta, his wife didn't understand either. When Maria Crolla had told Marietta about Alfonso's new business partnership with the grocer, Ralph Valvona, she had been very dubious.

'Why would a man of his age get involved in a business he has no experience of? Valvona knows about importing food and wine; he's done it for thirty years. Alfonso has no idea about cheese and wine except how to eat and drink it!'

'But Maria, Ralph Valvona will be around to do the buying, surely? Alfonso is a great salesman. He'll do well.'

'I don't know, Marietta. Don't tell anybody, but Alfonso has taken nearly all my savings to buy into the company. What was wrong with just selling ice cream?'

Cesidio knew now that Maria Crolla had been right to be concerned. Ralph Valvona had recently resigned, barely two years since the formation of the Valvona & Crolla limited company in 1934, and sold his shares back to Alfonso. From what they had heard, this had swallowed up the rest of his wife's savings.

Cesidio had a lot of time for Alfonso. They went back a long way. It was Alfonso who had helped him come across to Scotland from Picinisco, in the province of Frosinone, the village in the south of Italy where they had both grown up. He had given him his first job in Edinburgh and had helped him get started here in Cockenzie. It was with Alfonso that he had marched off to war in 1915. It had been such a proud moment when the Scottish crowds had cheered the Italian immigrants as they marched off to fight with the British.

To be perfectly honest, Alfonso had proved the better soldier; it had been he who had been promoted to corporal and recognised for his bravery. He had recently been honoured with an Italian knighthood and become a *Cavaliere* of the Italian nation. The whole Italian community in Scotland shared in his honour.

Cesidio had hated every day away from his family and had just done his best to keep out of danger. He was relieved those years were behind them and they had all survived. Yes, he admired Alfonso. Of all the boys who had come to Scotland, he was the natural leader. If anyone could make a success of that business it would be him: he was the only one who had the vision.

As he turned the corner from the old salt works at Brick Cottages, Cesidio looked out over the Firth of Forth and saw the fishing fleet lined up, waiting to come back into harbour. It would be a while yet before the tide would be high enough.

The *Bonnie Lass* was first in line. He could just make out the crew on board, busy sorting the catch, throwing any waste overboard. Flocks of gannets screeched piercingly, swooping and diving into the sea, fighting over the spoils. He noticed the fishermen never dodged the gulls. They were allies, hunter and scavenger.

He'd been up since five that morning and had already prepared 10 gallons of mix for the ice cream. He'd even peeled and chipped a sack of potatoes. He'd have time to sit for a bit until the boats came in. He strolled to the end of the pier, relaxed.

The morning haar had evaporated, revealing a spectacular sunrise. Golden shafts of sunlight dazzled the boats. It was going to be another fine day.

To the west he had a perfect view of the Forth Rail Bridge, its red reflection stretching across the firth. Further to his left loomed the silhouette of Arthur's Seat, the extinct volcano in the heart of Edinburgh. He raised his hand to cut the shimmer from the sea, and narrowed his eyes.

In the valley between Arthur's Seat and the coastline at Newhaven he could make out the Edinburgh skyline: the Castle in all its glory, its flag fluttering from the ramparts stretching over to the pillared monument on Calton Hill. In between he could see the silhouette of the North British Hotel and even the spire of the Scott Monument on Princes Street.

Reverend Osborne, the minister from the old parish church on the High Street next door to his café, had taken great pains to explain to him that the Romans had settled in this very area over 2,000 years ago, well before this latest wave of Italian immigrants had arrived. That had put him in his place. The reverend was quite put out that his collection plate had less money in it than Cesidio's till at the end of a Sunday night!

'Cesidio, they say the Romans looked across at the view of

Arthur's Seat and the Bay of Edinburgh and it reminded them of the Bay of Naples. They even say they were reluctant to return to Rome when their empire collapsed.'

'You can believe that if you like,' thought Cesidio, who was often nostalgic for his home country. This morning, however, looking at the magnificent view, he thought there might after all be some truth in it. He was almost a Roman himself; his family came from the mountains, high up between Rome and Naples and, looking at the view before him, he felt this was his home now; he too would be reluctant to leave.

It had been a remarkable summer: a heatwave, if you believed the headlines in the newspapers. It had been unusually dry, with temperatures as high as 95 degrees Fahrenheit, about as hot as he remembered when he had lived in Italy. His old father had not believed him when he wrote and told him how hot it was.

Apart from anything else, it was good for business. The holidaymakers from Edinburgh and Glasgow came in droves in July and August and they stayed out till it got dark, or even later. Along the promenade from Cockenzie to the next village, Port Seton, on a summer evening, it was just like the *passeggiata* at home. Families strolling with pushchairs, men enjoying a cigarette, kids eating ice cream and late-night feasts of fish suppers and 'pokes' of chips, all supplied by Cesidio.

The Cockenzie Café was the heart of the village, open seven days from nine in the morning till midnight. Business was booming. They had even had to take on more staff. Marietta had employed a young Scots girl called Margaret Davidson. She was still 14, just out of school and already proving to be a great help. She was getting on very well with his daughter Anna, who was just a year younger.

Hearing a commotion, Cesidio looked up to see the *Bonnie Lass* appearing round the harbour mouth. It was always an emotional moment when the boats came in. Even though they weren't his people, who could not be relieved to see them arriving home safely? No doubt it was a cold, wild sea out there. The fishermen had often told him of the terrible weather and dangers they endured out in the North Sea. He knew about the many lives that had been lost; sometimes even the men of a whole family at once. He never grudged the price of the fish. It was a hard-earned living.

By the time he walked round to the front, the pier was very busy. Most of the women had come down to see their men back safely and were gossiping and blethering together. The boats were high in the water. They'd have landed their main catch at Newhaven or Eyemouth and by the sounds of good cheer on board, they'd had a good catch. The Thorntree Inn would be busy tonight.

The skipper of the *Bonnie Lass* caught sight of him and called over to arrange a meeting. 'Aye, Cesidio. We'll not be a minute!' He had some nice fish to sell him, and a wee extra something for Marietta as well. She was a good-looking woman, Cesidio's wife.

The *Bonnie Lass* was the first to tie up. Cesidio went across to wait – he was keen to have first choice of the fish. He had a reputation of serving the best supper all along the coast, and that depended on the quality of the fish. He always bought a good-sized haddock; you couldn't beat a fresh haddock right off the boats, gutted and filleted, slapped in a simple flour and water batter and deep-fried in boiling hot melted dripping to a golden crisp. With a sprinkling of salt and a splash of vinegar, it was surely one of life's great pleasures.

Young Bill Brown was first to jump off the boat. A great friend of Cesidio's youngest son Alex, at 13 he had decided to try his luck on the fishing boats.

'Hi, Cesidio,' he shouted. 'The skipper says you've to wait. He's got plenty of fish for you.'

'OK, I'll wait. Was that your first trip out, Bill? How did it go?'

Cesidio was afraid of the sea. He couldn't even swim, even though he'd lived in Cockenzie for nearly 16 years.

'Aye, it was smashin''. My legs are a wee bit wobbly, but apart from that it was just great! You should try it!'

'Me? Never, you must be joking.'

'I'll be in later for a fish supper, Cesidio. I want to see if it tastes better when I caught it myself!' The whole adventure had made him very hungry.

Bill caught sight of his mother and ran off to greet her. The lad looked like he would fall over, his legs didn't appear to be working in rhythm with his feet. His face was blackened from standing too close to the boat's funnel, and his clothes were soaked through and covered with fish scales and bird droppings.

'Let's hope his mother has plenty water boiling to give him a good scrub,' Cesidio chuckled to himself.

One after another, the boats kept coming in round the harbour mouth. The quayside was filling up. As the pier became jammed full they nestled next to each other, jute bags thrown over the hulls to stop the paint scraping. The men hopped from boat to boat to cross the harbour and get ashore.

The local fishermen liked having the 'Eyeties' in the village. They came to the harbour every day and paid cash for their fish. The Italians were welcomed by a lot of trades. They bought local potatoes, usually at the harbour as well, as many a time there were potatoes being exported to Holland or Russia. To make their ice cream they bought milk and cream and eggs from the farms at the edge of the village.

Even better, the fishermen liked the Italians because they kept the café open on a Sunday night so there was somewhere for them to go when the pub was closed. Better still, his young daughters behind the counter were fascinating: dark-haired and vivacious. The fishing lads bought their cigarettes from the Cockenzie Café just so they could chat to Lena and Anna.

Cesidio saw his eldest son, Johnny, coming out of the ice store, loading a block of ice onto his barrow. He called him over.

'Good, son. Help me get the fish onto the barrow. Right, that's it. Back to work, we'll need to get these cleaned and gutted ready for tonight.'

Johnny was 17 now and had been working with his father for over four years. He was a great help, easily capable of doing all the jobs: gutting the fish; making the ice cream; frying the fish at night.

He was a young man now, nearly six foot tall, his thick brown hair framing a happy, open face with a genuine smile for anyone he saw. He had a wonderful sense of humour and had all the customers laughing and, without realising it, spending more money.

45

Cesidio patted his son on the shoulder as they walked back, contented, to the Cockenzie Café.

*

Later on in the morning Cesidio and Johnny were washing down the fish shed, all the preparation for the evening's trade complete. Six trays of filleted fish were lying on ice; four tubs of chips soaking in a stone bath of ice-cold water.

'Time for something to eat before we start,' Cesidio looked around, checking everything was ready. Hearing the horn of an automobile outside, he wiped his hands on a clean dishcloth and went out to see who had arrived. A horse and cart was more usual than an automobile here.

He was really pleased to see the new Valvona & Crolla van pull up right at his front door. It was Alfonso Crolla, just in time for a spot of lunch. The van looked very smart in its battleship grey with gold and dark green lettering. Cesidio had got the ship sign-writer in the harbour to paint it for Alfonso, and this was the first time he had seen the finished job.

To his delight, Alfonso's wife and young daughters, Olivia, Gloria and Phyllis, the youngest, were with him. They all climbed down from the vehicle, laughing and chatting, excited to be out of the city for the day.

'*Ciao,* Alfonso, Maria, *ciao.* Come in, come in.' He greeted them enthusiastically, kissing them all on both cheeks. It was about an hour and a half's drive down from Edinburgh, so it was a great treat to see them all. He took them through to the sitting room at the back of the shop.

'Marietta, Anna, look who's here!'

It was good to get some company; they sometimes felt isolated, away from the other Italian families in town. The girls immediately went off to sit together. After a refreshing lemonade and a catch-up Alfonso persuaded Marietta to come and choose from the goods he had in the van. He was very proud of his new acquisition and had great hopes for his new venture, his van delivery service.

'Well, Marietta, come out and see, you'll be amazed at the choice we have.'

Marietta really missed the Italian ingredients she had been used to as a young girl living in Italy, and although she could buy excellent locally grown meat and vegetables she really missed the more exotic flavours she needed to make her own home-cooking.

Outside a mixed crowd had gathered around the van: men who were on the dole and hung around the café anyway; a group of housewives, their aprons on and their hair tied up in printed scarves; the grocer from the Co-op across the road, interested to see what the fuss was about. A gaggle of barefoot bairns was running around the van, excitedly touching it, expecting it to shake.

It was a rare experience when any vehicle drove along the High Street and the Valvona & Crolla van looked particularly intriguing. None of them would ever dream of buying a single item from it, but they were all interested to see what was inside. Even the Reverend Osborne had come out from his kirk to see what was going on.

Kindly asking the spectators to move aside, Alfonso led his friends out proudly to his van. With a flourish, he opened the door at the back, climbed in, and let down the side shutter to present a travelling emporium. Olivia followed to help her father.

An overpowering pong of sweating cheese, sticky salami, pungent coffee and reeking garlic hit the crowd with a shock. They all took a step back as one, pulling faces and covering their mouths and noses to hide from the unfamiliar stench.

'Oooow. Ugh! What on earth?'

Half of them ran off, fearing they would catch a disease or be caught by the devil himself. Only the boldest hung around to watch as Marietta selected what she needed; she looked thrilled … no accounting for taste.

Olivia took the products Marietta asked for, wrapping them carefully in greaseproof paper: half a pecorino cheese, 12 links of fat, mottled pork sausages, a long, thin, powdery salami, its skin smelling strangely of ammonia. Alfonso passed down to Anna 10 long blue paper packets of macaroni, three bottles of Bertolli olive oil, a bottle of red-wine vinegar, 24 tins of tomatoes and half a dozen *fiaschi* of Chianti.

Anna passed everything to Margaret and Alex, who ran in

and out of the shop piling the treasure up on the counter. Cesidio stood watching, feeling pretty good that his wife could afford to choose what she wanted.

'Add an extra half-dozen flasks of Chianti, Alfonso. We don't want to be thirsty down here so far away from the city!'

Marietta had anticipated Cesidio would do that. If she'd ordered a case he would have said it was too much. It always worked if she ordered a bit less and let her husband add some more.

The selection complete, Alfonso locked the van door and they went back into the shop.

The crowd, encouraged by Marietta's enthusiasm, moved towards the van again. They all knew the tempting aromas that came from her kitchen at the back of the shop. She obviously knew something they didn't about making tasty food out of these pungent, unfamiliar ingredients.

Marietta went into the kitchen with Maria and the girls to sort the shopping and prepare some lunch. The men settled in the sitting room, chatting. Alfonso took his jacket off, rolled up his sleeves and loosened his tie, opening the neck of his shirt. He kept his black Homburg hat on; he was still working, after all.

'It's a relief to come out of the town. It's so hot in Edinburgh, it's impossible to work. You're lucky to be out here near the sea.' Alfonso mopped the sweat from his brow with his clean white handkerchief dipped in his cologne, Ashes of Roses, which he always kept tucked, fashionably in his top pocket. He had put on a bit of weight since he had taken over the food business. This was a cause of great frustration. A tall, fine-looking man, Alfonso had always prided himself on being well groomed, paying particular attention to his neatly trimmed moustache and smoothed-back Brylcreemed hair. His pin-stripe business suit, with white wing-collared shirt and narrow black neck tie, gave him the air of authority a grocer was expected to have.

He looked at his friend's white coat. He respected that, but was proud that he had taken a bolder step during his career.

'How is the new business coming on, Alfonso?' Cesidio asked his friend as if he had read his mind.

'Very good, very good, there are plenty of customers. I'm relieved that Valvona has retired. A partnership is never a good idea. It is always better to be master of your own destiny.'

There were a fair number of Italians now in Scotland, about 1,400 men at the census taken last year, nearly 6,000 in all; a decent customer base for any new business. Alfonso seemed to know most of them one way or another, most of them were related to him and a lot were already in his debt.

'Good on you, Alfonso,' thought Cesidio. 'Maybe it wasn't such a bad idea after all.'

'I'm trying to get my boys settled with their own shops. Vittorio is working mostly with me at the delicatessen at 19, Elm Row, and Domenico works in the ice cream shop in Easter Road.'

'That's for the best, Alfonso. It'll be better for them once they find a wife.'

'Cesidio, the Italian consul has asked me to invite all the ex-combatants to come to the Armistice Day parade in November. Will you be able to come?'

'Yes of course, *Cavaliere*!' Cesidio automatically saluted his friend, who he still saw as his superior officer. 'What do you think, Alfonso? Is the news from Europe making you worried at all? It seems that there is a lot of unrest across Italy.'

'It's nothing to worry about. It's just Mussolini keeping control of Italy. He won't let the country down. One war in a generation is more than enough. We know that, don't we, my friend?'

Cesidio nodded, 'You can say that again. Let's hope you're right. We don't want our boys going through what we had to.'

Alfonso looked at his friend. Their time fighting had been hard for them both, but even harder for their wives, who had been left abandoned in a strange country with young children and businesses to manage alone.

Maria called them through to the back shop.

'*A mangiare.*'

Cesidio stood up and put his hand on his friend's shoulder. 'Come on, Alfonso. Let's share a nice plate of macaroni and we'll open a *fiasco* of Chianti. You can tell me all about your new shop.'

After they had all eaten, Anna and young Margaret went behind the counter to mix the ice cream and fill the freezers.

Cesidio called through, 'Make some sliders for us, Anna. There's nothing to beat an ice cream to refresh you. Girls, would you like a snowball on top of a cone? Anna, give Olivia, Gloria and Phyllis what they want.'

The ice cream was soft and creamy, deliciously sweet, with just the right hint of vanilla.

As soon as the freezers were all full Anna came through and put her arms lovingly round her father's neck.

'It's so hot, Dad. Can we all go swimming this afternoon?'

Cesidio looked at Alfonso, who was a little flushed round the cheeks and would no doubt appreciate an excuse to relax a bit before driving home.

'Go on then, don't tell your mother. Take Margaret too, have a nice time. Johnny, you and Alex cycle the carts along and I'll stay here with Alfonso.'

The girls cleaned up and ran behind Johnny and Alex as they cycled their ice cream carts along to the Port Seton open-air swimming pool. It was very busy and in no time the boys had constant queues for their ice cream.

The girls hired costumes at the pool and they all spent the afternoon sharing the duties of selling ice cream and swimming in the pool. Between them all they made record sales.

On the way home that evening, Olivia sat at the front of the van beside her father.

'That was such good fun, Dad. We were in and out of the swimming pool and eating ice cream all day.'

'I wish we could live down here, Dad,' Gloria said excitedly. 'Their work is such good fun it feels just like a holiday.'

No one wanted to mention anything, but the smell of sweaty cheese pervading the van was almost unbearable on the winding roads back into Edinburgh. For all his bravado, the truth of it all was that being a grocer was proving a bigger challenge than Alfonso had anticipated. As if reading his mind, Maria shook her head.

'Well, Alfonso, it's all your own fault. You're the one who wanted to slice salami for a living! Now look where it's got us.'

'In a bit of a pickle,' shouted out Phyllis, making them all laugh.

'A bit of a *fiasco*,' retorted Gloria.

That was a joke too far. Her father was not amused and was quiet the rest of the way home.

Part Two

Arrangiarsi per sopravvivere

Do as one must to survive

Overleaf: Carlo Contini aged 15.

Chapter Six

POZZUOLI, JUNE 1940

For the past few years life had started to improve for Annunzi-ata.

Although she had had a little daughter, Lilla, who had died of measles aged three months, finally she was blessed with two healthy boys: Vincenzo and Ernesto. They were named after Carlo's older brothers who had died all those years ago.

Luigi had also managed to purchase one of life's newest luxuries: a radio. This became a source of great novelty to Annunziata and her neighbours: personal in-house entertainment!

To hear the music she loved in her own home was almost as good as looking at the view from her window. She could listen to Neapolitan ballads and opera, Caruso and Gigli; everything she was familiar with in the streets she could now hear in her own home. Carlo quickly learned to sing the songs, and serenaded and twirled her round the room like a young girl.

Like his father and younger brothers, Carlo's greatest pleasure, apart from Neapolitan music, was football. Listening to the excitement of a match live over the radio was intoxicating for the men, making them feel very proud of Naples and their country. Italy won at football!

However, as sometimes happens when there are moments of tranquillity in life, before you know it things begin to change. The radio, at first a welcome source of pleasure, gradually became one that generated worry and concern. Instead of listening to football, they became disturbed by the constant bulletins alerting them to the danger of impending conflicts, failed alliances and distant wars. Exhilarating music programmes were interrupted by Mussolini delivering hypnotic and ominous speeches and propaganda.

Before they knew it, the broadcasts of music and football were less frequent, replaced by patriotic anthems and a dull background murmur of male voices discussing interminable news.

When the first military aeroplanes were seen flying above Pozzuoli like a metallic flock of starlings, it had been very exciting. They had all run out into the streets, shading their eyes against the sun, straining to make out the bulky, shadowy machines in the sky. When it became a frequent occurrence, they turned away and went indoors, unsettled.

There were changes at school as well. Carlo could no longer play truant: there were constant registers and close supervision. It became compulsory for all students to attend the afternoon military clubs. It was impossible to sneak away, even to go to work.

Now he had reached his 15th year, Carlo was promoted into the Fascist Youth Combat Corps, the *Avanguardisti*. He was issued with a new uniform: black shirt, grey-green trousers, badges with Fascist emblems and an azure kerchief for his neck. A black fez added further inches to his height, now over six feet, a good head taller than most of his classmates. His *moschetto* was a scaled-down, fully functioning version of the Italian army rifle.

When Annunziata saw him in uniform for the first time she clutched her hands to her heart in terror. He was a child soldier!

'Carlo, don't grow. Stop growing. Don't listen to them at the *Avanguardista*. Don't join the army! You're still only a boy.'

At first, he had laughed. 'Don't worry, Mamma. I don't listen to any of it; it goes in one ear and out the other,' he said, pointing to one ear and then the other.

Fortunately, he was too young. It was the boys from the classes ahead of him that were being enlisted into the army. Carlo knew this was not the career path for him, but he was doubtful if he would have a choice.

One afternoon when he was making his way home after a training exercise, still dressed in his *Avanguardista* uniform, Carlo became uneasy. The shops had not re-opened after lunch. The street sellers in the piazza with their carts piled with vegetables and fruits were nowhere to be seen. The fishing boats in the harbour were all tied up, but there were no fishermen mending their nets. The coffee shop was closed, its green shutters locked. Even the door of the church was jammed shut. It reminded him of the day of Zi' Antonio's funeral. He wondered if someone had died.

When he arrived, Annunziata was very relieved to see him. His father was already home, sitting at the table with his four grandparents. The radio was on, playing military marches.

'We're waiting for news, Carlo.' His father looked uneasy. He had dark shadows under his eyes.

'Papà, are you ill?'

Luigi shook his head. 'No, I'm fine, Carlo. *Siediti, vicino a me.* Sit next to me.' He pointed to the chair on his left.

It was very warm outside. He left the door open to encourage a breeze through the room, some *aria fresca* from the balcony. They all sat there for the rest of the afternoon, talking, anxious, empty coffee cups lying unwashed.

Luigi smoked another cigarette. He smoked more than usual these days. The girls were all sitting on the bed in the corner with Vincenzo nestled between them. Annunziata was at her chair at the window, gazing out towards the islands, young Ernesto asleep on her lap.

The familiar beat of the Fascist anthem started again. Carlo sang it twice a day at school and at the club. He detested it.

Luigi leaned forwards and turned up the volume.

Annunziata crossed herself.

Even before the anthem had stopped, huge cheers rang out from an enormous crowd. A silence descended on the room; no one moved. Luigi reached out to move the volume dial again. The broadcast was from Rome. He gave the radio a tap, trying to get the clearest signal.

Suddenly they heard rapturous applauding and uproar, shouting for Il Duce. It echoed around Rione Terra, all the cheers from all the radios in every home. Then, after another interminable pause, they heard the unmistakable voice of their leader.

55

'*Soldati!* Soldiers! Sailors! Aviators! Black Shirts of the revolution and of the Fascist Legions! Men and women of *Italia*, of the empire, and of the kingdom of Albania! *Ascoltate!* Listen!'

He paused.

Silence. Not a sound to be heard. Not from the crowd in Piazza Venezia, where Mussolini was speaking, nor from the streets of Rione Terra, nor from any one of them in the room. Not even the dogs and cats dared make a sound. Not even the birds in the skies. Not even the waves lapping on the shoreline.

The whole of Italy was holding its breath.

'An hour appointed by destiny has struck in the heavens of our fatherland.'

The crowds erupted with fanatical, adoring cheers.

The room was silent.

'*La dichiarazione di guerra è già stata recapitata!* The declaration of war has already been delivered.'

An obscene outburst of exhilaration screeched from the radio.

'*Guerra! Guerra!* War! War!'

Luigi looked at Annunziata. Their fearful eyes filled with tears. Neither of them looked at Carlo; they couldn't bear to.

Mussolini stayed silent, letting the crowd vent its emotion. It was chilling to hear.

Carlo was stunned. He looked from his father to his mother. His eyes widened. He felt a knot in his stomach. 'What does it mean? Who will we be fighting against? Who will be our enemies? What will happen to me?' Questions raced through his mind. He couldn't open his mouth to say a word. He shuddered.

Mussolini continued, proclaiming Italy's fate.

'The declaration of war has already been delivered to the ambassadors of Great Britain and France. We go to battle … we go to war!'

When Carlo thought back in years to come he remembered clearly this was when the wailing started. His father dropped his head in his hands in despair. His grandmother dropped to the ground, beating it in anger. His sisters sobbed, horrified at the confusion around them. Ernesto awoke with the commotion and burst into tears.

The church bells started to toll, in Rome, in Naples, in Pozzuoli;

the horrifying clamour swept across the land.

They heard the crowd cheering and shouting.

'*Duce! Duce!*'

The men were all shocked, quiet and fearful. In the street below, in front of the harbour, a crowd had gathered. They were cheering as well, the ominous racket reverberating around the room.

'*Duce! Duce!*'

Annunziata came away from the window and closed the shutters. She looked at Carlo, still dressed in the uniform of the *Avanguardista*, with dread in her tear-filled eyes. Her heart was broken.

Her son was 15 years old. This war was for him.

*

No one slept that night. Sirens wailed across the town. The sky was ablaze with anti-aircraft searchlights scanning the heavens.

The next morning the sun was shining again: the sea was still glorious and the scraggy cats still played in the ancient ruins. Everything looked the same, but everything had changed.

Now the skies were full of aeroplanes: huge, prowling sinister carriers of armies, bombs and horror. Not only Italian planes but ominous German aircraft emblazoned with menacing swastikas and British bombers, flying so low Carlo felt he could reach out and touch them from the balcony. The radio brought news of the destruction they were already causing: Turin, Rome, Genoa had all been badly bombed within days. The aeroplanes were no longer a sign of wonder; now they were a symbol of terror.

The beautiful liners that had lolled in the warm waters of the Mediterranean appeared now dressed in battleship grey, their white and azure livery painted over. Their glamorous decks were stripped back, deckchairs and cocktail bars replaced by gun mountings. The larger fishing boats gradually left the bay, never to return. The smaller boats had to fish between the warships and aircraft carriers now anchored in the bay. As the sons of the town were enlisted into the army, the grandparents returned to the fishing boats to do the work of the absent youth.

Italy's new allies arrived in force.

The Germans evacuated families living in the wealthier homes on the seafront. Some of them moved into the already congested houses in Rione Terra. Some relocated into the mountains, finding shelter away from the coast. The soldiers requisitioned the splendid houses and set up headquarters.

Carlo, Vincenzo and his sisters watched from the balcony as a squadron of German Panzer tanks deafeningly lumbered along the Via Napoli, menacing and dangerous. Terrified, the girls began to cry.

Columns of German soldiers appeared, tall, blond, efficient, marching south to Naples. More stopped, now taking over the town halls and offices, hotels and boarding houses on the seafront. They came up to the Rione Terra, pushing doors open, barking orders no one understood and generating fear.

'Papà, why are they taking over? I thought these were our allies?' Carlo was confused.

'They're no friends of ours, Carlo.'

Within weeks the town was entirely under the authority of the German army.

Carlo became used to the sound of women crying: women crying in church; women collapsing in a faint when the post arrived; women at the station, screaming, being pulled from a train as it moved away from the platform, packed full of their husbands and sons. He had grown accustomed to the women of Rione Terra being in despair.

The senior classes of the *Avanguardista*, nothing more than an assembly of shambolic, inexperienced schoolboys, were enlisted. Lined up in the Piazza dei Golosi, following the First Battalion of Pozzuoli, they marched north out of town, their mothers lining the roads, terror-stricken.

At the *farmacia*, signora Carmelina's son, don Nicola, was called up to be a medic. He wasn't a trained doctor, but that was what he was assigned to be. He disappeared. Then his assistant didn't show up for work. One day signora Carmelina herself vanished. No one ever heard what happened to them.

Zi' Alf, now overweight and middle-aged, was commissioned to make boots only for the army, forbidden to use any materials for any other purpose. Seeing a gap in the market, the 'lost-shoe man', signor Perdutoscarpe, set up a stall on the pavement outside Zi' Alf's shop. He offered a selection of old, worn discarded shoes, single shoes without a partner, shoes with upturned, scraped toes and worn-down heels, shoes that had been left behind when people had fled secretly through the night. As the months passed his stall became busier. There was nowhere else to buy or get shoes repaired.

Fuel became scarce; the baker could only light his oven on alternate days, then only twice a week. Flour was rationed; he used maize flour instead and baked corn bread.

Not all businesses were challenged, however. The coffee shop in the piazza was busier than ever, full of soldiers all the time. Carlo and his sisters were forbidden to go in and had to use a longer route to get home. The tourist restaurants at the seafront became popular with the Italian and German officers, entertaining each other and their wives and girlfriends. They were a magnet for enterprising women of the town.

In the last few years Luigi had found good work on the construction of a vast fuel reservoir hidden in the hills behind the town. The workforce had wondered why such a huge reservoir was being built and why shipping carriers loaded with naphtha from Abyssinia had been systematically filling it over the last two years.

Now they knew.

When a letter arrived for Luigi he was not overly worried. Because of his trade, he had been expecting to be sent to the shipyards to help build warships. Instead he was ordered to show up at the Ansaldo Cannon factory, to make parts for German Panzers. He wasn't a mechanic, and he didn't understand the workings of the *Panzerkampfwagen*, but he had no choice. He had to do as he was instructed, ten hours a day, six days a week.

The town was being targeted by enemy aeroplanes; loud sirens went off every day. The school closed; there were no teachers left to teach. Carlo went to the *farmacia* every day and helped a retired pharmacist and an old sales assistant weigh out the potions and mixtures as best they could. He was uneasy, concerned what was going to happen to him.

Every evening when he came back from work he looked at his mother anxiously.

'Any letter?'

'*Niente*. Nothing.' She was always on edge now.

'Carlo, why don't you just stay home? They'll think you're a trained *farmacista*. They'll take you to the Front!'

'Carlo, it's such a relief you went to work at the *farmacia*. They'll need you here to manage the shop. They won't take you to the Front.'

'Carlo, why did you skip your training at the *Avanguardista*? Now they'll arrest you and put you in jail.'

She was beside herself with worry.

When the official letter addressed to Carlo Contini finally arrived Annunziata was terrified. She hid it in the drawer and waited till they had eaten their meal.

'Carlo, the letter has arrived.'

This was it. He would be called up to fight. He paled. He felt sick. He took the envelope and eased it open. He read it silently.

He took a deep breath, obviously relieved.

'It's OK, Mamma. It's OK,' he embraced her. 'I'm not being called up. I've been assigned to be an apprentice to build the *Panzerkampfwagen* at the Ansaldo factory in Pozzuoli. I'm going to work with Papà!'

Annunziata blessed herself. Her prayers had been answered.

'*Grazie*, Madonna. At least Carlo is staying at home with us and with Luigi in the same factory. At least I can feed him every night.'

Carlo whispered his thanks as well. He had started praying every day. It seemed to him the only help they could rely on now was the help of La Madonna.

*

This sense of relief was the last they felt that year. The war started to really take a hold.

They listened to constant radio reports of massive bombing raids by the British on the heavily industrialised areas in the north: Turin, Genoa and La Spezia, where the factories were arming the war. There was no let-up: the cities were systematically being destroyed.

The raids had now started in Pozzuoli, but the factories had been cleverly concealed and were difficult to target. Instead the bay, where the carriers were anchored, and Rione Terra itself, were being bombed. The raids were terrifying. As soon as they heard the sirens Luigi and Annunziata scooped up the children, and with Carlo behind helping his grandparents they all quickly made their way to take refuge in the tunnels of the Pozzuoli–Naples railway line.

They spent the nights together wrapped in blankets and coats with the rest of the townspeople: women and children, the old and the young. It was mayhem: crying, screaming, arguing, singing. They slept as best they could, then at four in the morning, before the first train to Naples was due, everyone left and returned home to see if their houses were still standing.

It became more dangerous; the population gradually left their homes to hide in the hills behind the town, and the narrow streets of the Rione Terra became deserted.

The grandparents still had vivid memories of the last war. Although the situation was dreadful, they feared it was going to get much worse.

It did.

Chapter Seven

It was early the following spring when the next shock happened.

When no one expected him, the postman came to the door again. He handed Annunziata another official letter.

'*Mi dispiace,* Annunziata. I'm sorry. It's a letter for Carlo.'

When Carlo and Luigi came home that night the whole family were waiting for them. They watched Carlo in deadly silence as he read the letter; the colour drained from his face.

'Papà, I'm being transferred to Genoa, to the Ansaldo munitions factory there. I have to report in three days.'

They all looked at each other. Genoa: where they had heard the factories were bombed almost every night, where the war was being fought most fiercely and where the Germans were in control.

Carlo read the order to his father.

'I have to train as a specialist *calderaio*. What does that mean, Papà? I don't understand.'

Carlo sat down at the table trying to steady himself.

'I'm not sure. I think you'll work on huge sheets of steel to make them high-calibre bullet-proof. They'll use the steel for German aeroplanes and tanks.'

Annunziata shook her head, frowning.

'But that's a man's job. I don't understand. He's just a boy. Look at him, he's just a child!' Annunziata was distraught.

Later that night, after everyone had fallen asleep in the house exhausted, with bombs falling all around them, Luigi lay down beside his wife. She whispered to him, terrified. 'Luigi, there must be some mistake. He's only fifteen. He's never been away from home, how can he manage without us?' Her mind was racing. 'What if he gets lost? What if he gets into trouble?'

What neither of them could bear to say was what they were both thinking: 'What if he doesn't come back? What if we never see him again?'

How could they even think of Carlo alone in a strange city, one that was in a war zone and under attack? How could they imagine him running for shelter alone, or, worse still, being hit or, God forbid, killed?

Eventually, absolutely worn out and exhausted, Annunziata fell asleep in Luigi's arms. Luigi couldn't sleep, he couldn't let this happen. He needed to think.

The next morning, he woke Annunziata very early. He had an idea.

'Annunziata, quickly, get dressed. *Vieni, forza!* We'll go to the factory. We'll go together, a father and a mother. We'll ask to speak with the *direttore,* face to face. We'll wait for as long as it takes. If we go together he'll help us. He won't refuse when he sees how distraught we are.'

Then he told her what he was thinking.

'I'll offer to go instead of Carlo.'

She looked at Luigi, her lip trembling. She nodded, shaking her fist to her mouth.

'OK, Luigi. You say you'll go instead if you have to.'

In his office, with a full-length glass partition overlooking the factory floor, Luigi and Annunziata stood in front of the *direttore.* He was seated in a black leather chair in front of an imposing desk. On the wall behind him hung a large image of Mussolini resplendent in his elaborate dress uniform, chin down, blue eyes glowering.

'Il Duce. Pah!' thought Annunziata, 'You fool. You've not made Italia great, you've crippled us.'

They looked desperate. A bedraggled man in a dusty jacket with worn trousers and workman's boots, his hat crumpled in his hands held down in front of him. A woman, past her youth, thin, greying hair pulled back from her face, her faded black dress ripped at the hem, a threadbare shawl round her shoulders.

Her eyes were keen. She had spirit. She looked directly at the man in charge, trying to understand him. Maybe he had a son. Surely he must know what she felt like.

Looking down on the factory floor, she was amazed at its vastness. Hundreds of men, very young and very old, worked in rhythm, the thudding and noise deafening even through the glass. At the far end, she saw rows of the colossal dark tanks, lined up in formation, menacing and powerful.

'The devil is here then, right among us,' she thought. 'He's here, using our own sons to do his deadly work.'

A shiver went up her spine. She crossed herself and pulled her shawl tighter round her throat.

The *direttore* shifted uncomfortably in his chair. He'd had hundreds of conversations just like this one since the start of the war: the same poor man and his wife, or a mother and a handful of children, or a grandmother with a crying baby.

A shiver went up *his* spine.

Every family was asking the same question of him. Could he save their son? But how could he save any of them? How could he tell them he hadn't even been able to save his own?

After Luigi had finished, the *direttore* stood up and came around to the front of the desk and put his hand out to shake Luigi's.

'Luigi, *signora*.' He acknowledged Annunziata with a slight bow of his head. '*Mi dispiace*, I'm sorry,' he took his handkerchief from his top pocket and mopped his brow, then put his arm behind Luigi and turned him firmly towards the door. '*Non c'e niente da fare*. There's nothing to be done.'

*

On the day of Carlo's departure, his family cried all day. From first light, when they all got up to watch him dress, till they saw him fading out of view, waving as the train carried him away, they cried till their tears ran dry.

Carlo's kitbag was filled to bursting with extra clothes, uniform, food – not that they had food to spare, but who knew when he would eat again. In his socks Annunziata hid the last jar of Nonna's apricot jam and the last jar of her *melanzane sott'olio*. In between his shirts she hid half a *salsiccia*. In a small bag she put some corn bread and an orange. In a handkerchief wrapped in newspaper she had hidden five sugared almonds, lovingly unfolded from the *bomboniere* from her wedding.

'Mamma,' Carlo objected, 'you can't give me all this food, there are too many here for you to feed!'

'*Figlio mio*, it's you who's going away. This will keep you safe. Here, take this as well.' Into Carlo's hand Annunziata pushed an envelope containing half of the family's ration cards. 'Take these. You'll need them. At least I'll know you'll be able to get a bit more food and you'll keep strong.'

The thought of the factory floor with all the machinery and tanks haunted her. If the enemy knew about factories like that in Genoa, of course they would do anything they could to bomb them.

Nonna Marianna was beside herself with worry.

'Oh Carlo, who's going to look after you? Who's going to feed you? How will you manage with your pasta not cooked the way you like it?'

'Nonna, I'll be fine,' said Carlo, trying to be brave. 'You've not to worry. I'll learn to cook for myself.'

At that, all his sisters started to cry all over again.

Annunziata was the last to embrace him.

'Promise you'll write every day, Carlo. Even if I don't get the letters, I'll know you'll be thinking of us.'

As he looked back along the platform as the train pulled away he saw his distressed family, huddled together, a sorry group among countless other similar distressed families. Vincenzo, his four-year-old brother, was standing slightly apart and had started to run after the last carriage of the train, calling to his brother.

'Carlo! Carlo! Come back soon!'

At that Carlo burst into tears.

Who knew if he ever would?

*

The journey took two days, with long waits at strange stops along the way.

Arriving on Platform 2 of the *Stazione Piazza Principe* in Genoa, Carlo was overwhelmed. The building was quite magnificent. He felt he had arrived in a cathedral, with its marble floors, huge, wide marble columns and vast cupola with shafts of light streaming down on the busy platforms. It was pandemonium, very crowded and noisy. It felt as if he was among the hectic hordes at the *Festa di San Gennaro* in Naples.

Huge trains were screeching into the station constantly, every inch of the space on board packed with people: families, children, vagrants, soldiers, passengers crammed in the aisles, leaning out of the windows.

He noticed young boys, even younger than him, precariously clinging to the roofs of the carriages, lying flat to avoid overhead wires. They jumped down just before the train stopped and disappeared into the crowd, the guards running after them, helplessly blowing their whistles. The crowds pouring from the carriages caused so much confusion there was no hope of apprehending anyone.

More trains were pulling out of the station, steam billowing from their funnels. The loudspeaker announced the destinations: Ventimiglia, Milano, Torino. They too were packed – with German soldiers, families, people overloaded with suitcases, *Avanguardisti*. Like Carlo, everyone was serious-faced and subdued. One train with what looked like an excess of priests and nuns was surely bound for Rome.

The platforms were all jammed with people, pushing against each other, aggressive, agitated. He tried to stay close to his group. He had met his new friends, Egidio and Angelo, at the factory at Pozzuoli. They were the same age as him and just as disorientated. There were 19 of them in all, each not yet 16 years old. None had travelled before, or even left the small towns or villages they came from. They tried to stay in line. A platoon of German soldiers marched past, disciplined, regimented, pushing them against the wall. Without hesitation, civilians and guards stood aside, like the parting of the Red Sea. No one was arguing.

So this was Genoa. Carlo felt foreign, alien. It was a completely different country, a different world. 'Madonna,' he thought, 'I'm an immigrant.'

The station smelled peculiar: steam, coal and oil mixed with urine, sawdust and cigarette smoke. It was full of strange voices and noise, whistles, commands, marching, embracing and kissing … life was raw in this mayhem, people were grasping at every minute.

There were a lot of Italian soldiers around, far more than they had seen in Pozzuoli. They were lounging, smoking, laughing and looking distracted or even bored.

'What have they to laugh about? Surely they don't want to go to war?' Carlo couldn't understand.

There were a lot of senior Italian military, captains and sergeants walking around in pairs. Unlike the soldiers, they were well groomed and dressed in spotless uniforms, almost like movie stars. Carlo noticed groups of exceptionally tall blond men dressed in long beige gabardines and smart trilby hats. They were looking around, watching all the time, cigarettes in hand, in no hurry to go anywhere.

There were also a lot of tramps sitting in corners, dressed in rags, beards and hair unkempt. He noticed a dishevelled woman, scruffy and barefoot, sitting on a dirty step begging. As he looked closer he noticed she had a baby wrapped in an old shawl, with some newspapers to add warmth.

Carlo felt his stomach lurch. 'Oh Mamma.'

It had been so hard to leave his mother. How would she manage without him? He had never realised till now how much he loved her. How much he relied on her. She had always put him first, always given him the best of everything. She always gave him his breakfast, his milky coffee and his Pavesini biscuit, the one from the market stall. At the end of the month, on pay day, she always made a pot of *ragu*, thick tomato *sugo* with slices of beef stuffed with garlic and parsley that had cooked so slowly it melted in his mouth. Oh, the smell of that *sugo*. His stomach cramped. She would roll out the pasta, cut it quickly into strips and after minutes cooking would serve it to him with the sweet *sugo* and soft, juicy meat.

'Oh, Mamma!'

He thought of the many times she had sat up at night waiting for him to come home. Marcello from the *farmacia* knew someone who worked in Cinema Sacchini. He sometimes gave Carlo free tickets. They were really tickets from the day before that he stamped with a *gratis* over the date, but it got them into the back row anyway. Carlo would go and get lost for an hour or two in a world of glamorous lives, music and excitement.

Then, when he wandered home, Annunziata was always waiting, watching for him from the balcony. When he arrived at the house she would have a quick plate of pasta *sciuè sciuè* ready for him, just so he would sleep well, dreaming of her instead of the pretty girls on the screen.

She washed all his clothes, scrubbed them on the board down at the fountain, carrying them back up to the house before hanging them outside the balcony to dry. He liked to look as smart as he could.

His eyes filled with tears again.

'*Madonna, aiutami!* How will I manage without my mother?'

Just then, a whiff of perfume caught his nostrils. He turned around quickly and walked right into the embrace of a tall, elegant woman, fully draped in a luxurious, knee-length fur coat.

Carlo took a step back, embarrassed, bumping into Egidio, almost knocking him over.

'*Mi scusi, signorina … signora?*' Carlo blushed.

She nodded gracefully, her deep ruby-red lips parting slightly to show a row of small, gleaming teeth. She smoothed her hand down her chest to straighten the fur on her coat.

'*Niente, caro,*' her voice was deep and slow, with a strange accent. She smiled at him, and touched his face gently with her cool fingers, her red-painted nails long and perfectly shaped, then turned around and slowly strolled away.

Carlo looked at her, her coat swinging seductively, her long stockinged legs with a seam stretching straight up, her narrow ankles perched in dark polished shoes with the narrowest of high heels.

Egidio nudged him, laughing, 'Are you in love?' he teased.

Carlo pulled himself together. 'No …' but he was hot under the collar. 'No, but I bet she's in love with me!' Carlo's thoughts of his mother went clean out of his head. Maybe this adventure would be fun after all.

Putting a stop to this nonsense the *capitano* of his group called the boys all together.

'*Attenzione!*'

He called their names to make sure they were all present. They'd started out as 20, but one of the boys had taken fright. When he thought no one was looking, he deliberately caught his finger in the train door as they left Pozzuoli. It caused a great commotion and he had to be taken off the train at Formia, and driven back to his mother … the first casualty of the war.

'*Avanti, soldati!*'

Carlo shivered. Now he was a soldier. Surely not? He was just an apprentice engineer!

'*Avanti! Marciate!*'

As they marched past the ticket inspector Carlo caught the alluring aroma of invigorating coffee. On his left he turned to see a busy café bar, open right onto the street, three baristas high on a platform shouting customers' orders out. The coffee machine whizzed and splashed and the smell took him right back to the coffee shop in Pozzuoli. At least something here was familiar.

He pulled his shoulders back and took a breath, trying to draw in as much of the coffee smell as he could. It gave him some courage; he was going to need it.

'I'll just have to play to my strengths,' he thought, 'and look for opportunities.'

He remembered his mother's last words to him before he left. '*Figlio mio*, don't look for worldly wealth. Riches and abundance are of no use. They can be lost in a moment. *Coraggio!* Just take one day at a time and do the best you can. That's all you can do.' She had taken him in her arms and embraced him, even though she was half his size. 'Write. Promise you'll write. *Non dimenticare di me, figlio mio.* Don't forget me.'

Carlo did write; long letters full of the detail of everything that was happening. He reassured her. Things were better than they had dared to hope. He and his friends were billeted at a hotel near the factory, all his meals supplied; more food than he could imagine. Contrary to her worries, they were being well looked

69

after; the Italian war machine was well fed!

'Of course, it's not like your food, Mamma, it's not even Neapolitan, but there's plenty of it. Don't worry, I'll not go hungry.'

After the initial disorientation, Carlo settled into a routine. He worked all day at the factory, learning sheet-metal cutting and specialist gun-making. The people around him were friendly and his troupe became like family to him. He was surprised, but not disappointed, to realise half the factory was manned by young women working alongside the boys as apprentices and mechanics. For the first time he had a lot of female company who were not his sisters or grannies. It was not at all unpleasant.

In the evening, they had free time to explore the city. There were relentless air raids and bombings but Carlo noticed how, oddly, they quickly became accustomed to danger. There were plenty of shelters, and concrete tunnels taking the roads through the mountains also served as effective protection.

He started to enjoy being away from home. For the first time he was free to do what he wanted, be independent, experiment. For the first time he wasn't surrounded by women, teachers and priests watching his every move. Once the boys' work was done, the bosses at the factory had no interest in them. For the first time, Carlo could do what he liked, with few responsibilities.

It wasn't long before he realised that in this industrialised northern city Neapolitans had a reputation for being fun-loving, romantic and great singers. He set about making sure he lived up to expectations. He took every opportunity to play to his strengths; to charm, to sing, and, when he picked up the courage … to love. Always the opportunist, Carlo decided it was time to be a man, but he wouldn't be telling his mother that!

The historic centre of the city was a constant adventure, with its intricate maze of alleyways and unexpected small squares with beautiful mansions nestling together, giving an impression of an opera set round every corner. There was plenty of opportunity to have fun.

They explored the narrow streets packed with soldiers on leave, plenty of girls and young people in cafés and bars. They ate food bought for a few *centesimi* at stands, eating it as they walked – crispy thin *focaccia al formaggio*, dripping with soft cheese, or cones of paper filled with *friggitoria*, deep-fried pieces of fish, washed down with a bottle of beer and a cigarette. The boys enjoyed their freedom for the first time.

Carlo loved exploring the port alone. In his uniform and his ever-growing self-confidence, he wandered amongst the guards, acting as if he had authorisation to be there. Before long he had contacts from whom he could buy cigarettes and wine, which he sold to his friends back at the factory.

The dangers of the constant bombings and attacks were exciting in themselves. Often their adventures were cut short by the heavy attacks of the British RAF, but hiding in the tunnels and shelters made them feel invincible. Life was for living after all, as his mother had always told him.

Chapter Eight

POZZUOLI, 1941

Annunziata was so relieved to receive Carlo's letters. At least he was safe and was being fed. She replied, with Ninuccia writing her letters for her. She told him the family were all well and they were managing fine without him. She told him Nonna Minicuccia and Nonno Vincenzo had left their home at the port and were living with them. It was better they were all together.

She told him young Vincenzo was helping his father in the evenings in the workshop. 'Carlo, he's just like you when you were four. Do you remember helping Papà?' And Ninuccia was helping in the *farmacia*. The family had taken over his duties, but it didn't mean she didn't miss him. None of them could sing or make her laugh like Carlo.

What she didn't tell him was that life in Pozzuoli had become unimaginable. The beautiful bay was crammed with warships and submarines. The water that had been so beautiful and crystal clear was murky and slimy with oil and grease. Food waste and effluent floated in the water, together with uncollected rubbish carelessly discarded. Rats brazenly ran along the seafront, gnawing on the fishermen's old ropes. Emboldened by the blackout, ravenous packs of wolves came down from the hills, prowling through the night, unchallenged.

Soldiers were everywhere. Annunziata kept the shutters closed all the time, hiding her girls indoors. The relentless threat of aircraft overhead kept them all constantly on alert. Planes meant bombs, and bombs meant homes smashed, broken drains and

72

roads destroyed. Many buildings around them had disappeared, ancient buildings that had stood for centuries and survived earthquakes were reduced to piles of rubble and dust. When people were trapped beneath there was no one to help. The men were all away or in the factories. Old women and children had to scrabble as best they could to attempt to rescue the trapped people. Often there was nothing they could do to save them.

The family stopped even trying to sleep at home. Before the curfew at sundown they would all go down into the tunnels along with the rest of the town. Huddled in the dark, close together to keep safe, ignoring the noise, the crying, the rats, the cockroaches, all to keep away from the bombs.

Gradually, the town shut down.

The schools were closed; there were no teachers. The churches were boarded up; the priests had gone. The shutters of shops were drawn down; there was nothing to sell. The food queues were longer, the rations less. The chickens stopped laying eggs, so they ate the chickens. The farmer's crops were destroyed, the fishermen were even banned from fishing.

To feed her family Annunziata had to be very resourceful. She added more water to her soup. There was no flour, so she bought polenta. She used beans, lentils and pulses, using wild garlic and herbs for flavour. She evaporated seawater to make salt. She grew plants on her balcony. She ate less herself to nourish her growing children.

One evening, when he came back from the factory, Annunziata noticed Luigi's hand was very red.

'Luigi, what's wrong? Have you hurt yourself?'

He hid his hand in his jacket pocket, 'It's nothing.' But over the next few days his hand became swollen. Annunziata made a poultice with her bread ration and secured it onto his hand with rags to try to reduce the swelling: they had no money for a doctor. Luigi still insisted it was nothing and went to work as usual.

A few days later, the *direttore* himself noticed the rag on Luigi's hand. He was still aware how difficult it was for Luigi with Carlo away.

'Luigi, it looks bad. Go to the infirmary now. I'll make sure Ansaldo pays the bill.'

After a long wait sitting in a room packed with wounded civilians – mothers with children crying, youngsters with bound heads, broken legs, cut faces – Luigi's hand was X-rayed. He returned home ashen-faced, with his whole arm bandaged.

'Luigi, what's happened?' Annunziata went towards him.

'The *direttore* sent me to the infirmary. It turns out I had an iron splinter in my hand. It was poisoned. They've cut it open and removed it. I'm so lucky, Anunziata. I could have lost my arm.'

Luigi didn't lose his arm; but he lost his job. His insurance pay-out was a mere quarter of his wage; now life was even more austere.

Annunziata started to visit the pawnbroker. Not that she had much to pawn – the frame that held the picture of Carlo's first Communion, the cabinet Carlo had made for her, the radio . . .

She did her best to keep the family's spirits up, but she was beginning to lose hope.

*

In Genoa, the war raged on. The air attacks continued unabated but so far there had been no direct hits on the factory. Carlo had not heard from his mother for a few weeks, and although he kept sending letters as he had promised he was starting to become concerned.

He had heard from a Neapolitan who had recently arrived in the factory that the situation in Naples and Pozzuoli was tragic. He was sick with worry. He felt so helpless.

One day, he was called into the *capitano*'s office. 'This is it,' he thought, 'I'm going to get bad news from home.'

'Carlo, I hear you've worked with wood before, haven't you? Do you know, by any chance, how to do French polishing?'

Carlo was taken aback. 'Yes sir, it was my first job.'

Obviously he didn't want to tell him he had learned when he was seven years old, working for an undertaker polishing coffins. Always best be economical with the truth.

'Excellent! I have a piece of furniture I found in the street, you know, a small cabinet. Come and see it and tell me what you think you can do. I'm getting married. I want to give my *fidanzata* a gift.'

Carlo had a look at the piece. It was a good-quality cabinet. His *capitano* must have found it in a good-quality ruin!

The *capitano* listed what he wanted done.

'The legs need repairing, the drawer is cracked, here, look. It needs new handles; the surface is all scratched. It's a big job. What do you think? Can you fix it?'

Carlo didn't comment. He put his finger to the side of his nose and tapped it twice.

'Leave it to me, *Capitano*. I'll see what I can do.'

Carlo found a small space in the back of the factory and, 'borrowing' the tools he needed, set to work. Every evening, after his meal, he went back to the factory and worked on the unit, sanding it down, mending the drawers, repairing the handles. He had noticed an old woodwork shop by the port so went there on his day off. The old man sitting outside with nothing to do was happy to give Carlo the spirits he needed to make the polish in exchange for a couple of packets of cigarettes.

In exactly seven days Carlo called on the *capitano* after work. 'Come with me, sir. Your cabinet is ready.'

The *capitano* couldn't believe his eyes. The cabinet was fully restored, all the details were replaced and best of all, it was shining and polished so highly that he could see his reflection in it.

'Carlo! You're amazing. My *fidanzata* will be so happy! Oh, I'm going to be very popular tonight!'

He gave Carlo five lire, more than Carlo had ever had in his entire life. He realised for the first time the advantage of being in the north of Italy. It looked like they had more money than sense!

Carlo had learned from Nonno Vincenzo that you should always wait until someone is in your debt before asking for a favour. 'It's all to do with timing, Carlo. If you already have them in your debt, they find it far more difficult to refuse!'

'I wonder, with respect, *Capitano*, if I could ask a favour of you?'

'Anything, Carlo, anything.'

The *capitano* had already found another piece of furniture he wanted Carlo to repair.

'If I grant him his favour,' he thought to himself, 'Carlo will be in my debt and he will help me again.'

Carlo had anticipated this and smiled. 'I've got him,' he thought, and made his move.

*

Luigi's hand wasn't healing. It had become infected and only Annunziata's bread poultice every night had stopped it getting worse. It was hard to use the bread for this when there was so little left to eat.

Zia Francesca and her husband Zio Paolo decided to leave.

'We're going to go to Napoli to see if it's any better there. We'll send for the grandparents if we can. It surely can't be as bad as here.'

This was a blow. Annunziata felt she didn't know how she would be able to manage. The girls had to stand in queues all morning, waiting to buy their rations of black, dry bread. Often by the time they got to the front of the queue there was none left.

Annunziata went with young Vincenzo every day searching for food. She went around Luigi's old customers: a lot of them still owed favours. They gave what they could – a handful of corn, a potato, an onion. She went to the grocer to ask for a loan.

'Sorry, Annunziata, you owe too much already. Maybe next week.'

She was mortified to be refused.

She went with the girls down to the seaside with a piece of wood and scraped through the sand as the tide went out. Nearly all the women in the town were doing the same thing. If they were lucky, sometimes they got a few clams or grabbed a few soft-shell crabs before they scuttled away.

Hunger became a habit. Annunziata's milk ran dry; she could no longer earn a bit of extra food as a wet nurse.

In the mornings, she'd leave Ernesto with her mother and go up into the hills behind Pozzuoli with Ninuccia and Rosetta. She taught them to collect herbs and roots, and to gather any fruit they could find. Sometimes they'd come across a shepherd with a few sheep. She'd ask for some milk and let the girls drink it there and then, like manna in the wilderness.

She couldn't even get Ninuccia to help her write to Carlo any more. She had no paper, never mind a spare *centesimo* for a stamp.

They were starving. They were not alone. The whole town was starving.

They even became immune to the air raids. Weakened by hunger, they simply stayed at home at night, unable to summon the energy to run to the tunnels. Annunziata and Luigi were at their wits' end. What on earth could they do?

Annunziata just prayed, trying to believe beyond every doubt and temptation that the Lord would look after them.

One night, she was so hungry she couldn't even sleep. She began to really despair.

'*Madonna, aiutami.* Help me.' Shaking her head, she covered her face in her hands, weeping silently. 'Maybe it would be better if a bomb dropped on us so we could be given peace at last.'

With this thought she fell into a fitful sleep.

In her dream she imagined a familiar sound. It reminded her of Carlo whistling. She felt a pang. If only she could see her son. Then she heard it again, louder this time. She was woken from her stupor by the sound of young Vincenzo shouting.

'I hear Carlo! It's my brother!'

The girls awoke and ran to the window, pulling back the black-out sacking. Vincenzo pushed between them and climbed on the shelf, reaching up to be able to see.

'Mamma! *Vieni!* Come! *Guarda!* Look, it *is* Carlo. *Veramente!*'

Annunziata pulled herself up and went to look out of the window.

The children jumped down and pushed past their mother, running full speed down the steps.

'Ma! Mamma!'

She wasn't dreaming. There he was. Carlo! It was her son, standing at the bottom of the piazza in a shaft of moonlight, her own Carlo strong, handsome and smiling, waving up to her and whistling.

'Mamma!' his voice cracked. The girls and Vincenzo arrived down and ran into his arms, laughing and shouting with delight. A policeman ran across shouting aggressively, 'Get indoors! Get indoors!'

No one heeded him. They were oblivious to everything except one fact.

Carlo had come home.

*

The favour Carlo had asked from his *capitano* was a week's pass to go home. It was unheard-of in the factory.

The following morning at work everyone was asking where Carlo was … he had already gone. He had planned this all week when he had been working on the cabinet; he knew exactly what he needed to do.

First thing in the morning he had gone down to the docks. He had already found out where the stores for the Italian navy were being loaded onto the ships. Here there was a good black market; with cash, you could buy anything you needed. He spent an hour dealing, dodging and paying with the money he had saved from his allowance and the lire the *capitano* had given him.

He bought as much as he could carry home. His sisters had given him half their rations; he would pay them back tenfold.

After a long train journey during which the other passengers were wondering where the beautiful smell of bread and cheese and *mortadella* was coming from, it was dusk by the time he arrived in Pozzuoli. Now, with his brothers and sisters running around his legs as excited as a flock of spring lambs, Carlo ran up the 178 steps to his mother.

He was shocked. His mother was so tiny, thin and gaunt. He saw his youngest sisters thin and pale, eyes wide with dark circles, black smudges in their sallow faces. Their clothes were tattered and patched, their hair shaved, their feet bare. Vincenzo looked like a street urchin. Ernesto, barely three years old, was listless and weak.

His father had become old since he'd left. His trousers were hanging on his braces, his unshaven face was stippled with grey stubble.

Luigi explained what had happened to his hand and that he had no work. Carlo had had no idea how bad things had become. He felt devastated.

'Mamma, why didn't you tell me how bad things were?'

His mother looked at Luigi. She thrust her chin out, her mouth down, her hands open. *'Non c'e niente da fare!* We manage as best we can. We were waiting for you, Carlo. We knew you'd come home.'

That night in their ramshackle room with the window left open to allow the moonlight to stream in, the stars scattering hope over the blacked-out town, they had a midnight feast, a feast like they had never had in their lives before or would ever have again.

They were 13 in all including Carlo, safe together: Annunziata, Luigi, Ninuccia, Rosetta, Annetta, Antonietta, Vincenzo, Ernesto and the four *nonni*.

Carlo looked at each one lovingly. How he'd missed them.

'Favorit,' Luigi beckoned with his cupped hand and scooped the air. *'Favorit,* Carlo, *siediti qui Figlio mio,* you sit here, *vicino a me.'* He motioned to his son to sit at the head of the table and he sat at his right-hand side. Vincenzo climbed up and sat on his father's knee next to his older brother, anxious not to let him out of his sight.

Carlo sat with the parcels of food in front of him and shared it out among his loved ones.

The smell of the cheese and the bread, and the salami and the coffee would never be so intense again. It filled their senses, imprinted survival and hope on their souls like the Blessed Sacrament itself.

He had found dried figs, anchovies, pine nuts, Genovese *trofie*, little rolls of pasta like squint cigars. He had olive oil and fresh lemons and big juicy pears. He had *torta di ceci*, a white grease-proof paper with two dripping slices of *focaccia al formaggio*, tiny juicy black olives and a stinky piece of dried cod. To crown it all he unzipped the side of his jacket and brought out a pack of cigarettes, a *fiasco* of Chianti and, finally, a bottle of Anisetta!

Carlo had brought enough food to fill their stomachs for the first time in months, enough food to save their lives.

There were really only small amounts of food – scraps of this, slices of that – but in their minds it was the feast of feasts, forever the meal to compare all meals to, the meal they would dream of re-creating, the meal that in all their lifetimes was always remembered as the best.

Carlo looked at his mother, 'Mamma, you were right. We should live for the day; there can always be a better one tomorrow.'

*

After a further six months' training in Genoa, Carlo was eventually billeted back to the factory in Pozzuoli. He had managed to save up a good amount of money by continuing to do furniture repairs and woodwork for the officers. They were disappointed to see him go.

'Enterprising lad, that Neapolitan. He'll go places.'

Carlo was sad to leave as well. Apart from the war raging all around them, he and his comrades had really enjoyed themselves. They had made new friends and experienced a very different, more sophisticated, way of life, one with more order and structure. They saw opportunities that were simply not available in the south.

This time returning to Pozzuoli he felt so different from the young boy who had left, what now seemed like a lifetime ago. He was proud of how he had coped. He had exceeded his own expectations.

The adventure had given him an appetite for more.

Leaving Genoa, the young men were shaken at the extent of the devastation and destruction they witnessed. They really hadn't understood how much danger they had been in.

'Egidio, look at all that. There are areas completely flattened by the bombing. I didn't realise what was happening.'

'We're lucky we survived,' Egidio laughed nervously.

Carlo was thoughtful. 'After the war, I'm coming back. I could make a life as a carpenter here, even start a business. With all this destruction there'll be plenty of work.'

'I'll come with you, Carlo. Or we might go to Torino. Ansaldo have a factory there as well, or we could join F.I.A.T. and build cars. We'll find nice girls and settle down.'

'*Ma, che sei pazzo?* Are you mad? A nice girl? Not for me. I'm a *gigolo*! A *scugnizzo*! No woman is going to get her hands on me!' Carlo had no ambitions to find a girl, nice or otherwise, and absolutely no ambition to settle down. He'd seen all the trouble that caused. He wanted his freedom. He had a taste for adventure. After the war, he was going to make his own way. After the war, he was going to conquer the world!

When Annunziata spotted the tall, very handsome, confident young man stepping down from the train she hardly recognised her son. Her heart filled with pride. She was relieved for Luigi as well. He was back at work but his hand was still not fully healed. They were very short of money and always short of food. How could one person earn enough to feed them all? It would be a great relief to have Carlo's wage coming in again.

She was also reassured Carlo was home to protect his sisters. Pozzuoli was extremely dangerous for them now. The military were everywhere. When the soldiers were hanging around in the alleyways the girls were terrified to go out. There were terrible reports of young girls being attacked, even abducted. Having Carlo home would bring good fortune to their household again.

Good fortune arrived even sooner than Annunziata had hoped for. As soon as he attended his first shift at the factory he was called to the *direttore*'s office.

'Well done, Carlo. I've had an excellent report from Genoa. You've made a great success of your training. You have the very skills we need. You'll receive a higher wage with immediate effect, which will help your family, I'm sure. This is yours. Well done.' He handed Carlo an envelope and offered his hand to shake.

'By the way, I've heard you're good at repairing furniture. I happened to find a small sideboard in the street. I was wondering …?'

As soon as he left the office Carlo opened the envelope. Inside was a cheque for an unusually large sum of money. Included was a statement explaining this was an accumulation of back payment of accrued allowances: for being away from his family, for training away from home and a bonus for completing his training. Having lived all his life from hand to mouth, Carlo had never even imagined he would get paid, or paid so handsomely.

When he went home that night not only could he give his mother a welcome windfall, they could celebrate that his new salary was now three times the standard rate. They could afford to put food on the table again. If they could find it.

Chapter Nine

Sometimes when terrible news breaks it is impossible to believe it. It is so implausible, so unexpected, it is rejected as fabrication, propaganda, fake. When the truth emerges the shock can be physically debilitating. Since the start of the war the situation had been extremely traumatic for the Italian women living in Scotland. Through no fault of their own they had become enemy aliens, trapped in a foreign country, treated with suspicion. Their menfolk had been taken from them, their lives had been destroyed.

Sitting alone in the front room of the flat in Brunton Place Maria, Alfonso Crolla's widow, was tormented by her thoughts. Dwelling on the dreadful events that had overtaken her life, she considered how in a moment you can lose control of your destiny.

For the rest of her days, such thoughts persisted and robbed her of her peace of mind. If only they had been somewhere else; had never emigrated to Scotland. But then her sons would have been in the Italian army and might not have survived. If only Mussolini had chosen a different path. But then the boys would have been called to fight in the British army. That could have been even worse. If only Churchill had not instructed the police to 'collar the lot', Alfonso would surely still be alive.

Her thoughts returned to 10 June 1940, the day they had heard the awful news that Italy had declared war on Britain. She remembered it was a Monday, a normal, everyday, common Monday that had ruined her life and the lives of her family and her community. How could she ever forget?

She had been working in the café in Easter Road, just a short walk along the road from their grocery shop on Elm Row. Her three young daughters, Olivia, Gloria and Phyllis, had been with her. The shop had been quiet, unusually so. Even though the weather had been lovely there hadn't been many customers. That should have been a clue. She should have realised something was wrong. She set the girls jobs to keep them busy: dusting the shelves, polishing the mirrors, filling the sweetie jars.

Alfonso had told her that they were expecting to hear news about Italy's position in the war any day now, but said she was not to worry. Britain was at war against Germany, but till now Italy had not been involved.

'Maria, Italy fought with the British, we are allies. I should know, I fought side by side with them in the last war. Il Duce will never take up arms against our friends.'

'Oh, Alfonso, I pray all the time that you're right. Could you bear it if our boys were called up to fight? They're shopkeepers, not soldiers.'

Maria had thought about this a lot. Poor Domenico had had glandular fever when he was a child. He had frequent bouts of illness and would surely not be accepted into any army. Vittorio had a weak leg and a slight limp. For the first time she was pleased her sons had small defects. As for Alfonso, he was too old now and, to be honest, she smiled affectionately to herself, a bit out of condition.

She reassured herself, she convinced herself that her menfolk were no use to any army and whatever happened they would all be left at home with her. Alfonso had told her to put it out of her mind, not to expect bad news. He was involved with the Italian consulate and the Edinburgh local councillors. If anybody had an idea of what was going to happen, it would be him. He wouldn't have let her open the shop and have the girls beside her if he had been concerned. He would have kept them at home, surely? Some of her Italian friends and relations had already left the country and returned to Italy. If he had had any concerns he would unquestionably have taken them all away and gone back to Italy.

As it turned out, by the time she had convinced herself her family was safe, it was too late. Already a mob of hooligans had swept down Leith Walk, smashing up all the Italian shops along the way. Then they came into the café and destroyed everything in front of her eyes; splintered the shelves, smashed the mirrors, shattered the sweetie jars. They pulled her and the girls out into the street and she stood with her arms around them, helpless. The street was crowded, jam-packed with the angry mob. She couldn't move to escape and had to stand among them with her young daughters, terrified, watching as the thugs ruined her livelihood.

It wasn't until then that Alfonso, Domenico and Vittorio arrived from Elm Row, dishevelled and distressed, obviously very shocked, unbelieving of what had taken place. That was the moment she heard the news she had been dreading: Italy *had* declared war on Britain. That was the moment that remained etched on her mind, when it really was all too late.

She could never forget the look on her husband's face. Her darling Alfonso was crying, holding her in his arms and weeping. Vittorio and Domenico embraced their sisters, trying helplessly to reassure them.

'Maria, *carissima, mi dispiace*,' Alfonso sobbed. 'I am so sorry, forgive me. You were right. You were right after all. Our Duce has betrayed us. He has deceived all of Italy. *Bugiardo!* He's a liar!'

Her poor husband, her dear Alfonso. He had put all his faith in Mussolini; he had been convinced by the rhetoric and propaganda that Il Duce was a force for good, that he was the leader to make his beloved Italy great. Maria had argued with him, pleaded with him, but he had not listened.

Now Alfonso understood the dreadful truth: Mussolini had duped them all. That very night Alfonso, Vittorio and Domenico were not called to fight for the Italian army as they expected. They were arrested by the British Government as enemy aliens and imprisoned. How could any of them know that they would never see Alfonso again after that fateful day? How could any of them guess that he would be deported with his friend Cesidio Di Ciacca and so many of his compatriots, and that the next news they would hear, weeks later, was that they had both drowned as the prisoner ship, the *Arandora Star*, sank in the North Sea on its way to Canada?

Maria's thoughts were interrupted by the sound of the key turning in the front door. She heard voices.

Olivia came into the room, quietly.

'Mum, Mum. Are you awake?' Maria opened her eyes and looked around.

Olivia was just 19 years old, tall and slim, perhaps a bit too thin. Her skin was flawless, smooth and clear with an olive complexion. Her large dusky eyes had a melancholy air about them which always saddened Maria to see. Her thick, glossy black hair was cut fashionably short, framing her face and enhancing her beautiful neck. Her father used to call her *Capa Nera* because of her lovely hair.

'She is such a beauty,' Maria thought.

Gloria, Olivia's younger sister, came into the living room behind Olivia, smiling broadly.

'Gloria, what is it?'

'Mum! It's wonderful news. You'll never guess who's here.'

Maria tried to stand up to greet the visitor. When she realised who it was standing at the door she fell back into her chair, shocked.

It was her friend Marietta Di Ciacca's eldest son, Johnny. She hadn't seen him since the start of the war.

'Johnny,' she took a deep breath and tried to compose herself. She stood up again and, moving across the room to embrace him, burst into tears. 'Oh Johnny. It's so good to see you, so good.'

She had thought Johnny was still interned on the Isle of Man with her sons Vittorio and Domenico. He had been there since he had been arrested, the same night her own menfolk had been taken three years ago now. He was the last person she had expected to see.

'Come and sit down. Come and sit down. Are you hungry? Get a drink. Gloria, get some drinks for Johnny. Make some tea. Have we got any coconut cake? Any shortbread?'

Anna was with her brother. She kissed Maria and sat down beside Johnny, not wanting to be too far away from him. Everyone settled around the large sitting room as near to their friend as possible, Maria sitting bolt upright now, alert.

85

'Tell me, Johnny. Are Vittorio and Domenico with you? Are they home too?'

'No, not yet, Zia, but they're both safe and well. They told me to come as soon as I arrived to let you know. They'll be released soon too, I'm sure.'

Maria looked confused.

'Mum, have you not heard the news?' Olivia sat beside her mother.

'No, what news? What's happened?

'Mussolini has surrendered. Italy has surrendered. We're no longer enemies of Great Britain.'

Johnny looked dazed rather than elated. 'I still can't believe it. After everything that has happened, he has surrendered.'

Maria blessed herself. She spoke very quietly.

'So, Italy's lost. It was all for nothing. It was all for nothing.' She shook her head, trying to absorb the implications.

Johnny came across and put his arms around her. He had tears in his eyes.

'I know, Zia. I understand. But we need to look to the future. It's good news. I was released last week. They knew this was going to be announced so a few of us have already been sent home.'

'What about Vittorio and Domenico? Do you know when they'll be out? Oh, I can't believe it. Does this mean my boys will be coming home?'

The girls were quiet, listening, grabbing any morsels of information they could. They had heard so little from their brothers over the last three years: a few letters, one telephone call. Every word from Johnny appeased the drought of news that had tortured them every day.

Johnny looked surprisingly well. He was much thinner then they remembered, and older. He looked like a man now, not the boy they recalled from the start of the war. It was a strange sensation, realising how they had missed three years of his life, and he theirs.

He was very handsome: tall, with dark curly hair over a broad forehead and a very attractive, wide smile. His brown eyes had a soft tenderness, already wrinkled with smile lines. He caught

Olivia staring at him, making her blush. Anna noticed the look.

'What age are you now, Johnny?' Maria had seen it too, and took note. Johnny would be a nice boy for her daughter.

Anna answered for him. 'He's nearly twenty-four, Zia Maria. He looks good doesn't he!' Johnny laughed. It was so good to be back amongst his friends.

'My Vittorio is twenty-five; Domenico twenty-eight. You're all young men now.'

'I know. We had a birthday party for Domenico before I was released.'

'Were you allowed to have birthday parties?' Olivia was amazed. The women knew nothing about conditions in the internment camp, but she had never imagined they would have birthday parties.

'You know, we were lucky really. It wasn't all that bad. It was sparse and well-guarded, but they left us more or less to our own devices. We had to keep the place clean, do our own washing, all that stuff. Best of all, we had to cook for ourselves. Zia, you'd have to laugh. The chefs in the kitchens were all the Italian chefs from the top hotels in London and Edinburgh. We had some good food, I can tell you. At least they knew how to season things.'

'What do you mean?' Olivia asked.

'When we first arrived we were given macaroni. I've never tasted anything like it! It was just boiled in water, no salt, and boiled till it tasted like porridge! We were really starving so of course we were glad of it. Once the chefs took over and started cooking it was a great relief.'

Maria squeezed his hand.

'Johnny, I'm so sorry about your father. Poor Cesidio and Alfonso – who would have imagined we would lose them both? I'll never understand it. It must have been so hard hearing you had lost your father while you were in the camp.'

Johnny was quiet. So many of the boys in the camp had lost their fathers; hundreds of them.

'Oh Zia. I am so sorry for you all as well. Zio Alfonso was always so good to us.'

They waited. He knew things about Alfonso and his father, Cesidio, and what had happened when they had all been arrested.

They had learned not to ask questions of the bereaved, to wait until they wanted to say something. It was as if their pain was easier to bear if it was kept private, not shared, repeated and diluted in other people's minds.

'Zia, you can imagine. We were all devastated. It's hard to talk about it. I know you want to know more. I've tried to share with my mother too, but …'

He fell silent, lost in his thoughts. He tried again; it was his duty to let them know something.

'We were so fortunate, Zia. We were all together, in a big hall. They were on a stage, British army officers. They read out the names to the whole camp, names of the men who had drowned. We didn't even know they had been on a ship till an hour or two before. We didn't even know that *one* had died, never mind over four hundred.'

Johnny's face was pale. He looked at Olivia. Anna held his hand. He knew it had been terrible for them as well. His mother had told him what they had been through.

'It was hideous.' He felt his anger rising. He took a drink of the whisky Gloria had set in front of him. He took a deep, sobbing breath. 'They just told us the *Arandora Star* had gone down and the following prisoners had drowned. Then they just started reading out names. We were all standing there, we could hardly hear, and they started reading out names in alphabetical order.'

He didn't want to say any more. He looked at his aunt.

'So, we just stood there and waited through the alphabet hoping our fathers' names were not going to be read out. I was with Vittorio and Domenico when we heard Zio Alfonso's name. I couldn't say anything to them. I was just waiting till the names beginning with D were read out.' Johnny went quiet. It had been horrendous. He was looking at Vittorio when he heard 'Alfonso Crolla' read out. Vittorio looked back at him, his eyes wide with terror. He told Johnny later that he was devastated to hear that his father had drowned, but looking at his friend waiting till the names starting with D were read, he was just praying that Johnny's father was not on the list, praying that his friend would not have to feel the pain that was tearing through his own body.

Johnny wanted to lighten the load for the women. He didn't

tell them about the dreadful horror and fear that they had endured. He couldn't tell them about it, and never would, not even when he was an old man with grandchildren of his own.

The subject was changed and some tea and pizza were served.

'Thank you for coming, Johnny. I'm so glad to see you.' Maria was still holding his hand, afraid that if she didn't actually feel him he would disappear. 'So, you really think my boys will be released soon?'

'I'm sure they will be. They have no right to hold us any more. They told Domenico he would be out first. He's been a bit poorly with his chest.'

'And Vittorio?'

'Not yet, but soon. Definitely soon.' He was not sure why he had been released first. Maybe because he was from Cockenzie, not the city. He knew the local policeman had kept writing to the authorities to support his application for release. He had been born in Italy and was an Italian citizen, but Alex, his younger brother, had been born in Scotland. Although Alex was arrested along with Johnny and their father, once the police had established this he was released. He had ended up serving in the RAF for most of the war, even though he was younger than Johnny. Maybe that was why Johnny was home now.

Anna tried to ease her *zia*'s concerns. 'Johnny's still under Home Office control. He has to work in the fields with me in Haddington.' She had been working in the Women's Land Army for the last two years. 'I'll have to teach him how to howk tatties.'

'What's that?' Gloria didn't know what her friend was talking about.

'Dig up potatoes. You're too posh for that, Gloria, but I'm a country lass and it doesn't bother me.'

'You're the most glamorous "tattie howker" I've ever seen,' Gloria laughed. Anna was always very stylish, and nothing like a country lass.

Once Maria had gone to bed, the young ones talked late into the night.

'So, Johnny, now that Italy has surrendered, what are they saying will happen? Will the Germans surrender next?' Olivia was desperate for news.

'I doubt it. The German prisoners-of-war we came across in the camp were different from us. They still believe in it, in their great plan.'

The girls were quiet. They were still afraid.

'Are you sure Domenico and Vittorio will be coming home soon?' Olivia was almost afraid to ask.

'I'm sure, I'm sure, there's no reason why not.' Johnny didn't want to reveal that he didn't know anything, and there was still no certainty for any of them.

Chapter Ten

While events took a turn for the better in Edinburgh, life in Pozzuoli was continuing more precariously than ever as the war raged around them. Almost two years had passed since Carlo's return from Genoa, and although the family had more access to money because of his wage rise, there were still severe food shortages and continual bombing raids. It was a daily struggle to survive. They too were desperately hoping for news that would result in a change for the better.

One day, in mid-July, Carlo had come back from the factory with snippets of conversation and rumours from the officers who hung about the coffee shop. The news was good. At last the Allies had invaded Sicily. Rather than being frightened or disappointed, the family were overjoyed. Surely if the British had landed, then maybe the end of the war was in sight.

Regrettably, it was not going to be that easy. As the reports from Sicily became more frequent, so did the bombing raids. The war was coming closer and was even more terrible than before. As the summer progressed, the situation rapidly deteriorated.

In a strategy to break lines of supply, the German army was systematically destroying the infrastructure of cities, roads and bridges. All medical support and medicines were being diverted to the army. Zia Francesca sent a message to warn them there were outbreaks of typhoid in Naples. The hospitals were full but there were no medical staff. The population had been abandoned, left to their own devices.

In Pozzuoli, without warning, the authorities had relinquished all responsibilities and simply unlocked the doors of the home for delinquent boys. Hundreds of neglected youngsters were left wandering the streets in rags, starving and abandoned. They brought with them an epidemic of lice and an increased risk of the spread of disease.

Food supplies collapsed; there was barely anything to purchase and what there was had hundreds of people scrabbling for it. Inflation was inordinately high, the lira lost almost all value. Each day Annunziata and Ninuccia went down to the piazza to wait with the crowds of emaciated women and children, desperate to get hold of any food they could for their families. Often, they had to return with nothing. Annunziata was distraught. She thought of the babies she had lost to pneumonia and bronchitis: when winter came her children would surely start to die. She looked at Vincenzo and Ernesto, their beautiful faces gaunt, their limbs wasted. She could not bear it if she lost them. This couldn't go on, surely?

It was on 25 July that Carlo came running up the stairs and into the room calling to his father.

'*Papà! Papà!* At last. *Grazie a Dio. Il Duce è finito.*'

'What do you mean? Is he dead? Have they killed him?'

'No, but just as good: the king has removed him from power and the police have arrested him.'

Annunziata beat her hands against her chest. She bent her head and, for the first time since the day Carlo had left to go to Genoa, she wept inconsolably. Mussolini had ruined her life. He had starved her children and stolen her husband's health. Finally, no more! No more from Il Duce!

A few weeks later, when Carlo and Luigi went to the factory as usual, they found a huge crowd congregated outside; the entire workforce, the managers, even the *direttore* himself.

The gates of the factory were locked and a sign had been haphazardly stuck on the front.

'*E FINITO. 8 SETTEMBRE 1943*'

The *direttore* climbed up on a bench and addressed them all.

'*Amici miei! Bravi Italiani! È finito!* Italy has surrendered. It's over! Go home, my friends. Go home to your women. Go home

92

to your daughters. Don't waste a moment. Good luck to you all. God go with you.'

A cheer went up in the crowd, drowning out the noise of the bells ringing. Carlo looked at his father. Luigi was alarmed: Annunziata was alone at home with the family. 'Carlo, you go ahead, quickly, run. I'll follow.' They embraced. Without glancing back, Carlo ran, dodging between the crowds of men rushing from the factory gates.

Annunziata was shocked when he arrived home, breathless and sweating. The girls all ran towards him. Vincenzo and Ernesto sat on the bed beside their grandparents, hugging them, confused by the commotion.

'We've surrendered. They've closed the factory; they've halted production.'

'Surrendered to whom?' Annunziata was confused. 'Who has surrendered?'

Luigi arrived just then, out of breath after struggling up the steps. Annunziata turned to him.

'Luigi, is that it? Is the war over?'

They had lived in confusion and mayhem for so long. It had seemed impossible that their beloved country should have aligned with Hitler and be fighting against their former allies. Everyone knew the Italian soldiers' hearts had not been in the war. It had never been their war.

'We have surrendered to the Allies. Already our soldiers are disbanding,' Luigi said, trying not to alarm them. He took Annunziata and Carlo aside and lowered his voice. 'I saw Italian uniforms discarded all along the sides of the road. But the Germans haven't surrendered. They are our enemy now, and they will be enraged we have deserted them. They'll be at their most dangerous. We need to stay altogether. We need to protect the girls.' He looked across at his four young daughters. 'Things are going to get much worse.'

The town was still full of German soldiers. They had been arrogant and aggressive but apart from hanging around the women, they had not caused any real harm. That was all about to change.

That night it felt as if all the combined power of the Allies was being unleashed on Pozzuoli and Naples. Bombs rained down incessantly, falling on the port, the factory, Rione Terra, illuminating the sky as if Vesuvius herself had erupted. The family huddled together in the overcrowded railway tunnel not daring to close an eye, as terrified of the crowd around them as much as of the bombs falling outside.

The next night the sirens started again, sounding even more urgent. The church bells rang out too. Everyone ran into the streets. Wave upon wave of RAF planes flew over, focused on destroying what remained of the jewel of the Italian fleet anchored in the Bay of Pozzuoli to prevent it falling into the hands of the Germans.

The Italian army had been demobilised, told to go home to look after their own families. The soldiers slipped away, hiding in the hills, making their way back. The Italian police force ceased to exist. There was no one left to protect the people.

The bombing was relentless. Houses were destroyed all around them, neighbours were killed. The water fountain was blown up. The church belltower collapsed.

There were no supplies at all. The rations that were allocated never appeared. They spent every day in a desperate search for food, anything to eat. They had suffered before, but nothing had prepared them for this. If they were not crushed under rubble or infected with disease, they would surely starve to death.

Annunziata and Ninuccia got up early every morning and stood in queues for hours, hoping for a single handful of polenta, a piece of black bread, an apple. But the queues dispersed before they reached the front as whatever food there was had already gone. What little money they had saved was used up in no time on the black market. More than ever, life became just a fight to survive.

No work, no food, no water, no soap, no security. And still a dozen mouths to feed.

Food supplies had been scarce from the start of the year, but there had always been a few people from the country coming with a few crops in season: some oranges, a few eggs, some pecorino.

Now no one came.

94

Carlo and his sisters scavenged in the bombed-out houses searching for discarded food – a few handfuls of rice, a half-empty bottle of wine, the dregs of a bottle of oil. They gathered anything they could find – old rags, lost shoes, pieces of leather. The departing Italian soldiers were abandoning their uniforms; they collected those as well.

The fishermen were still forbidden to fish, even during the day. They went out anyway, further away from the port but always in danger of being shot. Carlo would hang around the port waiting to see if he could buy anything from them.

Carlo and his sisters went down to the shore and walked as far from the port as they could, away from the German snipers. As the tide went out, following the seabirds that probed in the sand, they raked for clams, whelks and long razor clams. They were so hungry they would prize them open and eat them there and then, sweet and fresh, like nectar. Carlo used to do this for fun when he was a young boy; now he was doing it simply to survive.

Carlo would climb along the rocks and dive for sea urchins and *lumache*, snails, anything that moved. With Vincenzo and his sisters helping him he'd fill some baskets and take them to the one or two restaurants that were still open on the seafront. These were full of German officers now, some unsavoury women and officials of the government. Those types were always well fed.

They would go to the restaurant back doors and in exchange for the shellfish the chefs would give Carlo some money and some supplies: polenta, pulses, flour. Annunziata was grateful for anything they could find. She tried to be philosophical: 'If you don't have it, you don't need it.'

She knew the children were in pain with hunger. Her belly ached as well. She watched helpless as they became emaciated. How long could they go on like this? When would this all stop?

Scouring the hills behind the town brought scant rewards. Abandoned farmhouses occasionally revealed surprises: a scattering of brown fruit under a tree, an abandoned plant behind a shed, shrivelled tomatoes drying on withered stalks, some nuts, wild plants or *funghi* Annunziata could use to make soup.

Anything that didn't poison them nourished them. Hunger was now the enemy, typhoid and dysentery the threat, loss of hope the killer.

The Germans started to take control. They had no goodwill towards any Italians. The first instruction that caused serious alarm was a demand that everyone must register and carry a special ID card, with immediate effect.

Annunziata was dismayed. 'Carlo, I just saw some Germans in the street stopping a group of men. They were checking ID cards and making anyone they liked the look of get into a van. They're arresting all the strong young men.'

Carlo was eighteen now; he was very thin but he was tall and looked like a man, not a boy. He had been lucky so far, but how long could he rely on luck? Annunziata looked at her husband. Poor soul, he looked like an old man now. The Germans would not be interested in taking him. It was Carlo they would want.

Later that day Luigi came home panic-stricken.

'They're arresting all the men between eighteen and thirty-three. They're looking for Italian soldiers who're hiding among civilians and strong men to send to work camps.'

Carlo was petrified. He tried to put on a brave face but he had already heard that some of his friends had been arrested.

'Don't worry, Mamma. I'll make sure I keep out of the way. I know Rione Terra inside out. I know where to hide.'

They started a system of warnings, whistling to each other when they were moving around. They agree, as far as possible, that only Annunziata and the grandfathers would go out.

The late summer heat was unbearable. There were swarms of black flies and incessant mosquitos, biting and infecting them. Their room was infested with fleas. There was no sanitation, no running water; acrid smells of sulphur and burning were every-where.

The curfew was extended. No one was allowed out between 6 p.m. and 6 a.m. The Allied bombing was continuing with force but the people were now forbidden to run for shelter. They were simply shot if they were caught in the streets.

It was no longer safe to go to the railway tunnels anyway. They were full of people living there permanently, with constant

German patrols arresting any able-bodied men and abusing the women. So at night they tried to sleep at home as best they could, ignoring the explosions and the buildings shaking. If they died, they'd die together.

They heard from a friend that Francesca's husband, Paolo, had been arrested in Naples. She had no idea where he was being taken. Rumours suggested factories and prison camps in eastern Europe.

One day Ninuccia came home crying. She and Nonno Ernesto had been in a queue trying to get bread.

'The Germans stopped in a truck in the piazza. They asked to see all our papers. They just took any young men, dragged them onto the lorry, which was already half full of other men. They had guns, and ...' She went quiet.

'What? Ninuccia, tell me!' Annunziata demanded.

'The man in front tried to run away.' She started to cry again. 'They shot him. They just shot him in the back.'

Nonno Ernesto arrived soon after. 'Carlo, stay inside, whatever you do. There are checkpoints everywhere. It's no longer safe for you to go out at all.'

Carlo looked at his mother.

'Carlo you'll need to hide. We'll hide you. We'll keep you safe.'

Carlo spent the next few weeks hiding from the German soldiers who came around Rione Terra, shouting and banging on doors.

Carlo moved around and hid in discreet corners of *ngopp' 'a terra*, turning familiar corners and heading back to end up behind the soldiers so they couldn't find him. He remembered his tricks of hiding from Il Professore and laughed to himself, sardonically. He could never have imagined then what was happening now.

Finally, some good news arrived: the Allies had landed in Salerno and the invasion had begun on the mainland. Nonno Ernesto had fought with the British in the previous war.

'These are our true allies. This is the beginning of the end,' he tried to reassure the family. 'We just need to wait.'

Four days later Annunziata brought home a copy of a leaflet that was being posted on the walls all over the town. She couldn't read it but she had seen other women crying in front of it.

'What does it say?'

Carlo read it. 'It's from the new German commander of Napoli. He says it is compulsory that three thousand men report for work tomorrow.'

'Can you imagine? They think you are going to work for them?' Annunziata had never felt so angry. 'Work for them? They don't want you to work. They want to kill you. What a mess! What a waste! Mussolini, Il Duce? A proud fool, nothing else; only interested in his own skin, his own woman. Not even interested in his family.'

Annunziata was so overcome with rage, she lifted her only remaining plate and smashed it furiously against the wall. She was defiant.

'Germans, Nazis, they will *not* destroy my family!'

The next day was 23 September. A grey German truck drew up at the bottom of Rione Terra, just outside their window. Crouching at the balcony, they could hear an announcement from loud speakers.

'Today there will be a full evacuation of Pozzuoli and Rione Terra. All citizens of Pozzuoli must leave the town now and move at least fifteen kilometres away from the sea. All citizens must leave now. Quickly! *Forza! Schnell!*'

It was repeated in Italian, Neapolitan and German.

They looked at each other, confused. Luigi understood.

'This is it.' They all embraced. 'We have to leave.'

Annunziata looked around, shocked. Luigi took control. 'Come on. Quickly wrap what you can carry in sheets. Let's go. It can only be better than staying here. The war is nearly in Napoli now. It's time to go.'

They collected the few things they had, wrapped their clothes in torn sheets and tied them into bundles with pieces of string. They filled their coat pockets with their meagre food supplies, hardly enough to last a day.

'Carlo, put this old coat on. You need to walk bent over. If they notice you're taller than the rest of us they'll take you. Girls, rub mud on your cheeks, and look as grubby as possible. If we look dirty and diseased they'll leave us alone.'

Stunned, they filed out of the room.

Annunziata stopped at the door with Luigi. They looked back at the room that had witnessed their lives for the last 25 years. He embraced her.

'Luigi, do you think we'll ever come back here?'

He didn't answer. He didn't know.

They slowly made their way down the steps, barefoot, their clothes threadbare. With their worldly possessions in a few bundles on their heads, hand in hand they joined the long line of ragged families heading the same way.

'Where are we going, Carlo?' Vincenzo took his big brother's hand.

'We're going north, Vincenzo.' And under his breath, so he didn't frighten the boy, 'Towards Germany.'

*

Once they were clear of the town, Carlo carried Vincenzo on his shoulders, trailing behind the long straggle of dishevelled refugees. His father walked behind the girls, watching them carefully lest they were snatched. Ernesto and the grandparents were perched on the back of Zi' Alf's cart, among the bundles of their belongings. Tullio, Zi' Alf's youngest son, led the donkey, its head bent down, struggling to keep its footing on the broken road.

Annunziata, weakened from months of hunger, looked exhausted. Her face was gaunt, lines of worry creasing her parched skin. Her hair was faded and grey. She had borrowed scissors from Don Gennaro and cut their hair short. Try as she could, without soap or water how could she keep her family clean?

Her black dress was in rags, infested with lice and covered with dust. Her feet were wrapped in scraps of old rags bound with strips of leather round her calves. She pulled her tattered shawl over her head to cover her shame; she had never been so filthy and unkempt.

Annunziata looked at her family. They were all the same. She gripped her hands together, trying to find courage. She would not weaken. She thanked God they were still together.

She looked at Carlo and thrust her chin forward, trying to find strength. He understood what she was thinking. He gripped her hands between his and looking into her eyes as he tried to reassure her,

'*Mamma, non ti preoccupare*. Don't worry. They won't beat us. We'll find somewhere safe to hide in the hills. We'll get through this. Trust me.'

He looked over her head at his father; neither of them was convinced.

German soldiers drove past in convoys, pushing them off the road, spitting or yelling at them to get out of the way. A bedraggled line of old men trailing mangy, emaciated children and worn-out women with babes in arms were of no use to a retreating army. Aeroplanes flying overhead swooped down like giant vultures, checking the convoy, looking for soldiers or fit young men. Whenever he heard their drone, Carlo dropped down, hiding Vincenzo beneath him.

Looking at the hundreds of people ahead of them, all equally desperate, Carlo was horror-struck. The whole of Pozzuoli needed to find places to hide. He was afraid for them all; he was afraid his luck had finally run out.

They were given a few baskets of dry black bread on the way out of town, but other than that they had nothing to eat. They drank water from any streams they passed, although many were contaminated by bloated, decaying corpses. All along the road, villages lay destroyed and abandoned. Fields were scorched and burnt, farmhouses demolished, still smouldering after being set alight by the retreating army. Carcases of starved animals lay rotting at the sides of the paths.

'This is hell on earth. The devil is at work,' Annunziata whispered to Luigi, shaking her head and crossing herself. They were moving northwards along the coast road, retreating with the enemy.

'At least we're moving away from the Front. The fight will be behind us.' Luigi tried to reassure Annunziata. They were in the open air, which was a relief after the oppression of the last weeks spent imprisoned in their own home. News came that Naples was under siege, the Germans had surrounded it and there was no food at all. The citizens were starving. Poor Francesca was still trapped there.

By late afternoon they could go no further and stopped, exhausted, by the side of the road. They had already fallen well behind the convoy. Looking around, Carlo noticed a farmhouse further up the hill, away from the road. He spoke to Tullio.

'Come on, Tullio, let's go up the hill and see if we can find anything.'

'*Sta' attend'*, be careful, Carlo,' Luigi said, exhausted. What kind of father was he? He was not even fit to climb a hill to look for shelter for his family.

The two boys scrambled up the hill, keeping a lookout all the time for any Germans. The farmhouse looked deserted.

'Be careful,' Carlo whispered. 'Someone might be hiding inside.'

As they got closer they saw it had been set alight. The windows at the side were still smouldering, the air acrid and foul. The door was ajar.

'Wait here, Tullio. I'll check.'

Being as careful as he could, Carlo went inside. The room was empty, the table and chairs overturned. The remains of half-eaten food lay rotting on the floor. A chicken scrabbled in the corner. He tried to catch it but although emaciated it was faster than him and escaped.

He called to Tullio, 'It's OK.'

They looked around the room. They couldn't find anything to eat; everything had been destroyed or burnt. Despondent, they went out to the back of the house. All around, the land was scorched and smoking.

'They want us all to starve, Tullio. They're deliberately destroying everything in their wake.'

Tullio looked upset. How could they go back with nothing?

Just then he caught a familiar scent in a breeze. He took a deep breath.

'Carlo, can you smell that?'

They walked round to the west side of the house. There, in a corner, sheltered from the wind, a tenacious fig tree still clung to the stone wall, overladen with ripe sweet figs, abundant like manna from heaven. The smell made them delirious.

Carlo looked at Tullio. 'You first. *Mangia*. Eat.'

Sitting under the tree they gorged on the luscious sweet figs, the juice sticking to their unshaven faces, the intensity of the sugar reviving them and making them laugh with utter relief.

'Maybe we'll be saved after all.'

Energised, they checked around again and found a few items of clothing, and in a cupboard in a small outhouse they found a small, dry pecorino cheese and two flasks of wine hidden behind a dusty wicker basket. They filled the basket as full as they could with figs, layering them with green fig leaves. They had a beautiful gift to take down to their family.

'Tullio, make your way down with this, be careful. I'll just scout up there and see if I can find anything else and I'll follow you down. I won't be long.'

Tullio made his way down while Carlo scrambled further up the hill. When he got to the top, he lay on his stomach, checking around to making sure there were no soldiers or signs of danger. Seeing nothing, he got to his feet and turned around to get his bearings.

'Madonna!' he was overwhelmed.

In front of him was the vast expanse of the glorious blue sea. Looking south, he could see the Bay of Pozzuoli, sweeping round past Posillipo and the wide glory of the Bay of Naples. Vesuvius, mighty and magnificent, smouldered angrily. To the east, he could clearly see the islands, as far south as the island of Capri. The spectacular orange sun reflected across the sparkling waves. Here, high above the stench below, the air was clean and fresh.

Then, as the glare of the sun faded and his eyes adjusted to the blaze of light, he saw that the sparkling lights gleaming all over the ocean were not just refractions of sunlight but were in fact a small battleship and a fleet of landing ships. His caught his breath. The were flying American flags.

Carlo sank to his knees and with his face in his hands he wept with relief. 'Madonna, you do hold us all safe in your hands. *Grazie.*'

Chapter Eleven

MONDRAGONE, OCTOBER 1943

They slept by the side of the road, huddled together for warmth. Throughout the night, they watched in awe as wave upon wave of Allied planes flew overhead and relentlessly bombed the German front lines. The sky was ablaze. By the next morning all the German soldiers had disappeared, callously abandoning the defenceless refugees.

Relieved to be left to their own devices, Luigi's and Zi' Alf's families continued their slow walk, choosing to take the longer route inland along the small country roads, avoiding the checkpoints stationed along the main coast road. They came across groups of disbanded Italian soldiers unsuccessfully disguised in ill-fitting civilian clothes with giveaway army boots or heavy leather jackets. Most were very young, not much older than Carlo or Tullio. They told them they had been instructed by their commanding officers to go home, but without maps or local knowledge they were unsure which way to go.

Further into the hills there was less destruction than near the coast. Some farmhouses were still occupied. The farmers were in a better situation, and still had some crops. They managed to get some food; at least enough to keep them going.

Eventually, after four days, they reached the outskirts of the small farming town of Mondragone, about 24 miles from Pozzuoli. The town had been the Italian army's southern headquarters. About 25 miles further north flowed the River Garigliano, which the farmers alerted them formed the Gustav

Line, part of the German defensive barrier.

Luigi knew the town of Mondragone. The farmers used to come into the piazza at Pozzuoli to sell their mozzarella. Sensing a chance for safety and too exhausted to move further, the family sought refuge in an abandoned farmhouse in the hills above the town. The boys set about lighting a fire; that night Annunziata made a hot meal for the first time in weeks. In the grounds of the farmhouse they dug up some onions and potatoes. She boiled them together with some wild herbs and made some hot soup. With some black bread they had managed to buy on the way they sat together and ate. The unusual warmth in their bellies was soporific and, one by one, the children huddled together and fell asleep.

Luigi spoke with Carlo, whispering so as not to waken the others.

'Are you sure it was the Allies you saw? If so we should just wait here. I think we're about four kilometres from the coast, far enough away from immediate danger. We'll be able to get by for now.'

'I'm not sure, Papà. Maybe I was just dreaming, hoping.'

'That'll do for me. We need to dream. We need to hope.' Luigi put his arm round his son.

'How long will we need to stay?'

'Who knows? The Americans are fresh into the fight, the Germans are alone now and without our army they're severely weakened.'

'I wonder what's happened in Genoa. I used to go and see our aircraft carriers anchored there. They were so majestic and powerful. I think I'll be a sailor one day.'

Luigi smiled at his son.

'Carlo, you're always dreaming. Never stop. We'll stay here for now and wait. It should be easier to find food. We'll take a day at a time, it's the best we can do.'

'Maybe we'll find one of the farmers who makes the mozzarella.'

'We'll see.'

Luigi had already noticed a lot of carcases of buffalo rotting in the fields. He wouldn't be surprised if the Germans hadn't already destroyed the herds. They would leave nothing to help their enemy.

Later, when he lay down beside his wife, Luigi dared to share his hopes. 'Annunziata, I feel we'll be all right now. I'll be able to work and we'll get by till the war is over. The children will have a chance to recover their strength. Let's pray it's not too long.'

When he bent over to kiss her he smiled. She was already sound asleep.

*

Over the next few days they managed to trace the owner of the farmhouse. Luigi arranged to rent it in exchange for some carpentry. The farmhouse was comfortable. They had water and soap. Nonna Minicuccia took over the job of scrubbing them all down, one by one, Luigi included. Nonno Vincenzo built a big fire and in a milk pail they found he set about boiling all their clothes to disinfect them.

At last life settled down. It was still difficult, but at least in the countryside they could get vegetables, milk and corn. They even managed to get some eggs. Luigi found it easy to get work for Carlo and himself; during a war repairs were always needed.

The war raged around them and although the bombing didn't stop, it was no longer right over their heads. More and more refugees kept arriving from the south. The news that came through from Naples was chilling. They heard that people were so hungry they had smashed the fish tanks in the museums and eaten the exhibits in desperation. The Germans had ransacked the city, bombed the Chiesa di Santa Chiara and destroyed the harbours. Finally, when a young man was shot in the back on the steps of the museum, the citizens had had enough. They took up arms themselves and revolted, even the street urchins, the abandoned *scugnizzi*, and fought against the enemy. Over four days at the end of September the population chased the enemy out. The Germans set the city on fire and fled.

Carlo was enthralled by these reports.

'I wish I'd been there with them, I would have fought with them. *Bravi ragazzi!*' When the Allies entered the liberated city on 1 October they had been welcomed with great celebrations and cheers from the impoverished citizens.

'It's nearly all over, we just have to hold our nerve till the Germans pass through Mondragone. By the sounds of it they'll not stop; they're running scared.' Luigi hoped he was right.

Over the next few weeks they noticed the German soldiers were moving north. Apart from the senseless burning of farms and the destruction of any Italian war equipment, they seemed to be more interested in getting away than harming any more civilians. Luigi had been right about one thing: the retreating army destroyed all the buffalo herds as they moved north, wiping out centuries of cheese production.

It gradually became apparent to Luigi that they were no longer in enemy territory. The German Front now became entrenched at the Gustav Line, while the Allies encamped on the beach at Mondragone. Luigi's family, along with most of their relations and neighbours from Pozzuoli, were suspended in no-man's land.

Life fell into a surreal routine. Luigi got more work, Annunziata cared for her children, but although they felt relatively safe there was no opportunity to return home. They didn't even know if their home was still standing. They were anxious to find out what had happened to Zia Francesca and her family, but there was no way of knowing where she was, or if she was even still alive. They resigned themselves to settling where they were until the war was over.

*

Carlo had heard that the Americans were massing at the coast around Mondragone. He was bored and looking for adventure. One day, while helping his father repair a broken window, he casually announced, 'By the way, Papà, Tullio and I have borrowed a scooter. We're going down to the train station at the coast to see what's happening.'

His father didn't want him taking any risks. He tried to deflect him. 'Carlo, I need you here. There's a lot of repair work to do.'

'We'll just go and have a look.' Carlo needed to build an argument. 'If I eat another plate of polenta I think I'll die of boredom. It would be a shame if after all the adventures I've had so far it was boredom that got me in the end.'

His father couldn't help but laugh.

'And, Papà, hopefully we'll be able to get hold of some cigarettes.'

Luigi hadn't had a cigarette for months. He looked at Carlo and tried to look severe, 'OK then, but be careful!'

Balanced on the scooter, Tullio riding at the front, Carlo standing behind, they sped off down the hill to the station. The two were dressed in their best clothes, an assortment of items they had scavenged from the departing German and Italian soldiers: thick gabardine trousers, boots that were worn through at the soles and had cardboard inside to stop the water getting in, a green army jacket with all the badges and epaulettes torn off. Carlo had a leather belt, wrapped twice round his waist to hold his trousers up. At least they had clothes now. His grandmothers had started a small trade in repairing and de-branding discarded uniforms and had taken great delight in dressing the boys.

Tied onto the scooter between Tullio's feet was an old basket filled with some of the treasure they had been collecting: German badges and stripes, a cigarette case with a skull and crossbones engraved on it, a leather bread bag and a gun sling would surely fetch a good price. The boys were excited. Oblivious to the fact that the war was still not over, they felt that their lives were starting again.

As they hurtled down the hill, freewheeling to save fuel, they saw some American soldiers walking in twos, heavily armed but relaxed, smoking cigarettes, keen to talk with the locals. They were stopped once or twice and asked to produce their papers. The Americans laughed at their scooter, which, though a chariot to the boys, was just a broken-down, rusty old wreck.

As they approached the town centre they could see the sea. Sooner than they had expected they came right up against what looked like the entire American army.

'*Mannaggia!* Tullio! Look at that!'

Spread in front of them for as far as they could see were hundreds of khaki-coloured tents lined up like an entire city made of canvas. Milling around were thousands of American soldiers.

'*Dio!*' Tullio stopped the bike, 'Oh dear. I hope they're friendly!'

'Hey, lads! What you doin' there?'

A tall black American stationed at the checkpoint of the camp engaged his rifle and walked towards them.

Jumping promptly off the scooter, they immediately put their hands up.

'*Ciao, amico,*' Carlo kept his hands up. 'We just came to say hello.'

Without speaking a word of English, they managed to converse with the soldiers. An hour later they were chugging back up the hill with the basket in the front of the scooter empty of their German loot and filled instead with useful booty: tins of Spam, Camp coffee, Hershey's chocolate and bags of sugar. Best of all, they had Camel cigarettes! On top of that, they each had a new pair of shoes, as well as several pairs of different sizes for their brothers and sisters, who, as Tullio pumped the horn to announce their arrival, all ran out to greet them. Vincenzo overtook them all and Ernesto scrabbled behind, barefoot, trying to catch up. Even Luigi put his tools down and came out from behind the farmhouse. It had been a long time since they'd heard Carlo sound so happy and optimistic.

Carlo laid out all his treasures on the kitchen table. Using the key on the tin he opened the tin of Spam.

'What on earth is that?' Annunziata was not sure of the smell.

'American meat.'

They had not tasted meat for five years.

Carlo got a teaspoon and, lining his brothers and sisters up in order of age with the youngest, Ernesto, first, he fed each of them a spoonful of the sweet, aromatic paste. They all pulled faces at the unfamiliar flavour. He gave a spoonful to his mother, who smacked her lips, the spice, salt and sugar enlivening her jaded taste buds. She nodded approval.

'*Non c'è male.* It's not bad.'

Carlo finished the last two teaspoons himself, scraping the sides of the tin not to leave a drop.

'Carlo, why do you get two spoons and we only got one?' Vincenzo was not sure this was fair.

'Because Vincenzo, *fratello mio,* I am the breadwinner in the family and I need to have the most energy.'

That made sense. Vincenzo turned to his sisters. 'Carlo's the breadwinner. We need to look after him!'

This started a daily trip for Carlo and Tullio to hang around the American encampments and see what they could do to be helpful, and what they could barter from their new friends. They also saw English and Scottish soldiers, and a lot of Polish and South African troops. The boys started to pick up words in different languages, and heard the beat of their first American music. Carlo recognised a lot of Neapolitan tunes sung with English words. He was quick to pick up verse and made the Americans laugh as he sang along.

Becoming more self-assured, they explored further afield. It wasn't long before they came across German troops who were equally bored, languishing at the other side of no-man's land. They were just as keen to trade and before long Carlo and Tullio were trading with the enemy, selling American cigarettes for cash. Life was getting better by the day.

*

One morning, at the start of the following January, Tullio and Carlo got onto their scooter and headed down to see the Americans as usual.

There was a growing tension among the soldiers, as there now were frequent battles to try to break down the German front line, which was entrenched about 30 miles north. The ancient monastery at Monte Cassino had become the German stronghold and it was proving almost impossible to overthrow.

Turning a corner at the bottom of the hill they pulled up quickly. The field before them, which had been prepared for spring planting just the week before, had become a vast military camp for South African troops. It was covered as far as the eye could see with khaki tents and an impressive collection of heavy tanks and military vehicles. They had never seen this many troops assembled. The two young men stopped to watch, curious about the different uniforms.

'*Carlo, attenzione!*' Tullio whispered anxiously to his cousin. Two soldiers were approaching them. The pair took a step back, ready to jump on the scooter and make their escape. Another man came forward, even taller, with a big white smile beaming from his very black face.

'*Ciao, amico! Ciao,*' he seemed friendly. He made a gesture to hold something up to his mouth and pretend to drink.

'*Rooi. Rooi?*'

The boys didn't understand at first but with gestures and smiling and laughing they thought they had a clue.

'I think they want wine!' Carlo repeated the gesture asking, '*Vino? Vino?*'

The man nodded, very enthusiastically. '*Si Si … Vino – rooi.*'

The man flashed his hand three times with his fingers spread out and pointed to a colour on their flag.

'*Quindici,*' Tullio shouted. 'They want fifteen bottles of red wine!'

Relieved to have escaped trouble, the boys agreed to come back the next day with the wine.

The only problem was, there was no wine. The retreating Germans had taken what they could carry and the rest had long since been drunk by anyone who had had the good fortune to find a bottle.

They went to visit the Americans as usual and returned home loaded with cigarettes and tins of Spam for Annunziata, all the while trying to work out a plan.

'So, Tullio,' Carlo said, once they had eaten some bread with beans on top, 'let's think about this. I've had an idea. What is wine?'

'Grapes squashed and turned to alcohol.' Everyone knew that. 'But there are no grapes.'

'OK, I know, but wait. What does alcohol turn into?'

'I don't know. I just drink it!'

Annunziata was listening.

'Mamma, what does alcohol turn into?'

'*Aceto!* Vinegar!'

'Exactly. And … who makes *aceto*?'

Annunziata started to giggle. 'Signora Richetta … Signora Richetta sells wine vinegar.'

One of the farmers' wives had a cache of wine that she had

managed to hide when the Germans had passed. Unfortunately for her and for the boys, it was just starting to turn to vinegar; she was doing a great trade selling it anyway. Carlo thought some of it might well still have some alcohol in it.

Annunziata looked at Luigi. She turned her face to the side, turned her lips down and nodded to her husband. She was so impressed with Carlo. In her eyes he could do no wrong.

Carlo handed Tullio six cigarettes, 'Tullio, give these to signora Richetta and ask her for a litre of her old wine. Hurry!'

Carlo had been thinking of his days at the *farmacia*. He remembered that any concoction of ingredients that they had mixed to make a medicine or tonic had nearly always been sweetened with sugar to disguise the taste and make it palatable. They had amassed plenty of sugar from the Americans, more than they knew what to do with.

When Tullio returned with the old wine, Carlo tasted a little, and grimaced. It tasted strongly of vinegar but it was still high in alcohol. On the kitchen table they started to experiment to try to blend a recipe. After a few failed attempts they decided on a formula: vinegar diluted with one quarter water and enough sugar to make it sweet.

Good. They took half each and agreed they'd do some market research. They would let both their families taste their wine, not telling them where it had come from, and see their reactions.

Luigi hadn't had a glass of wine for over a year. He had been busy all afternoon and had not seen the goings-on in the kitchen; he assumed Carlo must have brought it from the Americans.

He held it up to the light: it was a bit cloudy. He sniffed it inquisitively: it had an unusual aroma. He tentatively took a sip, swirled it in his mouth and swallowed it. He tasted a second mouthful, Carlo watching anxiously to see his reaction.

He nodded approvingly. '*Non c'e male!* Carlo, not bad at all.' He drank down the rest and held his glass out for a refill.

Carlo winked at his mother. She burst out into her infectious giggle.

'*Bravo*, Carlo. *Bravo!* Now you just need to think of a price!'

The next morning, an hour later than usual, Tullio, Carlo and the scooter were racing down the hillside. Balanced between

Tullio's legs was a wooden crate with 20 odd bottles and flasks of their new wine. They took a detour past the American camps and headed straight to the South Africans.

The soldiers saw them coming and, hearing the clatter of the bottles as the scooter went over the rough path, they came forward, smiling.

'*Ciao, amici.*' Carlo put his best salesman face on. They had closed the bottles with an old capping device that the farmers used to make their tomato preserve, and only at the last minute had he remembered a bottle-opener: he was well prepared. He opened a bottle and handed it to the tall black soldier.

'*Assaggi, soldato.* Taste it. It's my father's favourite,' he signalled with his finger in his cheek and twisted it round indicating in Neapolitan sign language that it was good. '*Buono? Si?*'

Tullio joined in the sales pitch, taking a lead from his cousin. They had told the truth: it was both their fathers' favourite. It was the only one to choose.

The soldiers passed the bottle around and smiled, putting their thumbs up and saying '*Gooei.*'

Carlo nodded and agreed, '*Gooei! Gooei!*' He turned to Tullio. 'Maybe that means wine in their language. Who knows. Just repeat what they say.'

Before long a lot more soldiers had come round to see what was going on. They kept handing notes to the boys, and before long all the bottles were sold.

Carlo and Tullio waited to see the outcome. Soon the soldiers were all laughing and joking, and within 20 minutes they were all quite drunk. Even more soldiers came out to see what the noise was about.

Carlo and Tullio were soon driving back up the hill with the empty bottles rattling in their wooden crate, a pocket full of notes and orders for another 40 bottles of their sweet wine.

The South Africans stayed three weeks. Carlo and Tullio made two deliveries a day and their trade got better and better. The only downside was that they hadn't noticed the soldiers paying with rands. They stopped off at the market in the town and immediately spent all the money on cigarettes, clothes and cans of food.

After that, they insisted the South Africans paid in dollars and before long they had also set up a stall in the market themselves, trading contraband cigarettes to the public. Carlo and Tullio made a lot of dollars, splitting their profits equally.

In the meantime, Luigi had also built up a reputation for producing the best carpentry. There was plenty of work and he had managed to save enough to rent a small yard in the town. People were coming into the countryside from Naples to trade broken doors and window frames from bombed palazzi for food to take back to the still-starving city. Luigi told Carlo to stop going down to the armies and help him instead, but Carlo was having too much fun to start working in just one place.

'Papà, it's just for a few more weeks. I've heard all the soldiers will be moving north soon.'

Neither Carlo nor his family understood that while they were seeing a gradual return to some sort of normality, the soldiers Carlo and Tullio had made friends with were being sent to the front, where many of them were to lose their lives.

In fact, the garrisons stayed encamped there for a further four months, as the Battle for Monte Cassino raged at the start of 1944. In the most devastating battle of the war so far, tens of thousands of Allied and German soldiers horrifically lost their lives.

*

After the awful slaughter of Monte Cassino, the armies moved north towards Rome and the front line of the war finally passed beyond Carlo and his family. From the early summer of 1944 they had their first real chance of hope and life settled into a new pattern. Thankfully, they were not so hungry now; Luigi was working a lot and as there was still very little cash in circulation, they were usually paid with food. They had a few chickens and even a goat, which pleased the girls although it took time to learn how to milk it. In the mornings, Annunziata still went up into the hills with Ninuccia and picked wild herbs. She knew where to find wild mushrooms, and if she came across any shepherds, could buy some warm fresh ricotta and soft pecorino.

It was not until the autumn of 1945, when the war was over,

that with huge relief and an unexpected sense of regret, the family discussed whether it might be safe to move back to Pozzuoli. Luigi had built up a good business and they decided it was best that he settle in Mondragone temporarily with the grandparents and the children, leaving Carlo, Nonna Minicuccia and his mother to make their way back home, not sure what they would find. Luigi and the family would follow if there was a decent home to go to. The war was over and now, along with millions of other families, it was time to build their future.

Part Three

Un colpo di fulmine
The thunderbolt

Overleaf: Carlo Contini aged 27.

Chapter Twelve

It took almost five years after the end of the war for the Italians in Edinburgh to feel they could begin to put the past behind them. Almost every single family had lost a father or brother, and in most cases it was the eldest son or daughter who had to take over as head of the family. The mothers, especially those like Maria Crolla who had never learned to speak English, had to depend on their children to manage their lives. By working hard and not being distracted, they managed to build up their businesses, many of which had been on the brink of collapse.

Although his brother Domenico was older than him, it was Vittorio Crolla who had become the driving force in the survival of the family business. As soon as the brothers were released from internment on the Isle of Man, Vittorio had realised that a lot of the Italian businesses in Edinburgh had been damaged during the war. Sensing a market, the first thing he did was to invest in a shop fitments showroom in Montgomery Street Lane, just behind the Valvona & Crolla shop at 19 Elm Row. This had been a lucky move. His timing had been perfect. Within months a Government health regulation had made it law that all milk had to be elaborately heat-treated before it was used to make ice cream, and Vittorio was on hand to help his fellow Italians to follow the regulations. He was not minded to be thankful to the Government for anything, but he had to admit the Company enjoyed an impressive increase in trade supplying the necessary equipment.

Now that Valvona & Crolla were also the agents for the Frank

Ford fish ranges the firm was firmly established as the source of equipment for all the Italian businesses on the east coast.

Vittorio had just completed his stock count of the ice cream equipment in the showroom and was about to prepare his orders for the summer season. His assistant, Miss Dennison, came into the showroom slightly flushed and excited.

'Mr Crolla, that's young Johnny Di Ciacca downstairs asking if he can see you.'

'Johnny? Of course, please ask him to come up.'

To stop himself dwelling on unwelcome thoughts Vittorio enjoyed working with a backdrop of Beethoven or the soaring strains of Maria Callas, much to the disapproval of Miss Dennison, but he turned the music down to receive his visitor.

After the usual banter and asking after each other's families, Vittorio enquired how the new equipment was working. Johnny had refurbished his own ice cream factory in the Cockenzie Café, a substantial sale for Vittorio.

'It's been a learning curve, Vittorio, but it's marvellous. I can produce forty gallons of ice cream in one batch, in a quarter of the time. If we get a good summer again we should be able to pay off the last of the debt by the end of the year.'

'Excellent. It was worth the investment then.'

'It's good for you as well, Vittorio. I'm going to need more stock. I need five cases of ready-mix ice cream powder, six ice cream scoops and a pack of a thousand toffee-apple sticks. My mum makes them nearly every day; the local kids can't get enough of them.'

'How do you manage to get enough sugar, Johnny? The rationing is still quite tight.'

'There's always a way, Vittorio. You know that!'

As Vittorio was collecting the order Johnny had a chance to wander round the showroom. It was impressive, he had to admit, with everything anyone needed to create an up-to-the-minute ice cream parlour: pasteurisation vats, gleaming stainless steel freezers, dry-ice inserts, marble tabletops and anything else you could imagine. He even had a choice of various giant ice cream cones to stand outside the shop door, together with posters to encourage children to 'eat more ice cream'.

In the corner, Johnny noticed a very smart ice cream tricycle with two freezers.

'These look very good, Vittorio. I'll think about ordering a couple. I've applied to the local council to take some stands down the coast. If I get the licence I'll definitely need them.'

Miss Dennison brought in a spluttering, hissing Bialetti coffee pot. The invigorating aroma filled the showroom.

'Have you thought of selling coffee in your café, Johnny? I've been reading it's all the rage in London.'

'Not really. I don't think it will catch on. Our customers just want tea.'

The men sat down to complete their business, and Vittorio poured them both a nip of Muirhead's blended whisky. Johnny got out his wallet and counted out ten large Bank of Scotland five-pound notes towards his account.

Vittorio licked his fingers and checked the notes in front of Johnny, carefully writing out a receipt with a carbon copy to give to him.

'How is business now, Vittorio? It must be good. That's a very smart car you have outside.'

Vittorio was very proud of his new car, a black, shiny Citroën Traction Avant. It was stylish, understated and just a bit racy, with its long bonnet and large headlights. Vittorio liked to make a statement, discreetly letting the other Italians think he was successful. There was nothing wrong with engineering a degree of jealousy. It helped encourage competition.

'Things are steady, Johnny. You know, after the war we never thought we would be able to keep the business going, but things are starting to settle down. Thank God for the heat-treatment regulations! Keeps business brisk.'

Their time together on the Isle of Man had left them with a lot in common. Before the war had started they had been carefree young men with everything to look forward to. Now they were the heads of their families, with brothers to manage, sisters to marry off and widowed mothers to fuss over. What they really wanted now was to find wives for themselves, to let them feel carefree and young again. At least there were plenty of available girls to choose from.

On the way out, Vittorio let Johnny have a good look at the Citroën; he sat inside and admired the luxury leather seating and wood veneer dashboard. As he drove off in his old car he reflected on how well Vittorio was doing and resolved to visit the garage on the way home to see if they had any promising deals.

Once Johnny had left, Vittorio decided to walk home from the shop. It was a lovely day and near enough lunchtime. He still remembered longing for his mother's cooking when he was in the prisoner-of-war camp. Now, every day was a miracle to him: that he could walk home whenever he wanted, and Maria's kitchen would be there, warm and familiar, smelling of his favourite food. As he opened the door he took a deep breath and savoured the aroma of tomato and garlic. His favourite of all time was *sagne e fagiole*, pasta and bean soup. What a feast she could make with a tin of tomatoes, a handful of dried borlotti beans, some flour and a few eggs.

Domenico and his sisters were already there and urged him to hurry up. 'Sit down, man. We're starving, waiting for you!'

During lunch Vittorio spoke to Domenico. 'I saw Johnny this morning. He's looking well. They're expecting a busy summer.'

'Aye, aye.' Domenico was enjoying his soup.

'I've been thinking, Dom, we've done well with the new equipment, and there are good orders coming in for the fish ranges.'

'Aye, aye.'

'I've been thinking of buying a new van. How would you like to start taking the van round all the ice cream shops and seeing what we can sell? We've not done that since Dad used to travel around. I think we could start again.' Vittorio wanted to make sure they got a good share of the money the ice cream and fish-and-chip shops were making, and to make sure they continued to supply the Italians and their ever-expanding families with all their requirements. It was prudent to make a move to keep control of the market.

'Aye, that's good, Vittorio. I could take a selection of pasta, olive oil, wine and coffee. I'd get a good bit of trade going.'

'While you're at it, you can make sure they all keep paying their instalments for the equipment they've bought. Good. I'll go to the garage this afternoon.'

If he hadn't waited to have a snooze after lunch he would have been in time to see Johnny driving off in a brand new blue Rover.

'Now that the licence to sell a wider selection of liqueurs and spirits has been approved, I need to go down to London to see what's going on and get new supplies for the shop.'

Maria was instantly worried. 'Do you really need to go? Will you take the train?'

'No, I think I'll drive. I want to give my car a good run.'

'Drive to London alone? For the first time! You'll get lost. Where will you stay? It'll be so busy.' She hated it if the boys were away from home for any length of time.

'I hope it will be! I'll stay near Piccadilly Circus. I'll be in the thick of things! See what's going on.' For the first time in years, Vittorio felt a sense of freedom and the courage to start living again.

'Remember, be careful, Vittorio. Whatever you do, someone will see you and tell me!'

So much for that sense of freedom!

*

Vittorio was bound up with his thoughts as he drove alone down to London. He couldn't help reflecting on how his life had been changed so drastically by the events of the war. His personality was driven to explore, to read and learn. He might have become a philosopher or gone to university. But his choices had been removed. After all those wasted years of incarceration, now, at the age of 36, he needed to make his own way.

He had never imagined he would be a grocer all his life. Valvona & Crolla was Alfonso Crolla's vision. His own ambition was so different from his father's. He had dreamt of being a scholar, maybe to marry and have a family. Instead, he'd been left to carry the burden of a run-down shop with no stock, no funds, not even a reputation. How could he justify building up a business of Italian imports when the Italians had been so reviled in the last few years? Surely they would always be dependent on their own compatriots as customers, and they would end up no further forward than their ancestors back in Italy, up in the mountains. What would a

Scotsman want to buy from him? He felt overwhelmed with doubt.

He broke the journey with an overnight stay in York. At dinner he was served a Yorkshire pudding the size of a soup plate swimming with gravy. Typical English food. He had to admit it was very tasty. In bed, though he was tired, he was unable to sleep. His mind was racing, full of questions with no solutions.

He must have slept after all, as he woke surprisingly refreshed. His full English breakfast was a revelation: a plateful of fat, juicy pork sausages that were sweet and moreish, crisp, streaky bacon and fresh hen's eggs, soft and runny in the middle. The warm, home-made bread and creamy salty butter washed down with a good strong cup of Yorkshire tea cheered him no end. They did know how to make a good breakfast in England.

As he was packing up he picked up the George Bernard Shaw novel he'd been attempting to read the night before. A couple of lines caught his eye on the page it had fallen open on: 'If you cannot get rid of the family skeleton, you may as well make it dance.'

'That's it!' he thought. A smashed immigrant's shop at the top of Leith Walk might be regarded as a liability, a dead end in the capital of Scotland. But he would make it dance! He'd make it into the best shop in Edinburgh. No, the best shop in Scotland! That would show them! He'd make it so exciting and packed with everything from all over Italy and Scotland; he'd make it a great success.

Forza Italia!

*

Vittorio arrived in London late, well after eight, and took a room in the Regent Palace Hotel in Piccadilly. They took his car and parked it for him. He was impressed by their customer service.

After a quick supper, he went straight to sleep. He had a meeting organised with one of his suppliers, Giordano, in Windmill Street in Soho early the next day.

The next morning he was amazed how busy London was. Everyone seemed to be preparing for the Festival of Britain exhibition: flags and banners lined the streets. He was impressed with the sense of space, the wide streets and luscious greenery. Walking around before his meeting, he had to take his coat off: it was much warmer than Edinburgh. He walked along Regent Street and behind Liberty, the renowned department store, into Soho. He had never seen anything like it. The place was booming. There was far more trade going on here than in Edinburgh, which was only just starting to recover. There was building work going on everywhere, repairing war damage. The windows in the shops had beautiful displays: very classy and quite unlike anything he had imagined. He knew of some Italian grocers in Soho and Clerkenwell. He'd go around and have a look later. He was always on the lookout for ideas.

His appointment was at 11 a.m. and he suddenly realised he would have to hurry. He hadn't realised how vast London was. A bit flustered, he arrived a little late. The building was impressive, a four-storey art deco warehouse the length of four buildings, with full-length Greek columns and large frosted-glass windows.

He felt a bit out of his depth: he was just a grocer from the other end of the country. But he rang the bell and went into the reception. He spoke in Italian. 'Signor Crolla, *da Edimburgo*.'

'*Buongiorno*, signor Crolla. Signor Giordano is expecting you. Please come this way.'

The young dark-haired Italian girl spoke with a strong Cockney accent. She led him through a doorway behind her desk to a lift in a long corridor. It climbed slowly up four floors to the top of the building. At each landing, Vittorio caught a glimpse of vast areas piled ceiling-high with cases of wines and spirits. When the girl pulled the gate to let him out, Ercole Giordano was waiting for him.

'Vittorio, my friend! How good of you to come down and see us; how is your dear mother? I was so very sorry to hear about Alfonso. *Condoglianze*. Come, come.'

Ercole Giordano was an established importer of Italian wines and spirits founded in London in 1934, the same year Alfonso had joined with Ralph Valvona to form their limited company. He had been to Edinburgh to meet with Alfonso many times before the war, but had not been back since. He was definitely prospering.

They talked about the experiences of the war, about the hardships they had endured and about the way forward.

'Vittorio, don't despair. We must move forward. There are plenty of opportunities: trade in London is booming! The British soldiers who came back from Italy had an exhilarating experience of the country. For the first time they enjoyed the pleasures of our Italian food, our Italian coffee, our Italian wine. Now that's all they want! They got a taste for the good life and they want to enjoy it here. It'll take a few years, but we're on the way. The restaurants are open again and busier than ever – Quo Vadis, Quaglino's. Go, you'll be amazed who is queuing up to get inside.

'And you know, word travels. The market will grow across the country, even up to sunny Edinburgh, you'll see!' He burst out laughing. He was exaggerating of course, what salesman doesn't? But he was sowing the germ of an idea in someone he hoped would be a good ally in spreading the success of his own business. 'Now, my friend, come over here, I want you to taste something.'

*

That evening, after he had eaten at his hotel, Vittorio went out to try to relax a bit. The meeting had been good, well worth the journey. Ercole had let him taste some Cinzano vermouth from Turin. He hadn't tried it before – he didn't really like vermouth – but Ercole said it was going to be the next big thing; the women were all drinking it in the London bars. He had just taken on an agency for it. Vittorio couldn't see a market for it in Edinburgh. The women there drank at most a sherry on a Sunday evening; they weren't out drinking in bars like Pierce's next to his shop in Elm Row, that was for sure. It would take a while to change that!

He lit a cigarette and drew a deep breath. He crossed the road and turned left, behind the hotel towards Soho. The streets became narrower, and although there were plenty of lights in the pubs and diners he passed, it was quite dark and grimy. Under the flickering gaslight, it took him a while to realise that the cardboard boxes at the shop corners were sheltering people: men and women, even a few children. It took him aback. They had some tramps in Edinburgh, old soldiers or wounded servicemen. He even knew a few of them: they had a habit of coming into the shop on a Friday morning with their 'broo' money to buy a quarter bottle of whisky or vodka. But here there appeared to be a vagrant on every doorstep. He was shocked at the numbers, and it was now very cold.

'Gee'z a fag, guv!' One of the tramps stretched out a hand.

Vittorio put his hand in his pocket and gave the man the last three cigarettes he had and a couple of matches. The next man asked for the same. Vittorio gave the man a shilling. He turned left onto a busier street to try to move away, bumping into a couple of girls standing smoking at the corner.

'I beg your pardon,' he said, embarrassed.

'Want some company, luv?' The girl took his arm.

Vittorio, pulled away, shocked, and stumbled off the pavement, trying to walk away, pretending to be nonchalant.

Oh dear! London was different at night, that was for sure. Looking up, he saw a sign for the Windmill Theatre and thought he might go in and see a play or hear some music. When he went through the door he was greeted by a youngish lady perched on the desk, brash blonde hair piled high on her head, scandalously short dress tight at her chest and very long fishnet-stockinged legs crossed. She rocked her high heels suggestively up and down and smiled.

'Want to come in, ducky?'

Vittorio turned and fled. When he was safely back in his room he sat on the bed and mopped his brow. 'Oh my God,' he thought. 'That was a close shave. What if my mother found out?'

*

The next morning, Vittorio returned to Soho to visit some more of his suppliers. In the morning light the streets were far less sinister and he felt a fool for having been so nervous the night before. A street market selling fruit and vegetables was bustling with housewives with shopping bags haggling over prices. There was a wonderful array of exotic shops, delicatessens, new-fangled coffee shops, restaurants of all kinds: Italian, Turkish and Greek.

Round another corner he was amazed to walk into a street where most of the shops and restaurants were Chinese. There was a whole new mix of people, with languages and cuisines from every corner of the globe. It was just what he was looking for.

Driving back north after his three days in London, Vittorio had so many ideas he wondered which he should concentrate on first. By the time he reached home, he had decided he'd try them all.

Chapter Thirteen

It was late April and the weather was the same as always at this time of year: pouring with rain. Vittorio and Domenico were busy behind the counter.

They had a handful of customers, mainly Italians wanting freshly ground coffee and packets of pasta. On the pavement outside the delivery from Giordano's, 50 cases of mixed wines and spirits, had just been unloaded and stacked at the door, covered with a green tarpaulin, ready to be removed to the basement later on.

The driver was waiting inside for his usual mortadella panino. He looked forward to it from the moment he started up the A1 to deliver to Valvona & Crolla. That panino was always on his mind the whole of the journey: the crispy, chewy bread, the saltiness of the finely sliced sheets of pink and white mortadella; the kick of sweet, dark coffee to wash it down. It was worth coming all the way to Scotland just for that. If he were asked on his deathbed what he'd like for his last wish, it would be a mortadella panino from Valvona's.

The shop door was wedged open, the fragrance of rich coffee roasting wafted enticingly up Elm Row. A tall, distinguished-looking gentleman had been walking up and down the street, continually glancing at a crumpled piece of paper in his hand, and squinting at the street numbers. He looked a bit lost.

To his eyes it was a scruffy street; quite busy with the usual fruit shop, butcher's, fishmonger's, chemist and bootmaker. There was a public house at the corner, but nothing that looked remotely like a wine and spirit merchant.

The man checked the address in his hand again. Yes, it said 19 Elm Row. This must be it, however unlikely it seemed. Under the ragged green awning he eventually saw, printed faintly along the grey hoarding, a sign in grey and gold Romic Bold: 'Continental Produce'. Just as it dawned on him that this dishevelled shop front was indeed Valvona & Crolla, metal shutters were firmly pulled down. He heard the front door close and a key turn.

He checked his watch. It was 1 p.m. Lunchtime. He noticed a sign sellotaped onto the shutter:

'There is no love sincerer than the love of food.' (GBS seconded by VC)
    Buon apetito ... Back at 2.30 p.m.

'Ha!' he thought. 'This'll be it. Typical Italians! Their stomach comes first!'

When Vittorio opened the shutters after lunch there was already a modest queue of customers waiting outside. At the far side of the pavement he noticed the tall man with striking blond hair and piercing blue eyes, an impeccable moustache and a goatee beard. He was smartly dressed in a grey and black pinstripe suit with a high-neck white wing collar and a tight bow tie. He sported a bowler hat and a rolled-up umbrella.

'He looks shifty,' Vittorio thought to himself. 'He must be a lawyer.' He motioned for the customers to come in.

'*Buonasera,* apologies for keeping you waiting. We'll be with you immediately.' Spotting a well-dressed lady from Morningside, a regular customer, he bowed slightly. '*Signorina bella,* come in, come in, you're very welcome. Gentlemen, you will excuse me if I serve this young lady first.'

The 'signorina' was a well-groomed wife and mother of four, not a day under 40, but as the best-looking woman in the shop she was given pride of place. Her smart navy suit was nipped in at the waist and, Vittorio noticed, her skirt fell fashionably just below the knee. She had a short fur jacket and a small blue hat perched to the side of her pretty face.

'My dear, if you don't mind me remarking, you look particularly fetching today.'

The lady smiled, and even blushed a little. She didn't at all mind him commenting; her husband never noticed, unless she hinted, and even then she didn't think he really saw.

'Mr Crolla, may I have my usual half-pound of Polish boiled ham, and a quarter-pound of French brie. And I'll have a half-bottle of sweet sherry, if you have one.'

While their assistant, Mrs Glen, started to attend to the other customers, Domenico arrived from checking the delivery was all as it should be. He had three boxes in his arms which he had selected from the pile.

'Signorina, so lovely to see you. You are just the sunshine we have been missing this morning. I hope my brother is looking after you well?'

The lady simpered and smiled and looked particularly enchanted with the ham slices Vittorio showed her before wrapping them up. The bottle of sherry was wrapped and packed discreetly and not referred to again. The 'signorina' knew they only stocked full bottles, but it was an understanding that she preferred to ask for a half-bottle and would of course have to take what was in stock.

Vittorio noticed that the tall gentleman had come in and was now standing at the top of the shop watching the proceedings.

The shop was small, very long and narrow, with excessively high Georgian ceilings, shelved on either side right to the top. The rough wooden floor was covered with sawdust. The wooden counter at the door was most likely an old set of drawers for linen from a department store. The glass display at the front was filled with spaghetti and macaroni, laid out between layers of tissue paper as if they were treasure.

The shelves were filled with all manner of groceries: bottles, packets and jars, each labelled with a card or piece of paper with a description and price. There were few empty spaces; every inch was filled with something unusual and tantalising. Small bags of spices hung like streamers from nails on the high shelves. Anyone standing underneath them waiting to be served was assailed by the exotic smells of cardamom and cumin, chilli, paprika and saffron.

A heavy metal bar was suspended precariously across the width of the shop, sporting strings of salamis, fresh pork sausages, dripping somewhat onto the sawdust as they dried, and a collection of bulbous cheeses that glistened and sweated in the warmth. At the entrance, three large sacks of dark coffee beans lay open, their intense perfume filling the air. A set of red Berkel scales balanced precariously on an upturned wooden crate, a pile of black weights heaped expectantly beside it. Domenico was stationed there, blending and grinding to the customers' specifications.

Rationing and shortage of supply were still an issue, but by the looks of things here, the situation was getting better by the day.

The aromas of freshly ground dark roasted coffee, thinly sliced ham, pungent overripe brie, freshly baked bread, mortadella, pepper and spices were enticing. Alongside the acrid smoke from the waiting customers' cigarettes and cheroots, the alluring whiff of Vittorio's 4711, enhanced by a hint of Chanel No. 5 from the charming 'signorina' and the stink of salted *baccalà*, it was all a formula for the exotic. It felt like foreign territory, which to all intents and purposes, it was.

The mysterious gentleman raised an eyebrow: it was a very unusual shop. You definitely couldn't buy that smell in a bottle.

Vittorio finished his transaction with the pretty lady, and after packing her last purchases into her shopping basket wished her good day and acknowledged the waiting customers: all Italians he knew. He told them his brother would be with them shortly, which they were quite happy about; Domenico usually gave them an extra slice of something or a piece of cheese to eat while they were waiting.

Vittorio turned his attention to the gentleman. Everyone in the shop turned to see what would happen. 'Good afternoon, sir, welcome. How can we help you?'

In a very distinguished English accent with a strong over-layer of Polish, the gentleman offered his hand across the counter to Vittorio to shake.

'Mr Crolla? May I introduce myself? Sklar. Edmund Sklar. I've been sent from London by signor Giordano.'

Vittorio had been expecting a representative from Giordano's, but had not imagined anyone like this. 'So he's a salesman, not a lawyer!' he thought.

'Come with me, my friend, good to meet you.'

Vittorio directed Mr Sklar round the back of the counter, up a small winding staircase to a mezzanine floor filled with sacks of beans and pulses and spices and coffee, then up another staircase and into the offices above the shop. Through a warren of rooms and cupboards he took him into a large room at the front of the building and motioned for him to sit at the end of a bulky wooden table.

'Let me take your coat and umbrella. Please, sit down. Can I offer you a cup of coffee?' After an hour, Vittorio and the rep came back downstairs. The meeting had gone on a bit longer than expected.

'You see, Mr Sklar, I appreciate you have come all the way from London, but as I said to signor Giordano, we just don't have a market up here for a new vermouth. I have already received a case of each today with the delivery.'

'I appreciate that, Mr Crolla, but that's my job. I'm here for four days. Believe me, at the end of that you will have already sold out and be calling our London office to repeat your order! I have a plan. Leave it to me.'

*

The next morning, as the train crossed the Forth Rail Bridge, Mr Sklar was impressed with the magnificent view. The sun had broken through the clouds, and the reflection of the light on the river below was enchanting.

'This country looks promising,' he thought. 'On a morning like this I can understand why an Italian immigrant would consider settling down here.'

Mr Sklar's family had settled in London after the devastation of Poland in the First World War. His father had worked in the London docks and saved every penny he earned to educate his only son. Edmund Sklar had been sent to the best private school his father could afford, his father's ambition being that his son should train to be a lawyer. Instead, Edmund had started working with Giordano ten years ago. He would never fit into the professional class. Although his parents had done everything they could to give him an English upbringing, he would always sound like a Polish immigrant.

The train attendant pulled him from his thoughts.

'Next stop Dundee. All passengers leaving at Dundee, please prepare now.'

Edmund collected his small briefcase, his umbrella and his bowler hat and headed straight to the bar in the Railway Station Hotel. Oblivious to the lingering smell of stale beer, the barman, Jimmy, was polishing the beer pipes, waiting for his first customer.

Edmund took note of the bottles of spirits on display in front of the large mirror behind the bar: plenty of whisky, a Gordon's gin, a bottle of Jamaica rum and a bottle of Martini Rosso.

'Nice morning. Have you had a good journey?' Jimmy had noticed the gentleman descend from the Edinburgh train. 'What's your poison, sir?'

Jimmy kept to himself the thought that drinking at 11 a.m. was a welcome sale for him but a bad habit to get into.

'Good morning, my man.'

'That's a strange one,' thought Jimmy, not recognising the accent. 'What have we here then?' He had worked at the bar in the Railway Station Hotel Dundee all his life. He enjoyed the job, he never knew from one hour to the next who he would meet, and he had met all sorts.

Edmund took some time to look at the bottles gleaming and tempting behind the barman.

'I would like a Cinzano Bianco, if you please.'

'I beg your pardon?'

'Cinzano Bianco.'

Jimmy had never heard of it. The chap looked English but he sounded Polish; maybe it was a vodka?

'I have Smirnoff, sir, if that would suit?'

'No, thank you. Cinzano is vermouth, an Italian vermouth.'

Jimmy was at a real disadvantage now.

'I haven't heard of the vermouth you are looking for, I'm very sorry. Can I recommend a very nice Martini Rosso, refreshing with a shot of gin?'

'That's disappointing; very disappointing. Everyone is drinking it in London, you know.'

Now Jimmy was annoyed. He felt on the defensive and really wanted to tell this character that the next Aberdeen to London would be stopping at Platform 2 at 11.30 if he was that thirsty.

'I'm sorry, sir, we don't list that. I only have a Martini Rosso if you would like vermouth.'

'Martini Rosso is not to my taste, thank you. I'll have a whisky, if you please.'

Jimmy couldn't wait till the man had finished his drink. He saw him leave and wait at Platform 3. The next train was to Kirkcaldy.

'He'll be lucky to get a drink in Kirkcaldy, never mind a Cinzano or whatever it was,' he thought to himself. 'But better keep ahead of the times. That's how a good bar works. I wonder if they do have Cinzano in Kirkcaldy! I'd better make some calls.'

He had no luck with any of his regular suppliers, until one said, 'Why don't you call Valvona & Crolla? They're the Italian specialists; they'll know where to get it from.'

Edmund Sklar stopped at every railway station bar at every railway station on the east coast and ordered the elusive 'Cinzano Bianco' at each. Sure as fate, after each visit the telephone rang in 19 Elm Row. Mrs Glen couldn't keep up.

'Mr Crolla, that's the Aberdeen railway hotel barman wanting to know if we stock Cinzano … all styles.'

Vittorio's order book for Cinzano was bulging full.

Vittorio and Domenico loaded their new van with the dozen bottles of each style of Cinzano along with pasta, oil and cheese, and Domenico was sent off on the mission.

'Good luck, Dom. Do the business! Remember, cash only. No tick.'

'Aye, Vittorio, aye.'

A week later, Domenico sold all the Cinzano and came back with an order book full for more, but only half the cash.

'I've to go back next month with more stock and I'll get paid then, Vittorio.'

Never mind, there was enough cash to place another order with Ercole Giordano. Vittorio was impressed. That salesman Sklar really knew his job.

'You see, Domenico, you have to create a market in order to sell. We need to remember that. We need to create the market!'

Chapter Fourteen

COCKENZIE, JUNE 1951

'Anna, are you ready yet? We'll miss the tram if you don't hurry.'

Margaret Davidson stood at the front door, waiting for Anna Di Ciacca to check her hat in the mirror. When Anna turned round her friend tried not to look shocked. After a sharp intake of breath she turned to the door.

'Come on then, never mind missing the tram. If Johnny sees you like that he won't let you go at all!' Under her breath she mumbled to herself, 'Never mind Johnny; if her mother sees her, she'll lock her up.'

Anna went ahead down the stairs outside the house, taking her time. Her new heels were much higher than she was used to. She'd been into Edinburgh with Margaret last week, and in Jenners department store had chosen the perfect outfit for today. She was all in black, naturally, but her suit was just darling. It had a pencil skirt, two perfect inches below her knees, and a tightly fitted matching jacket, nipped in at the waist to accentuate her curvaceous figure. She had the jacket closed over her lace chemise and a light silk scarf arranged modestly round her neckline, secured by three strands of freshwater pearls. She wore short black leather gloves and a nifty little hat perched on the pile of her thick dark hair, tipped to the right with a veil of lace just skimming her deep brown eyes. Her full lips were carefully painted with her favourite Montezuma Red lipstick from Elizabeth Arden.

Putting her head around the front door of the shop she shouted her goodbyes and walked away before her mother could catch sight of her, calling over her shoulder, 'Don't worry, we'll be back by ten.'

'Nine!' her mother called back, exasperated. 'Be back by nine!'

Anna's Blue Grass perfume left a heady, but silent, bouquet in her wake. It was Margaret who replied to Marietta. 'We'll be back by nine, I'll make sure. Don't you worry. At least you've got Betty working late to help you.'

Betty McCran was a particularly pretty girl from the next village. Fresh-faced, with a very engaging smile and attitude, she preferred order and neatness to Italian chaos, but most engaging of all, she had a great sense of fun. Nobody had any idea, but Alex had taken a fancy to her; he hadn't had a chance to consider his own options in the romantic department as yet, he'd always been so busy covering for his sister and his friend Bill Brown.

Betty had started work last year, when she was 15, the same age Margaret had been when she had started. Margaret was 30 now, and even though she was a year older than Anna, she would never consider wearing lipstick, definitely not Montezuma Red! She and Anna had worked together since that day all those years ago when Anna's father had given her the job. They had six other staff working with them. Betty was a great help; they all got on, and when Betty was working, Margaret could have an afternoon off with Anna. Margaret had been very saddened by Cesidio's loss in the *Arandora Star* tragedy. She always felt grateful to him for giving her such a chance in life.

'You know, Anna, there was never a gentler man than your father. I don't know what he would have thought about you and your fancy lipstick.'

'My dad loved me and he would just be happy for me.'

Anna didn't mind Margaret teasing her; she respected her advice. The two of them were often out together: at the 'Scratcher' in Prestonpans to see a film, shopping in Edinburgh or even taking the train to Glasgow. In Edinburgh they usually met up with Vittorio's sister, Olivia Crolla, who was just a little younger. Anna's sister, Lena, was married now and living in Glasgow; she already had a daughter and was expecting another.

Today they were in fact meeting Olivia at the North British Hotel on Princes Street for afternoon tea, a favourite haunt of the girls; the tram conveniently stopped at the door. They used to go with Marietta but as they had got older they preferred going alone. Lena's wedding had been held there last year so the concierge, Mr Johnston, knew who they were and was very happy to allow the young ladies to come in unchaperoned. When they arrived he bowed and doffed his hat, Anna sweeping through the revolving door in her own inimitable style.

The porters gave her a formal welcome, but winked at each other with approval, as she swept past. 'Good afternoon, Miss Di Ciacca. Miss Crolla is already through in the Palm Court waiting for you. Hello, Margaret.'

Despite his name, Mr Johnston was Spanish, a man who had worked in the North British Hotel for over 20 years. Through hard work and attention to detail he had worked his way up to the position of concierge, which he took very seriously. A compact man, he was always exceptionally well presented, with everything arranged to give an impression of precision. His dark hair was neatly trimmed, his face clean-shaven. His flaring nostrils perched over his pursed lips gave an air of hesitancy; his beady eyes missed nothing.

He knew Miss Di Ciacca and her family very well; he had enjoyed being on duty for Lena's wedding. He also knew Margaret and her family. He and his wife lived in a small cottage in Cockenzie, just off School Lane. When he was not working he always looked forward to an ice cream slider from Di Ciacca's and a promenade by the West Harbour. There was something charming about the fishing village. It was why he had never thought of returning to Spain.

Of course, he knew Miss Crolla as well. She often served him when he went to Valvona & Crolla to purchase miniatures of liqueurs and whiskies. He had a nice sideline going with the buffet guards on the Flying Scotsman. The shop had the very best selection of miniatures, with an entire window display which was a source of constant interest to passing pedestrians. It was not a place you would just pop into; you really had to know about it, and have a requirement to go in. It was slightly secretive, with its grey metal shutters; he remembered they had been installed at the start of the war.

Mr Johnston would never forget the night when Italy had declared war. That was when the trouble had started for the Italians. He had arrived home in Cockenzie on the last tram. It was a warm evening in June and not yet dark, twilight, the longest night of the year. On the way down School Lane he had noticed a crowd at the bottom of the stair at the Cockenzie Café. He'd heard there had been trouble in Edinburgh so he'd walked down to see what was happening.

He was taken aback by what he saw. An ominous Black Maria was waiting at the bottom of the stairs outside the shop, its engine running. A plain-clothes officer was standing at an open door. He was armed.

'What's going on?' he asked the others gathered there.

'We don't know. There's two policemen upstairs in the Di Ciaccas' house.'

Just then the door opened at the top of the stairs. Cesidio Di Ciacca and his young son Alex came out and made their way down the steps. They both had their jackets on. Mr Johnston noticed Cesidio was carrying a small battered brown suitcase.

Two city policemen came down the stairs behind them. They pushed the man and boy into the car and jumped in beside them, one in the back, the other in the front beside the officer.

Marietta and her girls came out and stood watching. Johnny, the older son, was behind his mother. They were all crying, distraught. Mr Johnston couldn't understand what was going on. Alex was just a lad, just 14 or 15. What were they taking him for? Why were they taking Cesidio? He'd lived here at least 20 years, the same as him. That was the last time Mr Johnston ever saw Cesidio.

'My God,' he'd thought. 'I'm an immigrant, the same as them. I've got a Spanish passport. I could be next.' He turned and went quietly home to his wife who was waiting, very worried, at home.

It wasn't till the following morning that Mr Johnston had heard that a car had come later and taken Johnny away as well.

When he saw Anna now, a vivacious young woman, he couldn't help thinking of the small girl he'd seen crying that night at the top of the stairs. His own young daughter was about that age now. It didn't bear thinking about.

He was distracted from his memories by the arrival of another guest through the revolving door. That evening when he went home he reported to his wife all the details of the young women having a day out and what happened next.

'Who would believe it? There in front of me was young Alex Di Ciacca himself.'

'Is that the lad who was arrested when he was just 15?'

'Yes.'

His wife went quiet. Sometimes she was glad she'd never had a son. How could a mother cope with such worry?

Seeing her mood fall, Mr Johnston decided to share a little more gossip with his wife to distract her.

'You'll never guess who was with young Alex! A tall Scots lad, very kind-faced, with a big, wide smile. I think they knew the girls were there already.'

'Who was it? Someone I know?' Mrs Johnston was intrigued.

'It was none other than Bill Brown, the fishmonger. I think it was a rendezvous!'

Mrs Johnston was enchanted.

'How exciting! Well I never. I wonder if it's Anna or the Crolla girl that's winching. Who'd have thought it. An Italian and a fishmonger! Now that's a good business move.'

Mr Johnston laughed. Trust a woman to think of that!

*

'Mum, that's David ready. Do you want to come and see?' David Coia had arrived from Glasgow and had been working all morning, not even stopping for something to eat.

Johnny called his mother from the public sitting room at the back of the Cockenzie Café. It was a good-sized space. It had been home to the family before they moved to the flat upstairs. It had a good, tiled floor and a nice fireplace. At the side there were two bright windows. They had recently re-tiled the walls in cream and blue to match the ones in the ice cream shop. They even had new electric wall lights. Marietta had bought 18 new tables with maroon Formica tops and coordinating red leather banquettes. The tables were arranged along each wall with the banquettes back to back so that each group of customers could have some privacy; young couples liked to come on dates. When it was busy you could also squeeze three people onto each instead of just two. Marietta always had an eye for the best business.

Betty had just set out the new printed menus, balanced between a clean bottle of vinegar and one of brown sauce, salt and pepper shakers proudly completing the display.

'Here, Mum. Come through. Come and see. Isn't it just the ticket?' Johnny was very excited but Marietta looked dubious. 'Mum, wait and see. The clever thing about a jukebox is the customers pay for their own entertainment. How clever is that? And we don't have to buy it, just rent it.'

'Hello, David, nice to see you. Well, are you going to show me how this thing works?'

'Here you are, Mrs Di Ciacca. It couldn't be easier. You just put a sixpence in here and press any buttons, a letter and a number, like this.' David showed her what to do, completing his sales pitch as she watched.

'I'll come every month and put the new records in so you'll always have what's up to date! Music is the way forward. It's the best way to keep your customers coming back.'

With the lights in the contraption flashing orange, green and red, the selection of black discs turned, and Marietta watched enthralled as an automatic wand stretched over like an arm and pulled a record and laid it onto a turntable.

She waited eagerly, asking her son, 'What song have I chosen?'

'Wait, you'll hear'

Within a few seconds the record started to play and the familiar lyrics of Patti Page singing filled the whole café.

I was dancing with my darling to the Tennessee Waltz,
When an old friend I happened to see.
I introduced her to my loved one and while they were
   dancing,
My friend stole my sweetheart from me.

Johnny took his mother in his arms and, giving her a huge kiss on the cheek, started to waltz her round the sitting room. She tried to make him stop then started to laugh as she relaxed in her son's arms. Before she could object, Bobby Dates, the man who helped them gut the fish, stepped in and gave her another twirl round the floor.

By the time the music stopped Marietta was pink in the face, flushed and laughing. When she turned round the room was full; the music had brought plenty of people in from the street. Everybody clapped.

They all pushed forward to get a closer look at the Wurlitzer Jukebox, and before long one of them had put a sixpence in to play another song. They never stopped all night; Johnny, Marietta, Betty and Jeannie Heriot found themselves running a full café with music and dancing and great fun. They hadn't laughed so much for years. They served fish suppers and pies and milk shakes, a ball of ice cream in a glass of milk with a squirt of raspberry sauce and a paper straw, with a profit margin multiplied by three!

The customers were enthralled, playing music non-stop and, as Marietta changed yet another half-crown into sixpences from the till, she caught David winking at Johnny.

It was half past ten before the café emptied. David left to drive back to Glasgow, after showing Marietta how to open the back of the juke box and take out the money. She was amazed.

'I told you it would be a roaring success!' Johnny had been planning this for months; now he could pay for his new car.

They set about clearing the tables and washing all the glasses. Cigarette sales had doubled tonight. A lot of the young boys had had a smoke while they stood at the edges of the room watching the girls twirl and dance.

'Well I never! I just hope Reverend Osborne doesn't object! We'll become a house of ill repute!'

'Good, Mum, I hope we do. It's about time we all had a bit of fun again.'

Just as he started to sweep the floor, a car drew up outside, its headlights illuminating the inside of the shop.

'Who's that, Johnny? I hope it's not more customers at this time of night.'

Marietta looked at the clock on the wall. It fitted the new style of the place, with a young girl's smiling face with golden curls and a large ice cream cone, and the message 'eat more ice cream' underneath.

'Goodness, it's ten to eleven.'

'Hi, Mum, sorry we're late, we dropped Margaret off.'

It was Anna and Alex just coming into the shop, both very relaxed and happy and hoping to avoid any awkward questions about why they were so late.

Anna saw the jukebox first. She ran over to it, excited. 'Oh look, Alex. How does it work? Can we have a try?'

Not able to resist showing them the new gadget, Marietta put a sixpence in and pressed some buttons. Alex and Anna watched, amazed, as the records rotated and the selected one was placed on the turntable. The music that rang out from the machine was Beniamino Gigli singing 'Core 'ngrato', their father's favourite song. Anna hugged her mother. Both had tears in their eyes.

'Oh Mum. Dad would just have loved this.'

It wasn't until Anna had gone off to bed that Marietta got a chance to ask Alex who had brought them home.

'It was Bill Brown, Mum. I was out with him for the afternoon and we bumped into Anna and Olivia so we spent the evening together.'

'Where was Margaret?'

'Oh, she went off home in the tram.'

Marietta said nothing. This was what she had been afraid of. They had all known Bill all their lives, since he was a lad on the fishing boats. He'd grown into a fine young man and was great friends with Johnny and Alex. He had been a great support to her during the war when her boys had been taken away.

They might have a problem on their hands. Marietta had been watching Bill; he clearly had an eye for Anna. She had an idea they might be seeing each other already. That was definitely not allowed. Later, as Johnny was locking up the shop she took her chance to speak with him alone.

'Did you know Bill Brown brought them home?'

'Yes, Mum, but what can I do? Anna's almost thirty years old. She's a grown woman.'

'Please tell her, Johnny. I've tried to talk to her. I like Bill. He's a good chap. But he's not Italian, and he's not even Catholic.'

'I know, Mum. I know. But I'm not her father. It's not my job to tell her and she wouldn't listen to me anyway.'

'If only your father were here.'

'Well, he's not. And that's the problem.'

Johnny kissed his mother. 'You'll have to try and work out what he would want for Anna.'

She looked at him. 'We'll need to talk to a priest. I'll go and see Father Kevin. In the end it's up to him.'

Chapter Fifteen

'Why on earth do you want to be a nurse?'

Olivia was standing with her back to the fire. They had finished lunch and she had taken the opportunity to raise the subject of her future.

Maria had made a *sugo* with thin slices of meat rolled with garlic and parsley, served with home-made macaroni. They had all enjoyed it, there wasn't a morsel left. She made their lunch every day, but it was only on a Sunday, when they had a full day off work, that they could relax. The family always spent the day together. It was often the only time they could air their concerns and sort out any problems.

The remains of lunch were strewn across the table: crumbs of bread, splashes of wine, odd pieces of cutlery, empty coffee cups. Vittorio passed round the bottle of Anisetta. He always sat at the head of the table now. There were often some guests with them – a visiting supplier, a friend of one of the girls and nearly always one or two priests – although not today.

'Sister Anne suggested it. She said they were recruiting nursing assistants and if I joined it would give me a chance to see if I was good at it.'

'You'd be good at it all right!' Domenico was well aware of his sisters' skills. He really couldn't manage the ice cream business in Easter Road without the help of her and Phyllis. They both more or less ran the shop for him.

'But would you really want to do it?' Phyllis looked at her

143

older sister. This was the first she'd heard of the idea. Phyllis was the youngest of the family but she was 24 now. If Olivia went off to be a nurse she'd be left stuck in the shop alone. Gloria didn't do any work; she mostly looked after their mum.

'Olivia, you don't need to work in the convent,' Gloria was a bit worried. 'Are you thinking of becoming a nun?'

'No, not at all. Believe me, that's the last thing on my mind.'

The girls had been devastated by their father's death. They became inseparable, looking out for each other. Their mother had focused most of her maternal attention on her sons; she saw her daughters as support for herself, a habit of most Italian mothers.

Domenico thought he'd make a pitch for Olivia to work with him. Domenico had the job of managing the ice cream business, while Vittorio managed 19 Elm Row. Both felt the other had the easier job, but in fact neither had an easy time of it.

'Olivia, I really need you in Easter Road. I need the help even more now that I'm driving all over Scotland trying to collect debts.'

'Well, whose fault is that?' Vittorio was furious that Domenico kept giving all the Italians goods on credit. The shop's cash flow was causing him endless worries.

Olivia felt frustrated. She'd thought about this a lot and had been afraid she'd be put off. She was serious. She knew lots of Italian girls older than her stuck behind the counter, working long hours for their families and with no opportunity to lead their own lives. She wanted to be different; have a bit of adventure. Her brothers were getting to do exciting things. Why shouldn't she?

'Domenico, that's all very well, but I really would like to explore life a little. To try to be something different.'

Maria couldn't understand this at all. She tried every argument she could to deter her daughter.

'Olivia, darling, you need to be careful, you need to find a husband. You'll see no men but priests in the convent. You'll have a better chance finding a man behind the counter than in a hospital.'

Olivia was 27 years old; it was probably too late already.

'She might find a doctor.' Phyllis had always fancied marrying a doctor.

'Phyllis, mind your own business.'

The argument carried on all afternoon. By the end of it Olivia couldn't even remember why she wanted to be a nurse. She shrugged her shoulders. Her stab at independence would probably come to nothing. Sensing her surrender, Vittorio made his move. He tried to be forward-looking. The old ways might not be the best ways.

'Olivia, why don't we do this? Why don't you try the nursing, say three days a week? The rest of the week you can work in Easter Road. That way you can get a chance to see if you like nursing and you can still help Domenico.'

Olivia was a bit taken aback. She had felt almost relieved when she'd thought her attempt at independence had been unsuccessful, and now she had been handed a chance. What had she let herself in for?

Her mother also sensed her hesitation. 'Why don't you go out with Johnny Di Ciacca like he asked you? He's a nice boy. He's got a good business. If you don't choose a husband soon you'll end up on the shelf, *una zitella*, a spinster! You won't be young much longer.'

That struck a raw nerve.

'I'd rather end up on the shelf than spend my life stacking shelves, that's for sure!' Olivia had had enough. She didn't want to look for a husband; if she chose to stay on the shelf that was nobody's business but hers. The nursing idea was her way of finding a different life, just in case she did end up unmarried.

'I'll be a good nurse! The sooner I get out of here the better!'

With that she stormed out of the room and slammed the door behind her.

Phyllis looked at Gloria. They were both in exactly the same position: they'd better not take sides.

*

Olivia started work as a nursing assistant in St Raphael's Convent. She worked three days there then helped in the Easter Road Café the rest of the week. She had a half-day off on a Wednesday. It wasn't that bad after all.

It wasn't long before she realised working as a nurse was not much different from working in the café. She was either cleaning up and taking people cups of tea, or cleaning up and selling them cups of tea.

'Remember, Olivia, in this life you're either a doctor or a patient!' Vittorio had an answer for everything! He felt he'd handled the situation very well.

'Mum, she'll be perfectly safe among the nuns. She won't get into any trouble!'

Maria wasn't convinced.

*

Olivia got into the habit of meeting Anna in Fuller's Tea Rooms on Princes Street on their Wednesday afternoons off. The tearooms were halfway along Princes Street on the first floor and had a magnificent view of Edinburgh Castle. The girls sat near the window, looking out at the gold and burnt orange autumn leaves. As they both lived in flats, they appreciated the wide-open spaces of Princes Street Gardens.

Anna and Olivia were not like each other at all. Olivia was a quiet, thoughtful girl. She dressed well, and in the new fashions, but with a more demure look than Anna. Olivia had had a few boyfriends but she was quick to tell the boys that she was not interested. She had a reputation for being cool and aloof, or even snobby. Not like Anna. She was a 'scorcher', as the boys in the Cockenzie Café called her. She was a gregarious girl, always glamorous in the style of the Italian movie stars she loved to see at the pictures. She loved 'painting her face', as her mother called it, with the new powders and lipsticks, and kept her hair piled high in the newest fashion. All the sales assistants in Jenners knew her as she was a frequent, high-spending customer. She enjoyed being recognised as an Italian girl in Scotland. She loved the slight sense of notoriety that went with her flashy outfits and high heels.

They had known each other all their lives and had both lost their fathers. They both had older brothers trying to look after them instead but this often felt frustrating. A brother should not be telling them what to do. They relied on each other a lot to try and make sense of their lives.

Olivia had noticed Anna looked very upset.

'What's happened, Anna? Is something wrong?'

Anna gave a sigh.

'My mother has forbidden me to see Bill again. Because he's not a Catholic we can never get married, so she says we're not allowed to be seen together. She says I'll get a "reputation"!'

Olivia had expected something like this to happen. Her own mother had gossiped with the other Italian women about the scandal of Anna going out with a Protestant boy. She'd talked about it with Father Montesi and Father Gallagher. It went without saying that a Catholic girl couldn't marry outside the faith.

Gloria had told her of a cousin who had married a Glasgow steelworker; her mother had thrown her out of the house. She refused even to see her grandchildren. Olivia didn't want to repeat this to Anna to make her feel worse.

'But I thought your mother liked Bill?'

'Oh *she* loves Bill. Alex loves Bill. Johnny loves Bill. It's just me who is forbidden to love Bill!'

When Anna mentioned Johnny, Olivia blushed. Anna was quick to notice. She knew that Olivia and Johnny had gone out together, after six months of manoeuvring by the two mothers.

'What's the blush for when I mention my brother?'

'What? Nothing. It's just hot in here, the sun's in my eyes.'

'Tell me, though. Do you like him?'

'Of course I like him. He's always very charming. I've known him all my life. We're almost cousins.' Olivia was emphatic.

'So, what happened on your date?' Anna already knew all about it as she had previously interrogated her brother thoroughly, but maybe Johnny had told Olivia something about Bill.

'It was very nice. He collected me at home in his new car and we went to the Café Royal for dinner.'

'Oh, that's nice. What didn't you like about that?'

'Nothing. It's just that we have nothing in common. We had nothing to talk about. In fact,' she hesitated to say this but blurted it out nonetheless, 'I thought he was a bit boring.'

Anna found that hard to understand. Johnny was far from boring! He was always laughing and joking and had a reputation of being the life and soul of the party.

'What happened after your meal?'

'We finished dinner and then Johnny wanted to go for a drink. I was a bit tired so we just went home.'

'And?'

'He spent the rest of the night talking to Vittorio about going to Glasgow for a football match, and that was that.'

That did sound a bit boring, Anna agreed. The conversation trailed off. They looked out of the window, neither wanting to say what was bothering them.

Although they had some freedoms, in practice the young women of the Italian community were very tightly managed by their mothers and brothers. They were not allowed to meet anyone outside the community, unless of course they were serving them in the shop or café. They were expected to look after their mothers: they had to do the housework, the washing, the ironing. Then they had to work for their brothers in the shops, not getting paid, but given pocket money if asked. Without exception they all went to Mass every Sunday.

Their brothers had taken on the role of their fathers and were even stricter. The biggest fear in all the families was the disgrace of a daughter getting pregnant outside marriage. As the Church forbade any contraception, this was a big risk.

'You know, Anna, I look at the girls in Jenners serving at the counters. They look like they have so much fun.' Olivia was despondent.

'Well, let's cheer ourselves up. I've got an idea.' Anna's laugh was so loud everyone in the café stopped what they were doing, teacups held frozen halfway to their mouths, to look at them.

'Oh yes?'

'I think we need to get away. Everybody is entitled to one week's paid holiday now. I think we should go on holiday. We could go to North Berwick or even to Millport. Anywhere, as long as we go alone; away from our brothers.'

'That would be lovely!' Olivia felt excited at the thought, but there was no chance. 'We wouldn't be allowed. We'd have to go with our mothers. Gloria went to Italy last year and Mother was glued to her the whole time.'

'Oh.' Anna went quiet. Olivia had a point. How would she be

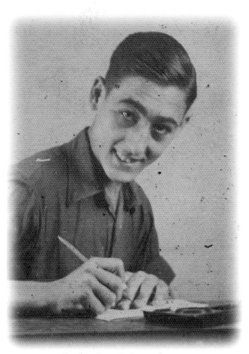

Carlo Contini aged 11.

Ngopp' 'a terra, 'the top of the land', Pozzuoli.

Pozzuoli.

Olivia Crolla aged 16.

Carlo aged 15.

The Crolla family, 1946. Left to right: Gloria, Olivia,
Domenico, Maria, Vittorio and Phyllis.

Above: The Di Ciacca family, 1936.
Left to right: Marietta, Lena, Anna
and Cesidio.

Right: Carlo in police uniform,
Naples, 1950.

Olivia aged 28.

Anna with Carlo's ice cream cart.

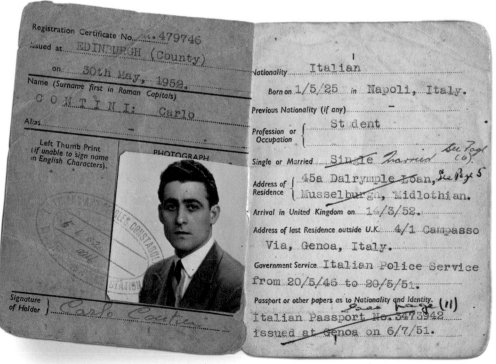

Carlo's registration papers, Edinburgh, 1952.

Anna and Alex Di Ciacca with and Olivia Crolla, 1950.

Lourdes 1952. Olivia, second left and Anna, far right.

Above. Bridesmaids Phyllis, Lidia and Gloria with Carlo and Olivia at the wedding lunch, 1952.

Left. Olivia and Carlo, 1953.

Johnny and Gertrude Di Ciacca, 1953.

Anna with Margaret and children.

Carlo behind the counter in Valvona & Crolla.

Vino Chianti

Extra Old Chianti Wine

Certaldo (Italy)

Importers :

Valvona & Crolla Ltd.

19 Elm Row - Edinburgh, 7 - Phone 556 6066

SLOVENIJAVINO - LJUBLJANA

RIESLING

CVICEK

1952

Produce of Yugoslavia

SHIPPED AND BOTTLED BY

VALVONA & CROLLA LTD.

19 ELM ROW · EDINBURGH · 7

Valvona & Crolla labels, 1952.

SICILIAN GOLDEN MUSCAT

Produce of Sicily

SHIPPED AND BOTTLED BY

VALVONA & CROLLA LTD.

19 ELM ROW · EDINBURGH · 7

VALVONA & CROLLA LTD.

19 ELM ROW · EDINBURGH · 7

SHIPPED AND B

VALVONA & CROLLA L

19 ELM ROW · EDINBURGH · 7

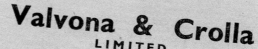

Valvona & Crolla
LIMITED
19 ELM ROW, EDINBURGH, 7

Telephone : 34049 (2 Lines)

Telegrams : " Chianti "

𝔍mporters of 𝔚ines
𝔏iqueurs, 𝔖pirits and
𝔠ontinental 𝔓roduce

> . . . the male
> Companionship of crusty ale,
> Cognac, as oily as a ferret :
> The faintly iron thrust of
>   claret ;
> Episcopal port, aged and
>   austere ;
> Rebellious must of grape, the
>   clear,
> Bluff confraternity of beer—
> All these are good, all are a part
> Of man's imperative needs that
>   start
> Not in the palate, but the heart.
>   —Louis Untermeyer

Above: Annunziata with family,
Pozzuoli.

Right: Olivia, Pozzuoli.

Left: Carlo, Pozzouli, 1955.

Above: Vincenzo, Pozzuoli, 1955.

Annunziata, Carlo and Luigi, Pozzuoli.

Left. Annunziata –
always wise.

Right: Philip and Vincenzo in
the timber yard, Pozzuoli.

allowed to get away? She wasn't even allowed to go out alone at night in Edinburgh.

They both went quiet again, distracted, looking out at the castle.

'Vittorio went to London to meet with some suppliers. Anna, you have relations in London, don't you? Isn't your Aunt Laura in Clerkenwell? How about we take the train to London to stay with her?'

'London! That would be so exciting. OK, I'll ask, there's no harm in that.'

They chatted all afternoon about the fun of a trip to London. They had read the magazines and seen pictures of the new fashions.

'We can go to Harrods. Can you imagine going shopping, wandering down Bond street, visiting the coffee shops?'

'We could go to Soho for lunch. I heard Vittorio talk about Soho all the time.'

'We could go to a show!'

'Let's ask.'

They left, excited about the idea of a trip to London, but both with serious doubts that they would ever be allowed to go.

*

When Anna and Olivia came into the tearoom the following Wednesday, the waitress recognised them and showed them to the same table.

'Have you seen Bill this week?'

'Just on Saturday in the shop. Oh, Olivia I think my heart is breaking. I just think about him all the time. I can't even sleep at night for thinking about him. I'm terrified he'll meet another girl.'

Olivia didn't want to say it out loud, but she suspected any young man would be tempted to just look elsewhere. There were plenty of lovely girls around, and eligible, good-looking young men were pretty thin on the ground.

Anna was quiet. She was quarrelling with her mother and brother all the time, and working in the shop every day and night. She was quite exhausted. Sometimes she wished she could run away.

'Did you ask about going to London? What did Vittorio say?'

'That's a joke! When I mentioned Soho and going to a show Vittorio nearly went mad! I don't know what's wrong with him!'

'Why on earth? He's just been. He came home safely didn't he?'

'That's just the thing: reading between the lines, I think he got into a scrape, or nearly did. He said categorically I was not allowed to go. He actually said, "There'll be no sister of mine walking the streets of London!"'

Anna raised an eyebrow. 'We didn't particularly want to walk the streets!'

'I know. What did your mother say?' Olivia thought if Marietta let Anna go she could try again to convince her mother.

'She said it was a wonderful idea and she would take us! That's not exactly going to be a holiday.'

'Oh dear. It would just be our luck if we ended up on holiday with both of our mothers!'

Both girls looked down at Princes Street below them. It felt like all the young people were laughing and joking, out shopping, having fun. It was so frustrating. Life looked so exciting for others yet it was passing them by.

The next week they met again. The crustless egg and cress sandwiches were their only consolation. The waitress brought them without even asking for an order.

'Any luck then, girls? Are your brothers going to let you go?'

'Not yet,' Olivia said.

'But they will soon!' Anna laughed. They were not going to be beaten.

'Bill came into the shop for cigarettes yesterday,' Anna blushed; she looked lovely and very happy, much happier than Olivia had seen her in the last few weeks. She leaned forward so no one could overhear.

'Oh, Olivia.' Anna gave a sigh. 'He told me he really misses me, but he doesn't want to quarrel with my family. I don't think he's got another girlfriend. I told him to try inviting my mother out and she would bring me too. That way I can get to see him.'

'Anna, listen, I've had another idea.' Olivia was animated, and excited. She had some good news as well.

'I've heard the nuns at St Raphael's are organising a pilgrimage to Lourdes. I spoke with Sister Anne. She said they need some nursing assistants. What do you think? It would be such an adventure!'

'A trip to France? Wonderful. Now you're talking! This could be the one! If it's anything to do with the Church, nuns and praying, the family can't possibly disapprove.'

They were absolutely right. In less than three weeks they were in Lourdes, chaperoned by a priest and four nuns, to nurse 20 patients who were all extremely ill and had come to pray for a miracle.

It was no holiday for the girls, but it was a miracle they had been allowed to go. The work started from the moment they arrived. They helped wash and dress the patients, serve breakfast, attend Mass, serve lunch, settle the patients for a rest and then at 3 p.m. follow a pilgrimage to say the rosary at the shrine of the Blessed Virgin. In the evening every patient had to be washed and fed, and at 9 p.m. they all went back to the shrine to say another three times five decades of the rosary.

The girls had never worked so hard in their lives. At the end of the six days they were absolutely exhausted, having worked 18 hours every day, fasted every other day and not set foot outside the sacred grounds. At the end of the pilgrimage they were given an hour off to go to the shrine of the Blessed Virgin to spend their last night in private prayer.

Kneeling in the dark, heads bowed and trying desperately not to drop off to sleep they looked at each other and started to giggle. The more they tried not to, the more they laughed till tears ran down their cheeks.

So much for the glamorous holiday in London, dressed to the nines, shopping in Soho, visiting the theatre and enjoying delicious, elegant dinners. Here they both were in a convent in Lourdes, working and fasting, chaperoned by nuns. And the best joke of all, they'd swapped their white overalls of the ice cream shop for the same white overalls as nursing assistants.

'So much for a holiday, and our break for freedom!' Anna gave Olivia an embrace.

Kneeling in the twilight looking up to the statue of the

Madonna they both prayed quietly, feeling amazingly peaceful and comforted. Olivia looked across at her friend, who was deep in thought.

'Anna, are you glad you came?'

'Yes, I suppose I am. It's made me realise how lucky we really are.'

It was very quiet and peaceful in the grotto.

'Anna, are you thinking about your father?'

'Yes. I think for the first time I feel he's at peace. Are you thinking about yours?'

'Yes, I feel the same.'

They both fell silent, deep in prayer.

'Anna,' Olivia bent over and whispered to her friend, 'what are you praying for?'

Anna looked up at Olivia. She looked so beautiful, bronzed and serene in the candlelight.

'I'm praying for a man, Olivia,' she said in a serious, quiet voice. 'And you?'

Olivia smiled, her sleepy eyes nodding in approval. 'Me too! I'm praying for a man too.'

They walked back to the convent in the moonlight arm in arm, looking forward to when their prayers would be answered.

Chapter Sixteen

The girls were right to feel relieved as they walked back to their rooms that evening in Lourdes: they had no idea how soon their prayers would be answered, and that the romantic love they yearned for was right around the corner! Although they didn't realise it, there were plenty of single young men around who had the same concerns, and Cupid had everything in hand.

In Pozzuoli, after she had had a glass of wine or an Anisetta, Annunziata loved to tell the story of when she was struck by *il colpo di fulmine*, the thunderbolt. She would laugh and giggle, happy that everyone knew the story but loved hearing her newest version, as it changed and became more fanciful every time she told it.

She swore that when she first set eyes on Luigi she was struck there and then by a thunderbolt of passion. Seeing them now, companions for the best part of their lives, few could remember when Annunziata and Luigi had not been a couple. They just were as one, and the years before their marriage were nothing but preparation for their future lives together.

It happened in Rione Terra when she was just 14 years old, but she remembered it as if it were yesterday.

'I was hanging out the washing on my mother's balcony, next to the church. I looked across at the balcony opposite and, when I saw Luigi, the thunderbolt hit me. I was amazed it was just Luigi. I'd known him all my life; he lived in the house opposite.'

She giggled as she remembered, 'But,' she turned her lips down and shrugged her shoulders then put her hand emphatically over her mouth and, kissing it, waved it across to Luigi, 'the thunderbolt struck and that was that. I was his *innamorata*.'

Looking at their lives, and the number of children they had produced, the thunderbolt had had a lasting effect. She wanted her son to understand; she didn't want him to make a mistake. 'Carlo, *figlio mio*, wait for the thunderbolt. Wait; you'll know when it strikes.'

Trusting his mother, Carlo decided to follow her advice. Sometimes he doubted it would ever strike. And what if the thunderbolt struck and he didn't know that was it?

He had plenty of choice. A lot of girls set their caps at him, and a lot of girls' mothers too. The girls were often very beautiful: young, fresh-faced, voluptuous. Carlo could not deny he had been tempted.

His father's advice was more direct: 'Be on your guard, Carlo. Remember, *tale madre, tale figlia*, like mother, like daughter.'

Between the two, he didn't know what to think. When he thought he liked the look of a pretty girl, the look of her mother put him off. When he liked the look of the mother, there was no spark with the daughter. He had flirted and flattered, but so far he had been too often disappointed or, luckily, had had a narrow escape!

His mother was always at hand with an opinion. If he asked her about a girl he had noticed she'd say to him, '*Quella!* Her!' Then skimming the back of her hand under her chin with a grimace, she'd write the poor girl off. That was enough for Carlo. If his mother was not impressed then there was no hope for the girl.

Annunziata cautioned, '*Aspetta, Carlo, figlio mio.* Wait. You're in no hurry. You'll know when *il colpo di fulmine* strikes.'

He had not seen even a glimmer of a thunderbolt so far. He thought about it often. If your life is predestined, and your path is laid out before you, how can you have the freedom to make choices? Does fate take control, or is it your own decisions that dictate your fate? He reflected on how fate had given him more than his fair share of good luck already.

He had been a baby when the first vaccinations that Mussolini had introduced had started to be administered. Because of that he'd fortunately avoided the diseases that had taken the lives of his older siblings.

He was 15 when the war broke out, so he narrowly missed being called up to fight. He could be dead by now.

Bombs had fallen all around him, yet he had managed not to be hit even once.

When they were told to leave Pozzuoli, his family had chosen to follow the column of refugees north instead of south. If they had gone towards Naples they might not have survived.

Even when the Germans were arresting young men in the streets, somehow, he had never been apprehended.

His mother was right: he needed to wait. He was surprisingly lucky, but he never dared believe it. He thanked the Madonna daily, just to hedge his bets.

And the Madonna had not let him down. Look at him now. Chance had brought him here, to Edinburgh. The previous year he had been invited to Scotland to the wedding of one of his police colleagues, who had met a Scottish girl and decided to marry. It had been a huge adventure, the first time he had left Italy and the first time he had had a holiday.

He had enjoyed the wedding but he hadn't known anyone apart from the few friends he had come with, including his close friend Gianni. Gianni was a smooth operator, a real networker who had the great knack of knowing how to get things sorted. Carlo had felt a little uneasy, at a disadvantage, which he did not like. However, he had spent the rest of his visit touring Scotland and had been charmed. When he went home he tried to describe the country to his mother. It had reminded him of the hills behind Mondragone: small farms with a lot of sheep rearing but still not too far from the sea.

He had spent a few days in Edinburgh, and Gianni had even found an Italian delicatessen which looked very like the grocer shop in Pozzuoli, with every space from floor to ceiling packed with all sorts of interesting items. Carlo had talked to the owners, two nice men whose family hailed from a remote village in the mountains between Rome and Naples.

The following spring, when he and Gianni along with a couple of their colleagues were offered an English language scholarship in Edinburgh for three months by his superior officer, they had jumped at the chance to return.

So now, here he was, immaculately dressed in the *grande uniforme* of the cavalry regiment of the Italian Police Special Forces, standing at the door of the Empire Ballroom in Edinburgh, surveying the scene. He thought, unexpectedly, about his glamorous Zi' Antonio. The memory of his handsome uncle dressed up in his fancy outfit and those black and cream shoes all ready to go dancing came flooding back. Poor Zi' Antonio; he'd have just loved to see this!

His three fellow officers came into the ballroom behind him, causing a bit of a stir among the people in the room. It was full of Italians, mostly from the south by the look of them, and of mixed ages. There was a generous selection of pretty young girls, most of them surrounded by enthusiastic young bloods.

Catching sight of himself in a gilt mirror on the wall, he straightened his tie. He did look good, he had to admit. His mother would have been proud.

It was a grand salon, impressive with three magnificent crystal chandeliers, the red lace curtains cascading over the great windows giving it an air of sultry decadence. Small round tables arranged around the edges of the room were already surrounded by groups of people, chatting and laughing, very much at ease. The four young men looked at each other. They had not expected this; so far Edinburgh had felt quite grey and austere.

On a high stage at the far end of the room, an ensemble was performing; five young men dressed smartly in fancy tuxedos and a pretty girl in a sparkling red dress. The music was very familiar, Neapolitan and southern Italian songs as well as a selection of the swing songs Carlo had enjoyed so much when the American soldiers were in Mondragone.

It reminded him of the parade at the end of the war when the Americans drove down the Via Toledo in Naples and everyone was cheering and clapping. His mother and he had gone to visit his Aunt Francesca and celebrate for the day; the crowds were so big it was if the whole of the south of Italy had been there. The bands played such exciting music, everyone was dancing and laughing; there was so much jubilation and gratitude that the nightmare of war was over.

Several couples were dancing; pretty girls swinging their skirts with young, fashionably dressed men, trousers with turn-ups held up with wide braces, jackets off and sleeves rolled up. They all looked very casual and relaxed.

At a long bar stretching along the left-hand side of the room, more men congregated, smoking and drinking, their roars of laughter ringing above the beat of the music.

Carlo's friends went off to get some drinks and left him at the side of the room. He lit a cigarette and looked around. He was surprised to see so many Italians together in Edinburgh.

Gianni came back with a drink for him and asked, 'Well, Carlo, what do you think? With our uniforms on we've got as good a chance as these *paesani*. Shall we try for a dance?'

Carlo motioned Gianni to go ahead. He didn't want to push himself forward. His mother always advised restraint in any situation where he might be at a disadvantage. He could just hear her voice in his head: '*Stai attento, figlio mio.* Just wait, pay attention before making a move. Always remember to make a good first impression.'

Carlo could speak very little English. The last thing he wanted to do was to approach a girl and for her not to understand what he was saying. He could hear a lot of dialect, but it was from the mountains, Lazio or Frosinone, not Naples.

He noticed a free table at the side of the room and went to sit down. Looking at the happy families, he felt a pang of nostalgia for his home. He rested his head on his arms and was lost in thought for a few minutes. He glanced absentmindedly at the dancers' feet. It was best to check the steps they were dancing before he took a risk on the floor.

And then it happened. *Il colpo di fulmine* struck!

Just like that, out of the blue when he was least expecting it, exactly as his mother had told him. He was shocked. He had noticed a particularly attractive pair of legs, with the seam up their stockings perfectly straight. Attracted, he raised his head to see what the girl with those legs looked like.

'I hope her looks match her legs,' he laughed to himself.

As he raised his eyes he caught the sight of the most beautiful face he had ever seen – the face of an angel, the face of *his* angel.

He pulled back in amazement. That was it: his fate was sealed.

Taking a deep breath, he stood up and leant against the wall, slightly overwhelmed by his emotions. As the girl waltzed past he saw her face again. She really was very beautiful. Thick black hair framed her unblemished olive skin. Her deep brown eyes had a distant look, her sweet lips upturned in a gentle smile.

She wore a white lace shirt with some pretty pearls at her neck. Carlo noticed her dark skirt was slightly longer than some of the others. She had an air of innocence and slight aloofness. He noticed she held herself modestly as she danced.

'*Mannaggia,*' he swore under his breath.

She danced away out of sight. He looked around for his friends. Carlo didn't want any competition here. They were all already dancing on the floor, very dashing in their navy-blue uniforms with red stripes down the sides of their trousers, their gilded epaulettes swaying with the music.

'*Aspetta,* Carlo,' he heard his mother's voice: 'Wait.' He took a sip of his drink, pressed his cigarette out in an ashtray and straightened his tie.

He waited.

When he sensed the end of the dance he moved across to position himself to catch the girl as she turned from her partner. He timed it perfectly and bowed respectfully in front of her.

'*Buona sera, signorina. Potrei avere l'onore di questo ballo?* May I have the honour of the next dance?'

He had forgotten even to try to speak English, and didn't realise till later that she had answered in Italian. The first hurdle had been passed.

The girl was very self-contained. She didn't smile or blush, but calmly looked at her dance card, feigning to check the list of names.

'*Grazie, ma mi dispiace,* I'm sorry, but the next dance is taken.'

'OK. That's just a first move,' Carlo thought.

'May I add my name to your dance schedule?'

She didn't check her card this time but looked directly into his eyes.

'I'm sorry; all my dances are taken this evening.'

Carlo bowed and turned away, ever so slightly put off. Her manner was cold, almost superior. He watched as a young man she obviously knew came across and kissed her on the cheek and took her hand towards a dance.

'Oh well,' Carlo thought. 'Not the one for me after all.'

He moved away just as Gianni approached with two girls, one on each arm.

'Carlo, *vieni*. It's the *tarantella*. We need you!'

Later in the evening, to his surprise, he started to enjoy himself. The men in uniform were popular and a lot of girls were coming to dance and chat with them.

Gianni winked at him. 'I told you we'd have fun in Edinburgh!'

Towards the end of the evening a new band took to the stage and started to play Scottish tunes. This was new to Carlo and he joined with Gianni and a pretty girl to make a set of three.

'Carlo, just follow me,' the girl advised. 'It's Scottish dancing. It's just like the *tarantella* but wilder!'

They joined another group of three and following the beat of the music, after a few minutes fell into an easy rhythm of jumping, dancing, twirling and clapping. Each time the round started again they dipped under their partners' outstretched arms and faced a new set of three.

As he bent down to go under the next three dancers Carlo came up directly face to face with the beautiful girl with the straight stockings. She looked directly into his eyes again and smiled in recognition, and they completed the next few minutes of the dance together. But then she ducked under his arms and swapped to the next set of dancers and was gone.

The room had now filled with dancers, maybe 300 in all. Swept along with the fun and excitement of the crowd, Carlo forgot about the beautiful girl for the rest of the evening.

*

That night he dreamt about Nonno Vincenzo. He was helping him in his workroom at the yard in front of the harbour where the fishermen mended their nets. He was at the end of the room, methodically polishing a small cot. It was made of old oak and had intricate mouldings and engravings. He worked on the patterns, trying to refresh them and make each one look as good as new again. His grandfather kept encouraging him, telling him to keep trying to get it right, to be patient, not to rush.

When he awoke, he thought he saw the girl's face looking straight at him.

Over the next few days she was always on his mind. He kept thinking about her beautiful dark hair, her disdainful look when he had asked her to dance, about the straight seams in her stockings. He didn't know why; she was just another girl. He was surprised at his reaction. He was not a kid, for heaven's sake. He'd met plenty of pretty girls; he wasn't an innocent after all. What was it about this girl that had touched him so profoundly?

In his mind he heard his mother's voice, speaking to him, 'If it means that much to you, do something about it.'

Even though she was a thousand miles away he answered her aloud.

'*Hai ragione, Mamma*. You're right, Mum. I will.'

Chapter Seventeen

Carlo needed a plan. He had only 10 weeks or so left of his course in Edinburgh. He needed to create an opportunity. If he didn't find out who this girl was and how he could meet her soon, his time would run out. He was a stranger in a foreign country and couldn't speak the language. It was like looking for a needle in a haystack.

The trouble was he didn't have a lot of free time. His English lessons were in the evenings at Melville Place, six until eight, Monday to Thursday. He was learning, but slowly. Apart from the few weeks he had spent in Scotland the previous year, his only other experience of English was from music and songs, and of course the American soldiers he had come across in Mondragone.

When he had been selling to the Americans he had learned some words: 'guys', 'dude', 'Spam'. The problem with learning in a classroom was they were teaching him what they called the 'King's English'. Out in the streets of Edinburgh he heard everything but the King's English, and when he tried to speak it with an Italian accent he could have been speaking Chinese for all the good it did.

He was studious, and to make the most of the opportunity he worked even harder. He studied every afternoon to complete his homework and then late into the night. He tried to talk with as many Scottish people as possible. As usual, Gianni was his main source of advice.

'What you need, Carlo, is to get a job with the Scots. It's the only way you'll learn.'

'That would be great, but my visa states I'm not allowed to work.'

'That's just a formality. If anyone asks you anything just say "No speekie de Eenglish!" They expect you to say that anyway. It always works!'

So, Carlo started working in the mornings in an Italian biscuit factory. Zaccardelli & Cervi was based at the bottom of Broughton Street, not far from the Roman Catholic cathedral. Carlo was impressed; they were an enterprising outfit. It was run by two brothers, Adolfo and Anthony Zaccardelli, and their partner, Mr Cervi. The factory worked six shifts a week, making every conceivable confection to sell with ice cream.

Since he had arrived at the start of February the weather had been dull, wet and bitterly cold, Carlo was amazed that anyone at all in Scotland would even consider eating ice cream.

The workers in the factory were all locals. As he got to know them his English improved. In class they had to keep correcting him for using slang and blasphemous language. How was he supposed to know?

'It's "Do you know?" Carlo, not "*Dae ye ken?*"'

'No, Carlo, "*Go and bile yer heid*" is not the same as taking your leave of a person.'

At work, Carlo particularly enjoyed helping Mr Milroy, who made the specialist sugar confections for the factory: mallow cones, chocolate oysters and marshmallow snowballs. Carlo watched him weigh out the ingredients to make the soft sugar filling which, he realised, were similar ingredients to those he had used to make the *mallo pastille* all those years ago in the *farmacia* in Pozzuoli.

Once he'd made the mallow, Mr Milroy would push it through a machine and the small balls of fluffed white meringue were drizzled with a steady stream of melted dark chocolate. As soon as the chocolate solidified they were rolled in luxurious desiccated coconut to make the snowballs.

Carlo tasted them just once. They were so sweet, how was it Mr Milroy made 20 dozen every day? Who was eating all this sugar?

Still, he was distracted at his classes and his job. The girl from the Empire Ballroom was always on his mind. He asked around about other Italian dances but Gianni had discovered there weren't any until the summer; Carlo would be back home by then, it would be too late.

One day, after his shift, he walked up to St Mary's Cathedral and hesitantly went in through the high, imposing doors at the top of the steps. What a vast, cold space to pray in. My God, was this a Catholic church? Had he come into the wrong building? There were no statues, icons or any of the images he was familiar with in churches in Naples and Rome. Even the Cathedral of San Procolo in Pozzuoli was fabulously decorated in gold and art, unlike this place.

It was so dark and lit with only a few glittering candles at the far end of the aisle. He made his way up the left-hand side to a small side chapel. He noticed a statue of Our Lady of Lourdes. In front of it was a small rack with several lit candles flickering. He took a farthing out of his pocket and, taking a candle, lit it and put it in the middle of the top shelf. He knelt and prayed, '*Madonna, aiutami*.' His own mother was far away; his Holy Mother would have to help him instead.

That Friday night he went with the Zaccardelli boys to the Empire Theatre to 'the dancing'. It was full of Scottish girls and boys and was great fun, but Carlo was distracted. He'd never find the girl here. She would never be allowed to come to a place like this, he was sure of that.

Then his luck changed.

He bumped into Alberto, one of the boys he had met at the Italian dance at the Empire Ballroom.

'Alberto, at that dance we went to, did you see the girl I tried to dance with?'

'I didn't notice, Carlo. What was she like?'

Carlo described the girl: tall, dark-haired, beautiful.

'I don't know.'

'She was very distant, a bit standoffish if anything.'

'Oh, that sounds like Olivia Crolla. If it is, watch out!'

Another of the lads, Anthony, was listening. 'Yes, she's a tricky one; she's a bit aloof, a bit unapproachable.'

'Yes, that's her!' Carlo recognised that description immediately.

163

The boys laughed, slapping him on his back. 'She's definitely a looker; she's had plenty of suitors. You've got good taste but I think you're punching above your weight! I think she's too fussy for the likes of us.'

The boys laughed. They knew Olivia. She was beautiful but she was the least friendly of all the Crolla girls.

'You've no chance, Carlo. She doesn't like boys born in Italy, she thinks they're on the make and doesn't trust them.'

'Poor chap that gets her. She'll be a handful.'

'Try her sister, Gloria. She's a much gentler soul.'

Carlo was not put off. This made Olivia even more alluring. He was going to take a chance.

'Do you know where she lives?'

'She works with her brother in an ice cream shop on Easter Road.' Carlo took this in and went off to dance with a Scottish girl to put them off his trail. He didn't want gossip about him arriving before he had had a chance to find her.

So her name was Olivia. Olivia Crolla. What a beautiful name.

He danced on air but with not a thought for the girl in his arms. At the end of the dance he said his goodbyes to the boys and went off home.

Now he had his first lead. His plan was working.

*

Carlo was living in a rented room with another Italian family in Musselburgh, 20 minutes outside the city centre.

The next evening he had no lessons. After his meal he took a tram into Edinburgh and headed straight for Easter Road. He started at the top and walked down, seeking out Italian shops, looking into each one. He was surprised how many there were. They were the only shops that were still open, their windows bright in the gloom, twinkling like a festoon of flags decorating the length of the street.

After the eighth shop left him with no success he felt discouraged. The boys had been right: he had no chance!

He kept going but, having walked about two miles over the best part of an hour, right down one side of Easter Road and halfway back up the other side, he decided to head for home. This was a wild goose chase.

It was starting to rain. It was very dark and there was no light from the waning crescent moon. Apart from some groups of youths going in and out of public houses, the streets were deserted. It was getting chilly. Carlo put his collar up to protect the back of his neck from the biting wind. He saw a small shop with a narrow entrance on the left and an illuminated 'Player's Cigarettes' sign hanging outside.

'Oh good, I'll get some cigarettes.' He opened the door and stepped into the brightly lit shop, the doorbell tinkling, announcing his entrance. The shop was warm and cosy, and smelled alluringly of vanilla and coffee. He noticed a small, welcoming seating area at the back. He turned to the counter, reaching into his pocket for some money.

And there she was, the beautiful girl from the dance: Olivia, the *bellissima* Olivia. *Il colpo di fulmine* had struck again.

'Good evening, what can I get for you?' The girl showed no sign of recognition but was cool and polite.

'*Ciao, signorina,* how nice to see you again.'

The shop was small and neat, with a marble counter and a tidy display of sweets and cigarettes. It had an ice cream freezer and a long tube displaying a fan of ice cream cones and a large display of snowballs, just like the ones from the factory.

Now he was struggling to know what to say. He thought about telling her he helped make those cones and snowballs, but he didn't think she'd be that impressed. He felt like a schoolboy.

'Twenty Players Navy Cut, please.'

The girl turned away to get them. She was dressed in a spotless white apron. Her hair was tied tightly back from her face, with just a strand loose, falling over those lovely eyes.

When she turned round again the light caught her face. They were alone in the shop. Carlo thought she looked even more beautiful than he had remembered. He needed to play for time.

'And … a box of matches, please.'

Carlo had matches in his hand with the money he had pulled from his pocket. She put the matches on the counter, looking pointedly at the ones in his hand.

'That'll be three and six, please.'

Taking the money from Carlo she rang up the till and counted the change in a business-like manner, and with a 'Thank you, good evening', turned away to do another job.

Carlo found himself outside the shop, unable to find any excuse to stay longer.

At first he felt dejected, but at least he'd found her. He couldn't believe his luck.

Standing under the light of the window he opened the packet of cigarettes and, tipping the box into his hand, shook one free. He tapped it on the back of the packet and slipped it between his lips while he reached for a match. Sheltering the flame from the draught he slowly moved towards the window. He glanced into the shop as he straightened from lighting his cigarette. She was working away, wiping the counters, oblivious to his trembling and excitement. He lingered, savouring the moment.

'This is it. This is the real thing. I'm in love!'

Carlo had no doubts. This was the girl for him. He took another draw of his cigarette and, reluctantly, walked back up the road.

'OK,' Olivia Crolla,' he thought, 'you want to play hard to get? You've got a fight on your hands, my darling girl. You don't know who you're dealing with.'

*

The next day Carlo waited at the factory for Nick, the delivery driver, to come to get his snowball order.

Once this was done Carlo could go home. He wanted to work out what to do next.

'What do you need today, Nick?'

'Not much, Carlo. I'm just going down Ferry Road, Newhaven and back up Easter Road.'

'Ah,' thought Carlo, 'that's lucky.'

'Can I come with you today? I'm keen to see the route you take. You might need some help, and I can drive.'

'Why not? In fact I might be busy next week as I've to go to the west coast so maybe the bosses would let you do my drive then.'

'OK. I'll just be a minute. I'll get my coat.'

Carlo quickly went to the gents' changing room and took his overalls off. He combed his hair and gave his teeth a rub with his finger, rinsing his mouth with cold water from the tap. He thought of his mother. 'Mamma, wait till I tell you how the water just comes from the tap. And it tastes good too!'

He splashed his face. 'And wait till I tell you about my darling Olivia.'

The girl was now 'his Olivia'.

Nick was waiting outside on the main road. The Zaccardelli Cervi delivery van was painted elaborately red and green, majestically inscribed with gold and red branding, an image of a pretty blonde child grinning as she went to lick a large mallow cone filled with ice cream.

'Nick, can you wait a second? I just need to get something.'

Carlo popped into Lyndsey's the chemist next door. Mr Lyndsey already knew Carlo. He had been interested to have a look at a Scottish *farmacia* and had had a few conversations about the work he had done in Pozzuoli.

'Can I have a splash of your 4711, Mr Lyndsey?'

'Help yourself, Carlo.'

He raised his eyebrows and waved his hand so Carlo could have a splash from the cologne sample bottle. The chemist smiled to himself.

'What are you up to, Carlo, are you off chasing a girl?'

'You might just be right!' Carlo laughed and, feeling confident, shouted back, 'Wish me luck!'

'What a lad!' Mr Lyndsey had taken a shine to Carlo. He was amazed how much he knew about dispensing. He'd even thought he could give him a job once his English improved.

When he climbed into the van Nick spluttered at the strong smell of cologne. Carlo was definitely up to something.

'Nick, can you start your deliveries at Easter Road?' Carlo looked at him, smiling disarmingly.

'Why not?' Nick was not one to stand in Cupid's way. Everyone had heard the gossip. Carlo, the Neapolitan looker, had set his cap at the Crolla girl. Well, good luck to him. There'd been many a lad at her door over the last few years, and she hadn't softened once!

Carlo jumped in and out of the shops dropping off the orders while Nick waited outside in the van. The tin boxes of wafers and the flat boxes of snowballs were delicate. You couldn't drop them on the way in or the wafers would break. He had to go into some of the bigger shops two or three times.

When they got to the little ice cream shop at 119 Easter Road, Carlo reached for his coat.

'OK, Nick, I'll take the order in here and I'll let you get on.'

Nick winked at him and put his thumb up into the air. He burst out laughing. 'What a chancer! Good luck, lad, you'll need it!'

Carlo carried three boxes of wafers and a box of snowballs stacked on top into the shop. The bell rang as he pushed the door open. He could hardly see across the top of the stack so when he put them on the counter and stepped to the side he gave Olivia a start.

'Oh, it's you! When I saw the van I thought it would be Nick.'

Well, that was a start. At least she was acknowledging that she recognised him. Carlo smiled charmingly as he made his move.

'*Ciao, come va?* How are you?' Carlo resisted calling her '*bella*' though that was his natural instinct. 'Here, let me help you put these boxes away.'

'No. No, thank you.' She was quite abrupt. She didn't want this Neapolitan gigolo getting behind the counter.

'May I introduce myself? My name is Carlo, Carlo Contini.'

Carlo stretched his hand out across the counter. She put her hand in her pocket.

'Very nice.'

'I'm working in the biscuit factory while I'm studying.'

'Very nice.'

Oh dear. This wasn't getting anywhere.

'I'm here from Napoli to learn English.'

Nothing. Not even a yawn!

'I was wondering if you would care to come out with me for an afternoon on your day off.'

'Thank you, but my afternoon off is busy.'

So that was a no. Carlo tried again.

'Well how about Friday? Or next week? Are you free to come

out with me any time next week?' Maybe this was a bit desperate.

'No, thank you, I'm busy all next week.'

Carlo took a deep breath. It was probably no good; he would need to try another approach. He couldn't think of a reason to hang around.

'That's a pity. Never mind, maybe another time. Have a nice afternoon.' He turned to leave the shop, very disappointed.

And as luck would have it, at that moment, and with that exact timing, Carlo's luck changed.

Vittorio Crolla came into the shop.

'Carlo! My goodness. Fancy seeing you here. *Ciao! Ciao!* How are you?'

Vittorio put his hand out and gave Carlo's a good shake, slapping him encouragingly on the back.

'How good to see you. When did you come back?'

Confused, Carlo took a few minutes to recognise the chap, but after a few words it dawned on him. He had met Vittorio before, when he had visited Edinburgh the previous year. Gianni had taken him to the delicatessen at 19 Elm Row and he had had a conversation with Vittorio and Domenico about the various pasta producers in Naples. He just hadn't expected to see him here.

'I came back a few weeks ago. I got the chance of an English course for a few months so I took the opportunity.'

'Quite right. How nice to see you again. Why don't you come with me? Have you got time for a coffee? I'll take you to meet my mother.'

Of course. Crolla. Valvona & Crolla. Olivia must be Vittorio's sister! It was so obvious now, but it had never dawned on him.

'This is just the break I needed!' he thought 'She won't go out with me, but I'm going to meet her mother! Now that's the test. I hope her mother's nice!' Carlo's thoughts took an optimistic turn. '*Grazie Madonna!*' He managed to resist the impulse to bless himself.

Luckily, Olivia's mother turned out to be nice, very nice. She was worried about Carlo being so far away from home; they chatted all afternoon and by the time he made his excuses to go he had also made friends with Olivia's two younger sisters, Gloria and Phyllis.

'Carlo, come and have lunch on Sunday. We'll have time to hear all about your family and Napoli.'

On the way home everyone on the tram was looking at the handsome foreign boy. He looked as if he had just won the lottery.

He had. He had an invitation to Sunday lunch in his darling Olivia's house. And she didn't even know yet! He'd love to see her face when her mother told her. First round to Carlo!

He was already looking forward to Round Two.

Chapter Eighteen

EDINBURGH, MARCH 1952

On Sunday, Olivia took extra care getting dressed. For no reason really. She put on her new navy and white spotted dress with a Peter Pan white collar, and a narrow white leather belt pulled neatly round her waist. Her navy-blue coat had been a gift from her mother for Christmas and she decided on impulse to wear a small navy beret she had bought when she had been in Lourdes. As she left the house Gloria pinned a white winter rose on her lapel. 'We don't want you looking like a nun!'

It was a bright, fresh morning. A show of white snowdrops and a scattering of yellow and violet crocuses had burst through the moss under the trees of the London Road gardens. The girls jumped on a tram to go up to the cathedral at the top of the road and intended to walk back. Lunch was all prepared; they had been up early and the table was already set in the dining room.

Maria had asked the butcher to prepare a large chicken to roast. The bird's head and giblets had been removed, and Maria planned to use them to make a good pot of soup for lunch the next day. She had made a stuffing with eight beaten eggs and chopped smoked bacon, adding some generous handfuls of grated pecorino, finely chopped parsley and a lot of black pepper. She grated some nutmeg and tasted the mixture with her finger to make sure it was really tasty before filling the cavity of the bird with it, then rubbed the chicken with a lot of olive oil and more salt and pepper and added a few more slices of bacon under the skin and over the breast. She put the bird into the oven just as she left for Mass; if they got back from church briskly it would be nice and crispy, just the way Vittorio liked it.

As rationing became less tightly controlled, their Sunday lunches were becoming more and more enjoyable. Because they had food-related businesses, Maria had always found it easier than most to get hold of the ingredients she needed, and since Vittorio's trip to London they were starting to get more produce from Italy, which was a great joy.

Since she'd lost Alfonso, Maria had often thought of returning to Italy. She missed the mountains and the sunshine. Oh, to walk up *la montagna* and wander along the meadows. At this time of year, the spring flowers would be out and the air would already be deliciously warm.

She shook herself. It was no good dreaming. She couldn't leave her family, and they would definitely not go back. After the chaos of Mussolini, never!

But what had she here? Her life was very lonely without Alfonso. While the children were unmarried it was bearable. She had the job of feeding them all, which gave her great pleasure. Once they found partners and started families of their own she would become superfluous, especially if the boys married. She sighed.

Madonna! That was the last thing she wanted: a daughter-in-law. She would live with her sons, naturally. Her grandmother had lived to 102; it could be a long life to spend with a daughter-in-law. Maybe the boys would spare her and not marry.

*

Olivia was usually good at paying attention in church but today her mind was wandering all the time. Sitting in the fourth pew on the left between her mother and Gloria, it wandered.

It wandered through the creed: where was this Neapolitan from, exactly?

It wandered through the sermon: does he have any family?

It wandered through the long ritual of the consecration: how long will he stay in Edinburgh?

As she queued to go to Holy Communion, the choir started

singing 'Soul of my Saviour'. She thought of her father. Oh, if only her father were there!

'Oh Dad. You would tell me what to do.' The thing was, losing her father had broken her heart; she was terrified of letting it be broken again. Overcome with emotion, tears started to roll down Olivia's cheeks unchecked.

Noticing her moist eyes the priest nodded to her compassionately when he gave her the Host. It was not unusual for bereaved Italian women to cry during Holy Mass. Their healing would not be complete for many Masses to come.

When Olivia turned to go back to her pew she was startled. Waiting directly behind her, ready to go forward for Communion was the Neapolitan. She looked straight into his eyes. He saw her tears. She didn't blush; at least not until she was back beside Gloria in her pew. She had to loosen the collar of her coat; she had become quite hot.

After Mass, everyone greeted each other and chatted at the back of the church. When Olivia saw the Neapolitan making his way towards her family, she grabbed her sisters and called to her mother, 'We'll rush home to check the chicken doesn't burn.'

Carlo saw them running off.

By the time the door of their flat opened and Vittorio's voice was audible in the large round hallway, Olivia had had a chance to compose herself, ready to greet their guest.

The food was well received. Carlo really enjoyed a home-cooked Italian meal after all this time away from his mother.

'Signora Crolla, *grazie*. The chicken is really delicious; you have no idea how good.'

She really didn't have an idea. He had never tasted a chicken that was so juicy and moist and fleshy. He caught Olivia looking at him.

'It must be my state of mind. Everything tastes so delightful,' he thought, feeling a little hot under the collar himself.

At the end of the lunch, the girls brought coffee and a bottle of Anisetta. On the table were three empty flasks of Chianti, a half-empty bottle of Cinzano and a bottle of whisky. Carlo had brought a large, round quilted box of Ferguson's rose and violet creams for Maria, which she now opened and passed around.

Olivia stayed out of the way in the kitchen with Phyllis and washed every plate and pot she could find. Eventually, when there was nothing left to wash, she had no option but to come through to join the company. She sat at the corner of her mother's chair, and tried to look relaxed. The afternoon slipped away and by the end of the evening Vittorio and Maria had managed to find out just about everything they needed to know about Carlo.

At 7.30, Carlo looked at his watch and stood up, embarrassed.

'Signora Crolla, please forgive me. I have stayed far too long. You must think we Neapolitans have no manners.'

'Not at all; you're very welcome.'

He went over and bent to kiss Maria's hand, clicking his heels as he did so; perhaps a little bit over-the-top, but quite effective nonetheless.

'Thank you for a delicious lunch and your wonderful hospitality. I'll write to my mother this evening and tell her how excellent your chicken was and suggest your recipe to her.' This was over-the-top as well, because any chicken Annunziata had any chance of cooking would be one of the scraggy ones she kept in her back yard. Fit for laying an egg in the morning and not much else.

He went to Olivia and took her hand and put his head down towards it, just enough that she could feel his breath on the back of her hand, and not presuming at all that he had the right to lay his lips on her skin.

This had exactly the effect he had hoped for. He looked up into her eyes and with a warm smile in his eyes, declared in front of her family. 'Dear Olivia, now that you know a little of who I am, would you give me the greatest pleasure of allowing me to take you out? Perhaps we could see a movie on Tuesday evening? I've checked the listings; Mario Lanza is on in *The Great Caruso*. Would you enjoy that?'

There was no way out now. No excuse left. They all knew her diary was empty.

Blushing from her neck down to her chest, Olivia recovered her hand and laid it on her throat to stop her heart pounding.

'Thank you,' she replied, in what could only be described a husky croak. She cleared her throat, 'Yes, that would be very nice.'

'*Finalmente!*' Gloria and Phyllis burst out laughing and started clapping.

Poor Carlo had had to ask her five times before she accepted. He left the house walking on air.

'Got you! *Sono innamorato!* I'm in love!' On the tram all the way back to Musselburgh he was whistling all the Neapolitan love songs he had ever heard.

Hearing him sing the song '*A vucchella*' to himself, the people sitting on a seat opposite laughed to each other. 'Who have we got here? He thinks he's Mario Lanza himself!'

At the front door of the North British Hotel Mr Johnston's Mackintosh did little to protect him from the driving snow. Seeing the taxi drive up to the kerb he opened the oversized tartan umbrella and ran down the steps to welcome the passengers. He had to steady himself as a gust of wind almost knocked him off his feet.

He pulled the taxi door open and bent over, holding the umbrella high to allow the young lady inside to come out.

'Oh, Miss Crolla, it's you. How lovely to see you again. Mrs Brown and Miss Davidson have just arrived.'

Olivia smiled her greeting and, keeping under the umbrella to avoid getting wet, she ran up the steps and into the warm foyer. A blazing coal fire welcomed her as a young porter took her coat.

She was very excited to be meeting Anna for the first time since her friend had returned from her honeymoon. She went up the steps to the Palm Court.

Anna and Margaret were sitting in the far corner opposite the piano. Only a few tables were occupied. Apart from the tinkling of the music, the voices were subdued and *sotto voce*. The girls stood up when they saw Olivia and embraced her.

The piano player, reacting to their mood, started a Dean Martin tune. Anna recognised it: 'Powder Your Face with Sunshine'.

'That's just what I've been doing. Oh Olivia, I've had such a wonderful time.'

'Let me see you, Anna.' Olivia held her friend at arm's length. 'You look wonderful. Come sit down, tell me everything!'

Olivia wanted to know all about Anna's honeymoon.

There had been such a drama over the last year. When Anna and Bill had declared they intended to marry it was as if World War Three had started: Bill was not an Italian, he was not a Catholic, he was just not suitable. There had been so many quarrels and arguments, and Margaret had heard most of them. Marietta and Johnny were firmly set against it.

Finally, after yet another meeting with Father Kevin, the priest had come up with a possible solution. Bill had to convert to Roman Catholicism. Only then could Anna marry him. Bill went to all the classes and it was not long before he was baptised and confirmed.

'There you go, Bill.' Father Kevin had become quite fond of him. 'That's you in the fold. They can't put up any more objections now.'

This solution caught Marietta off guard. She wasn't really sure why she was objecting to Bill. They had known him all his life. He was a good friend of her two boys. He was hard-working; he had a business, so was not short of money. There was still the problem that Bill was Scottish. The Italian community were not likely to accept a stranger in their midst; it caused all sorts of problems. She'd seen it all before. Often it ended in divorce, another thing that was definitely not permissable. When you married, you married for life. For better or worse!

Marietta didn't want something so scandalous in her family. She had warned Anna. Johnny had warned Anna. But nothing would stop her.

Margaret thought to herself they really didn't want Anna to marry at all. She did most of the work in the shop and she would be sorely missed. Margaret herself would miss Anna but she was sure Marietta would take on other girls to help her. There were plenty lassies looking for work.

'Anna, tell me all about Rome. Was it wonderful?'

As she listened to Anna telling them about the Hotel d'Inghilterra and the Piazza di Spagna, about morning coffee and brioche in the Caffè Greco, the Vatican City and the Gelateria Ciampini, the food and the music, Olivia longed to go there herself.

'Oh, Anna, it sounds wonderful. Look at the weather here, I

can't believe it's snowing and it's nearly March.'

The afternoon tea of tiny sandwiches, warm scones with fresh strawberry jam and butter made them very jolly. They called to the waiter.

'Yes, Mrs Brown?' Anna's wedding had been in the hotel just a month ago so the staff all knew the excitement and drama of the event.

'Can we have some Cinzano Bianco, please?' She winked at Olivia; they had shared the story of Vittorio's plan to change the drinking habits of the Scots.

By the end of the afternoon Anna and Olivia were giggling and laughing. Anna had confided in Margaret that she was already expecting a baby. She didn't want to say anything to Olivia yet but she was very happy and contented. She hoped her friends could be as lucky as her soon.

'Now, Olivia, who is this handsome Neapolitan policeman I've been hearing about? What have you been up to since I've been away?' Anna had heard all about this Carlo from her mother and Johnny. 'I hear he has set his cap at you!'

Anna had waited until Olivia was a tiny bit tipsy before raising the subject.

'He's a policeman from Naples and he's been on duty in Rome. He'll know all the places you've been visiting.'

'Is he as good-looking as they say?'

Olivia didn't want anyone to get any ideas about Carlo.

'He's just a gigolo, Anna. Not for me. He's leaving in a couple of months anyway.'

Anna looked at Margaret. This was just a little bit too strong a denial.

'Nick, the Zaccardelli delivery driver, was telling us all Carlo wanted dropped off at Easter Road so he could have an excuse to talk to you, Olivia.'

Olivia looked shocked. 'Is there nothing I can do without everybody talking about it?'

Anna and Margaret burst out laughing and shouted together, 'No! Nothing.'

The piano player, listening to the conversation, picked up on the theme and started to sing,

I'm just a gigolo and everywhere I go
People know the part I'm playin'.
Paid for every dance, selling each romance
Ooh, and they're sayin'

There will come a day when youth will pass away,
What will they say about me?
When the end comes, I know
They'll say just a gigolo
Life goes on without me.

Anna and Margaret burst out laughing. Even Olivia couldn't help smiling. She had to admit Carlo was charming, and particularly good-looking. She hoped he was not 'just a gigolo'.

Chapter Nineteen

As with all courtships, especially those involving the passions of *il colpo di fulmine*, there can be uncertainties and setbacks. There are of course moments of delirium and delight, but feelings of insecurity and unworthiness can hijack the bravado in the cold light of day.

As a stranger in town Carlo was all too aware that all eyes were on him. The young suitor, though keen to express his emotions, was careful to advance with thrilling restraint. He was at all times vigilant. He understood the levels of propriety expected. This was a fine line.

Carlo was passionately in love. The young lady, though perhaps not that young at 28 years old, might have been regarded by some as being on the shelf. To Carlo she looked decidedly tempting; in fact his intentions were to lift her off 'the shelf' as soon as realistically possible.

He reflected on his course of action. He remembered his mother's advice when looking for a wife. 'Be nice to the mother and you'll get the girl.'

That was his strategy and it was easy enough to follow. Maria was a very good cook, and she seemed intent on feeding him every time she saw him. If he was not mistaken, he suspected Maria had a strategy as well.

Olivia was also well aware that all eyes were on Carlo. The small community of Italians in Edinburgh were from one remote village in Italy, and, as with all small villages everywhere, there was little or no privacy to be enjoyed. Now that she had accepted a first date with the Neapolitan, she knew everyone was watching to see her next move. If she put a foot wrong her reputation, which she had guarded jealously, could be ruined.

But Olivia's feet were firmly planted on the ground and she was determined to keep them there for as long as necessary. She had had many suitors in the past, though none had inspired any degree of emotion that had tempted her to abandon her reserve.

She had to admit, however, that Carlo was more attractive than most of those who had set their caps at her before. He did have a particular elegance about him, a special charm. But that charm was the very thing that caused her to be suspicious. He was Neapolitan, after all. And what experience did she have of Neapolitans? None! The closest she had come to Naples was a plate of macaroni.

She couldn't put her finger on just why she had even agreed to go out with Carlo. Most of their time together was awkward. His *Puteolano* dialect was impossible and his English was a mixture of everything he had picked up in the last few months, whilst he found her Italian dialect confusing.

He did have particularly attractive eyes, but all her suitors had eyes! He also got on very well with her mother, and that could be a challenge, she had to admit. Maria was not the easiest of people to find favour with.

Carlo had become very friendly with her brothers and sisters. She even wondered if Gloria fancied him for herself. She was younger than Olivia and just as pretty. Or Phyllis? She was the youngest of them all and she and Carlo got on like a house on fire.

Maybe Carlo was keeping them both happy just in case Olivia didn't want him for herself. Well, they'd better keep their hands off! The thought of him walking out with one of her sisters instead of her was not one she cared to contemplate.

What she really loved about Carlo was the way he spoke softly to her and the sound of his voice when he sang Neapolitan songs quietly to her when they walked out in the afternoon.

There, she'd admitted it: there *was* something she loved about him.

Carlo, for his part, sometimes sensing a softening of her attitude, would try to pull her towards him. Sensing this amorous advance she would stiffen and pull further away. When they were out together and Carlo gently laid her gloved hand on his arm, it stayed there for less than a few moments before it fell by her side again. When he put his hand on her back to assist her safe passage through a door, she stepped a bit quicker to move away from any contact. When he walked her home and bent to kiss her cheek at the end of the evening she extended her hand instead and shook his quite firmly.

He was being cautious but this was getting a bit frustrating! He just wanted to sweep her into his arms and kiss her passionately. Then she would know what she was missing. She wouldn't find him so hard to resist after that!

Carlo was getting nervous. Time was against him. His English course would be finished at the end of the month. He would be required to return to Italy very soon after that. He still didn't know if he had made a good enough impression on Olivia or if she was even interested in him.

He had to find a way of getting her to reveal her feelings. Once he returned to Italy he wouldn't be able to see her for at least a year. They could communicate only by letter. He couldn't bear the thought of that. He would go mad wondering what she was doing, where she was going, who she was going out with.

He had no time to waste, he needed to make his move. He still needed a plan.

'I'll use all my skills, all my past experiences. I'll get as many people to back me as possible. I need to become indispensable. I'll watch for every opportunity and take them all. Watch out Olivia! I'm going to become irresistible.'

The heat was on!

So when Carlo heard Vittorio telling Domenico that Johnny had ordered a new ice cream cart ready for the summer trade he seized his chance.

'Vittorio, I used to make ice cream carts when I was younger. You know my father is a trained carpenter.'

'Excellent. If you know how to make them that's perfect; it will save us buying them through an agent.'

Carlo hadn't made ice cream carts before but he was well trained in the art of making coffins. As far as he could see, a coffin with wheels would do the trick.

He secured a space in a garage in Montgomery Street Lane and every spare minute he had he worked on the cart. He worked in the afternoons after his job at the biscuit factory and before his English classes. He worked on his day off and on Sunday, stopping only if he had a chance to take Olivia out. Within a week he had built the best ice cream cart they had ever seen. It had an original design, about the length of a short man, with a very attractive pointed shape at the front, like a boat, he told Vittorio.

It had room for two freezers and the wood was particularly attractive, highly polished and shining. It was beautifully painted in the colours of the Italian flag.

'What a great job, Carlo. It's wider than usual, room for two freezers.'

'What a great design, Carlo. I'd like to lie down on it and have a rest!'

'It looks French polished, Carlo. Just like my best sideboard being taken to the customers. What a great idea.'

Carlo took all the praise he was offered, relieved his design had been accepted.

'They're all the rage in Napoli, you know.'

That was not an untruth, highly polished coffins were!

Vittorio was impressed. Carlo did a better job and charged less than his usual supplier. When Johnny saw it he was so pleased he immediately ordered another two. His payments for his new car were catching up on him and he had to make sure he sold a lot of ice cream!

'Carlo's definitely a talented and hard-working man,' Vittorio told his mother, careful to make sure Olivia was in earshot.

Carlo put aside every penny that he was making. He needed to become an attractive suitor. He still sent money every week to his mother – he was always aware that he was in a hugely better financial position that all his family at home – but he saved the rest. You never knew when you might have to produce an engagement ring!

Carlo went to Mass every Sunday. He made sure he went to

the same Mass as Olivia so they could direct their prayers to the Madonna in parallel. He didn't sit beside her, that would have been too presumptuous, but if her mother or sisters were there he would sit with them.

'He's a good boy, you know, Vittorio. He is always at Holy Mass and I see him praying at the statue of the Madonna,' Maria told Vittorio, taking care to make sure Olivia was in earshot.

Then, as had happened to Carlo in the past, just when he needed it, he had a stroke of luck.

Domenico became very ill.

Of course, Carlo was very sorry when he heard poor Domenico had to go to hospital for at least a month. This left everyone distressed but also in difficulties at work. There was not going to be anyone to lock up the shop at Easter Road.

'Vittorio, my lessons finish at eight. Would it help you if I went to Easter Road every evening and kept an eye on the shop for you? I'd be able to help the girls lock up and I'd make sure to bring them home safely. That way you'd be free to go with your mother to the hospital to see poor Domenico.'

'Carlo, that's very thoughtful of you. If you're sure you have the time that would be perfect. Mother will be eternally grateful.'

That evening Carlo appeared in the shop in Easter Road at ten minutes past eight. Making sure he was in earshot of Olivia, he spoke to her sister, 'Ciao, Gloria. Vittorio asked me to come and help you both while Domenico's in hospital. I've worked in a shop before so know a bit about what to do.'

How fortunate was this! Now he could see Olivia every single night.

Carlo became very popular with Olivia's sisters. They enjoyed the fun of having the company of a handsome young Neapolitan to entertain them every evening instead of their brother telling them what to do.

Finally, even Olivia started to enjoy being with Carlo. She became more relaxed around him and even thought of him as her young man. She looked forward to seeing him when he came to the shop after his classes. She got into the habit of having a plate of pasta ready for him, just in case he was hungry.

This was a good sign!

When they were alone together now, and he put her ungloved hand on his arm, she casually left it there. When he put his arm at her back to guide her through a door, she walked ever so slightly slower so that his arm could linger on her back just a little longer. When he moved at night to kiss her cheek she moved her face towards his so he could kiss her lips.

In fact, without intending to, Olivia had fallen in love.

Things were coming along just nicely.

On Sunday, when Father Gallagher saw the young Neapolitan who was wooing the Crolla girl light a candle at the statue, he was sure he caught him winking at the Madonna.

*

Before he knew it, the end of Carlo's English course was in sight. He was due to leave Edinburgh within days. He couldn't see how he could bear to leave Olivia. He was terrified he would lose her if he didn't make a move.

He had to find a way of staying in Scotland, at least a bit longer. He talked to his friend Gianni.

'Can you get a doctor to write a certificate for me to say I am ill and unfit to travel?'

The certificate was duly purchased and wired to Lieutenant Pelosi in Rome. A telegram came back by return.

'NOTED YOU ARE ILL. STOP. STAY EXTENDED 30 DAYS. STOP.'

After the 15 days were up he was still 'unwell' and had a further extension granted.

'Gianni, do you think there is any chance I'll be able to get more time to stay in Scotland?'

Gianni had done his best for his friend. 'I think your luck is running out Carlo. You'll have to speak to the consul yourself.'

The consul was sympathetic; he had known and respected Cavaliere Alfonso Crolla and wanted to do all he could to help his daughter. He organised an official telephone call to Rome. Carlo's superior, Lieutenant Pelosi, had seen it all before.

'Carlo, you know as well as I do the rules cannot be bent. You are an employee of the Italian Police Force. So many young men like you go abroad, see the opportunities and decide they want

184

to stay. I need to ask you this: is there a girl involved?'

Carlo had to tell him the truth.

'Well, my boy, it's your decision. I can authorise a further leave of absence, but you must understand, if you are not available for duty here in Rome by the 16th of June I will have no option but to accept that you have resigned from your position.'

This was a blow. Now Carlo was in danger of losing on two fronts. He could only legally stay in Scotland if he had a job or was getting married. If Olivia didn't want to marry him, or if she changed her mind, he would have lost his job in the police force, lost all opportunities of regaining it and lost all the advantage he had gained from leaving home and working so hard.

He would be forced to go back to Pozzuoli and start all over again.

Carlo took a deep breath and thought to himself, 'Attenzione, perdere Filippo e il panaro. Be careful Carlo, you're in danger of losing everything.'

He made his choice. He was determined not to lose Olivia.

The first thing he did was to write to his mother to tell her he would be staying a little longer in Scotland. He hinted that perhaps it was to do with a girl.

*

The following afternoon, when Carlo tried to explain to Olivia that he was considering resigning his position in the police force and finding a job in Edinburgh, she felt quite overwhelmed. She had only known him a few months. She did love him, or at least she felt she did. But how could he give up everything he had worked for and start here with nothing?

He told her that unless she gave him an indication that she wanted to be serious with him, that she wanted an 'understanding', he would have to leave and return to Italy.

It was very troubling for Olivia: how could she take the decision to make him do something so drastic? They still didn't really know each other. She went out alone and walked along London Road as she tried to think, and coming round the corner of Elm Row she stopped in front of the shop. Something drew her in. In the tall, narrow space with the shelves full to the ceiling, the salamis and garlic hanging and the smell of cheeses and coffee, she felt calmer. As she took a deep breath she was suddenly aware of the familiar perfume of her father's aftershave, Ashes of Roses.

She turned round, startled. 'Dad?'

It was her brother, Vittorio, standing behind her.

'Oh, Vittorio. I thought for a moment you were Dad standing there.'

Vittorio was just finishing serving the last customer.

'Olivia, sorry darling. It's just me I'm afraid. Here, check this for me and I'll carry out the boxes for this customer.'

He gave her the bill to check and carried the boxes, including two bottles of Cinzano Bianco that the customer hadn't even known he'd needed, but for some unexplainable reason was very glad to have.

Once the customer had gone out smiling and happy, Vittorio pulled down the shutters and turned the key in the door. He rang open the till and took out the pile of notes that were secured under the two metal tabs. He folded them and pushed them into his back pocket. He lifted the till drawer out and checked what was underneath; three large Clydesdale Bank five-pound notes.

He nodded to himself, adding them to his pocket. Stretching up he selected a bottle of Muirhead's whisky from the shelf above the till.

He turned to his sister and, encouraging her to follow him, started singing, '*Jamme, jamme 'ncopp' jamme jà.* Let's go, let's go, let's go to the top!'

Vittorio was making a joke. Carlo had been singing this last week and they'd all had fun joining in. Olivia followed him up the narrow stairs. She didn't feel like laughing.

'Vittorio, that's not funny. Please don't.'

Vittorio limped a little when he was tired. He was putting on a bit of weight and his trousers were a bit tighter than they used to be. He reminded her more and more of her father. As he climbed some notes fell out of his pocket onto the step. Olivia picked them up.

'Vittorio, you're always dropping money out of your back pockets. You should be more careful. Have you got money to burn?'

186

'You're right. I'd better be a bit more careful, especially if I'm going to have a wedding to pay for!'

Olivia pretended not to hear him. 'That's him teasing me again,' she thought. 'I shouldn't have come.'

In his office he sat down heavily in his old black leather chair, opened the bottle of whisky, poured a small glass and drank it.

'Do you want a wee dram? It'll not do you any harm.'

'No, thank you.'

Vittorio poured himself another and with his hands folded in front of his chest leaned back in his chair. He knew exactly why Olivia had come to speak to him.

'Well, what do you think? Do you love him?'

'Maybe I do. I don't know. I'm just not sure. I don't know anything about him. He could be making it all up. His stories are all a bit exaggerated. How do we know who he is? How can I know in such a short time?' Olivia felt awkward. She had never spoken to her brother about a man before.

'Well, you must know something. It's come this far. Let's look at what we do know.' Vittorio took the small stub of pencil from behind his ear and, turning over an envelope, started to write on the back all the things they were sure about this man who was turning their lives upside down.

'We know he's a policeman, registered in Genoa and well-regarded enough to be in the Special Forces. That tells us he is respected, diligent and that he doesn't have a criminal record.'

'Vittorio! That's not nice!'

'Well, it's a fact. We know he comes from Naples.'

'Not Naples, Pozzuoli!'

Vittorio smiled to himself, thinking, 'Huh, she's sticking up for him. That's a good sign!'

'Carlo said the people from there are a different type, more sophisticated than the Neapolitans.'

Vittorio looked at her, slightly taken aback. Olivia never knew a thing about either Naples or Pozzuoli till three months ago!

'OK. I take your point,' he scored out Naples and changed it to Pozzuoli. 'Better that than he comes from our own Picinisco! At least it's new blood!'

Olivia blushed. Most of the immigrants who had come from

the villages in their area were still marrying within the community. It was a constant source of discussion among their mothers and grandmothers. They were always worrying about intermarriage. The women knew the physical traits and weaknesses of every family and were careful to discourage marriages that were too close; they knew the consequences from bitter experience.

'Well, we girls can't win! Mum has made such a fuss about Anna marrying Bill as he's Scottish. It's a wonder there's any of us married at all!'

'So,' Vittorio thought, 'she's worried about not being married. That might make her a bit impulsive. I'd better be careful what I suggest here.'

'So, are you sure you don't want a wee drink?' Vittorio poured himself another nip to buy himself time.

'At least he's a Roman Catholic.'

Vittorio looked at her. She was building the case in Carlo's favour.

'You're right. He goes to Mass. He takes Communion.' Vittorio agreed with her, but reflected that it could be a front, just to impress them all.

'He prays to the Madonna. He writes to his mother.' Olivia found herself enthusiastically adding to the list of positives on Vittorio's envelope.

Vittorio looked at her, smiling, and wondered why she was even asking his opinion. She'd clearly already made up her mind!

Seeing Vittorio's look and suddenly aware she was sounding too keen she blurted out, 'But he's still an Italian!'

Olivia had always stated vehemently that she'd never marry an Italian. The boys came, charmed the girls and once they were married they disappeared back to Italy.

Now she was trying not to sound too keen. Vittorio was enjoying himself. He knew where the conversation was leading. He just wanted to tease her a little more.

'So what else? He's tall. He's good-looking. He dresses well. He likes his food. He likes our mother's food! That's a double bonus point!' He burst out laughing.

Olivia tried to be serious. 'But, Vittorio, why is he in such a hurry?'

'Well, he hasn't got much choice. He hasn't any right to stay here, unless he gets a job and marries.' Vittorio looked at her to see her reaction, deducing from her unblushing face that Carlo hadn't proposed yet. He was getting a good sense of what had been going on between them. He continued.

'If he stayed, he wouldn't have a job or any income. If that was me I'd be in a hurry to know where I stood!'

Olivia was all too aware: Carlo had nothing!

'Oh, Vittorio. What do you think Dad would have said?'

Vittorio reached over and took her hands in his.

'Olivia, darling. Since we don't have the luxury of Dad to ask, we'll have to make up our own minds.'

He looked at her, sorry that her eyes had welled up. He understood the raw pain she still felt. What *would* his father have done? He took a sip of whisky. It was obvious!

'I'll tell you what. I need to go to Italy, to Milan. There's a food fair there now and I was thinking it's the right time to start to see if we can find some new suppliers and import directly. Rationing is lifting and there's a real appetite for good food. I've always thought, if we're going to be grocers we need to be the best grocers we can be. So,' he watched her reaction carefully as he put his plan to her, 'I'll go to Milan. Then, when I've finished here, I'll drive down to Naples. I'll go myself to Pozzuoli and meet his family. Then we can make the right decision. I'm sure that's what Dad would have done.'

Vittorio liked Carlo, but there were plenty of nice Italian boys coming across looking for women. He needed to be careful for his sister; she was right to be cautious. No one really knew who Carlo was or where he'd come from. Some of the men coming to marry girls here were already married in Italy; all sorts of shenanigans were going on. Now she had made it clear to him that she was keen on Carlo it was his duty to make sure he was suitable for her. Carlo was 27. It could be he was married already. He could even have children. It was the right decision to go himself and find out what this was all about before it got out of hand. He had no intention of stopping at Milan. He would go straight to Pozzuoli. There was no time to waste.

Part Four

Pranzo è all'una
Lunch is at one

Overleaf: Carlo Contini aged 27.

Chapter Twenty

POZZUOLI, JUNE 1952

Annunziata had a premonition. Something told her their lives were about to change. She felt in her heart Carlo had already made a decision; he had chosen a new life. She had been waiting for this, she had seen it all before. So many young Neapolitan men left their homes in search of work; few, if any, returned.

She jutted her chin up and shrugged her shoulders. What right did she have to ask the Madonna for any more blessings? It was enough that Carlo would be happy. Her own future was charted now. There was nothing she could do to change that. And, in her experience, when the Lord takes with one hand he gives with the other. Look what had happened to her. Precisely when Carlo had decided to join the police force and go back to Genoa, her youngest child, Peppino, had been born.

Annunziata giggled to herself. She had been 44 and already a nonna twice over when she'd found out she was expecting another child. Ninuccia had already married and had two children. *Grazie alla Madonna*, Peppino was born healthy. He was six years old now; younger than his own nieces and nephews!

Since they had come back to Pozzuoli Ninuccia had moved into Zia Francesca's old room with her husband and children. After he had been arrested by the Germans Paolo had spent the rest of the war in work camps in Eastern Europe. They had all been so fearful for his life and were so very relieved when he had returned, worn and exhausted, but thankfully home safely. Rosetta was married and lived in another room. All four grandparents had moved back down to the port; they found the 178 steps *ngopp' 'a terra* a challenge and only a good meal would tempt them to climb them. Luigi had followed her back and they had returned to their old home. It was fine for now but the rumours were that the whole area was going to be evacuated as it was in such bad repair. She hated the thought, but they might have to go back to live in Mondragone again. Nothing was settled.

On top of that, Luigi's health was not good; his hand had never fully recovered from his factory injury and his legs were not as strong as they had been. A lunch and siesta every day were perhaps part of the problem. He never saw it like that: lunch and a siesta every day, what more could you want?

Vincenzo and young Ernesto, at 15 and 13, were both working with their father now, so that was a good help. Vincenzo was already almost as good a carpenter as his father. There was plenty of work: all the destruction heaped on Rione Terra could never be repaired, not even in a hundred years; the rebuilding and repair works were unending. As always, the real problem was money. Still no one paid with cash, always in kind.

To be fair, they gave more than they used to: now they would bring Luigi a whole fish rather than two fish heads. It was easy to cook. Annunziata would light a small charcoal burner on the balcony, wash the fish, slash the skin and rub the fish inside and out with salt and olive oil. She'd stuff the belly with fennel and lemon and sprinkle it all over with the dried fennel pollen she had harvested in the spring.

As it grilled and the aromas wafted down to the yard below, she knew Luigi and the boys would smell the chargrilled skin and just when the fish was cooked she'd hear their whistles, as they knew it was time to come up to eat.

If she was given a basket of tomatoes she'd cover them in boiling water, slide off the skins and seeds and make the rest into a sauce to bottle with a bunch of fresh basil and a clove of garlic. She always had tomato sauce ready for a quick plate of *spaghettini scieuè scieuè* if anyone was hungry.

She was grateful they no longer had to be hungry. It was good she had six chickens now in the back of the wood yard laying eggs every day; good that the shepherds often came from the mountains with fresh pecorino and the farmers had bought buffalo and there was plenty of fresh, creamy mozzarella.

She was very grateful to have food again; she hardly dared remember how terrible it had been when they were starving. But to get on in life and find a way forward, what they really needed was cash. As it was she still had to use all her wits to survive day to day.

Annunziata's youth had passed her by; she was no longer the local wet nurse. Nevertheless, young mothers still came to her, expecting her to help.

'*Balia* Annunziata, please. Are you sure you can't help? You fed my daughter, see how well she looks. Could you not take my boy? If you just try, the milk will come, surely?'

Annunziata would giggle, shaking her hands open, but empty, in front of her sagging breasts. She'd squeeze them just like one of the black horns on the fancy cars that now drove around the piazza all day.

'*Non c'e niente!* Beep, beep! They're empty! Get a bottle for milk. Put some bread in it as well. The baby will sleep all the time. Then,' she'd giggle again, waving her hand to show the mother to the door, 'you can look after your husband and make another baby!'

She took the precaution of 'forgetting' to tell the authorities that her 'babies' no longer required diapers. She was entitled to two dozen free every week. She claimed them and, serving the needs of the community, sold them on to older women in the town. Incontinence pads, she was well aware, could be very useful to women of a certain age.

When he had returned from Genoa during the war, Carlo had never told his parents how much he had enjoyed his time there – most of it, anyway. He had thrived away from the suffocating constraints of Pozzuoli. In a foreign city, no one knew who you were. No one was interested in what you did, where you went or what time you came home. In Genoa, every mother wasn't eyeing you up and trying to get you to marry her daughter.

Even now, all these years later, life in Pozzuoli had hardly improved; if anything, it was worse. There were still problems with sanitation and electrical supply. The black market was now endemic and there were signs of the *Camorra* taking control. It would take years to get the town rebuilt, if it ever was. The south of Italy would never be modernised. It was obvious to everyone – the north would always pull the best of the youth away. Why would you stay in a place like Pozzuoli?

Carlo's eyes had been opened: there was no going back.

Of course, there were opportunities for him in Pozzuoli. He could have stayed and worked with his father as a carpenter, or as a shoemaker with Zi' Alf, though somehow, he doubted he'd be welcome. Zi' Alf had always looked at him suspiciously since he'd smashed his shop window when he was a boy. He had been invited to go back to the *farmacia*, as neither signora Carmelina nor her son had ever returned after the war, but the life would have been too slow for him.

He was skilled enough to get work as a French polisher or even a coffin-maker, but even that market was less busy than it had been. Since babies and young children were now being vaccinated, more were surviving and far fewer coffins were required.

Carlo was a fully trained steelworker but the Ansaldo factory in Pozzuoli had been so badly damaged that the workforce had collapsed from 6,000 during the war to only 300 now. All the decent jobs were transferred to the north. A lot of his friends had taken work in the Ansaldo factory in Genoa, some in Turin with F.I.A.T. One had even gone to Pomigliano d'Arco to work with Alfa Romeo.

He had been tempted to join them, but he knew he could do better than a life enclosed in a car factory. He helped his father and honed his carpentry skills and waited.

When he was 22, just as Peppino arrived in the family, his opportunity arose. He saw a sign in the town about joining the police force as a trainee. He applied without hesitation. He suited the position perfectly in temperament as well as appearance: hard-working, tall, slim, elegant-looking. It was not surprising to anyone, not least his mother, that he got the job.

After a training period in Genoa he was sent to Rome, this time as a fully trained mounted police officer. It was a great position that offered board and lodgings, good health insurance, and on top of that, a wage packet every week! He found a whole new way of life with his group of fellow cadets and was at last enjoying a life of freedom and independence.

Carlo wrote frequently, telling his mother all his adventures, but mostly to send money to help his family.

Every Thursday Annunziata waited for the whistle of *il postino*. When she heard it, she would lower her basket from the window. As soon as he'd put her letter in it, she'd pull the basket up slowly so all her neighbours could see that her son had sent a letter. They all knew, of course, that she couldn't read the letters, but no one said a word.

First, she would open the letter, removing any money Carlo had enclosed, then carefully reseal the flap. She didn't want the family to know how much money there was; they would want to spend it too easily. They all knew she did this, and she knew they knew; if they needed money she would give it to them anyway.

She would then place the letter with the photograph of Carlo dressed in his full uniform astride his horse at the head of the table, where Carlo used to sit.

'*A mangiare! Oggi Carlo è con noi!* Eat! Carlo's with us today!'

On these days she would prepare Carlo's favourite food so she could bring him closer to her: *zuppa di chichierchie* or *vermicelli ai frutti di mare*. She would never make polenta. After the war had ended, Carlo swore he would never eat polenta again.

The letter would be read after Luigi had had his usual *mezz'oretta*. This was reasonable. 'You can't get excited on a full stomach!'

She would brew the coffee, now in the new Bialetti coffee-maker Carlo had brought her from Rome. It spluttered and splashed and propelled its thick, dark mysterious liquid up through the spout, just like the lava from Vesuvius itself. Alerting Luigi, the aroma would bring him back to the table, where he would smile contentedly as she poured the syrup into his cup. She would add a splash of Anisetta, and Luigi would stir in a little sugar to add the sweetness he enjoyed.

Since Carlo had been in Scotland on his English course, she hadn't heard from him as often. He still wrote every week, even longer letters, filled with more exciting news, but the postal service was erratic. Sometimes she got no letter at all, and then two or three arrived at the same time. When they did arrive she saved them like *dolci*, as a sweet treat to be enjoyed at the table together after the family had eaten.

There had been no letter for two weeks so, when the family heard the postman had delivered one they all congregated around the table, eagerly anticipating the news.

'Read it, Vincenzo, read it!'

Vincenzo took his duty very seriously and read the letter with care.

'OK, here we go …

'*Ciao, tutti.* I hope you are all well. I hope the sun is shining. Even though it is the end of May it is still cold here and it feels like the rain will never stop.

'Mamma, I love you with all my heart and I will always be your son. I am writing to let you know that I am staying in Edimburgo for another few weeks. I have permission from Lieutenant Pelosi. You see Mamma, I have met a girl …'

Annunziata's heart lurched. She sat down on Carlo's chair. This was it then. This was the premonition she had felt that morning.

She waited till the letter was all read and had been placed in the drawer, and everyone had gone laughing and joking back to their work, oblivious of their mother's reaction.

Luigi stayed behind. He took Annunziata's hands in his.

'Luigi, what will we do? What will we do?'

The next day, after a sleepless night when they lay together as they hadn't done for many years, Luigi and Annunziata went to see the priest. With his assistance they wrote a reply to Carlo's letter. They walked together slowly down to the piazza to the *ufficio postale*, just a few doors from the *farmacia* where Carlo had worked. It was a beautiful sunny day with cloudless skies; the smell of lemon blossom perfumed the air. Annunziata sat quietly on the bench under the lemon trees while Luigi went in to post the letter.

She could do nothing now but wait.

*

198

Annunziata went to her window to check the laundry. She smiled to herself. There were still plenty of children's clothes to hang out to dry in her home.

She bent over, stretching as far as she could to reach the clothes, folding and carefully laying them in the basket at her feet, dropping the wooden clothes pegs into her apron pocket as she worked. She quietly prayed to the Madonna as she went.

'Holy Mother, I abandon myself to thee.' There was nothing else to say. Her Holy Mother had always looked after her, and Carlo.

Once the last item of clothing was folded, Annunziata leaned on the balcony, resting. She looked across at the sea, and sighing, allowed her eyes to gaze into the horizon. The beauty of the panorama was still breathtaking; even though she saw it every day she never took it for granted. The sea was calm, small white waves making a lazy effort to be noticed. A sailor was rowing his boat to shore, a straw hat pulled over his face to shelter him from the glare of the sun. His naked chest was swaying with the boat as he pulled himself across the water, leaving a wake of white foam rippling out into the distance.

As he raised his head towards the shore his melancholic voice carried up towards her,

Quanne fa notte e 'o sole se ne scenne, me vene quase 'na malincunia

When night comes and the sun sets, a gentle sadness comes over me.

The sun was just turning to a glowing auburn, like a giant orange gleaming in the pale blue sky. 'Surely heaven itself is no less beautiful,' she thought, as the church bell for evensong rang out across the Rione Terra.

Her peace was broken by the sound of a car, a very unusual thing at this time of the evening. There were no ferries till the morning. She looked down to the harbour to see who was arriving. It was a dead-end past *'ngoppa al porto;* whoever was coming must be stopping there.

A large green car pulled up at the quayside. She watched as the door swung open and a man came out, stood up and stretched his arms and shoulders as if he had been driving a long distance. He was dressed in dark trousers and a crumpled white shirt with the sleeves rolled up. His shirt neck was open and he looked quite relaxed. She noticed his dark hair was thinning on top and he had a slight limp as he walked towards the water and watched the fisherman pulling into the shore.

The man waited till the fisherman jumped out of his boat then, after a short conversation, she saw the fisherman turn round and point up towards her. He waved and, climbing up onto the quayside and fastening his boat, shouted outside Luigi's yard. The man and the fisherman went into the yard together.

Annunziata shrugged her shoulders. It must be a customer from Naples, or a salesman.

'I hope he doesn't keep Luigi long.' She had made *seppie in zimino* and some *carciofi alla contadina*. At the market that morning Annunziata had bought some baby artichokes and some greens. Luigi had brought some cuttlefish from the boats at lunchtime and she had sautéed them in fresh tomato sugo. On the table she had put some sautéed greens and some *melanzane sott'olio*, the final jar of aubergines from the winter store. There was a jug of water and a jug of wine out too.

'Antonietta, set the table. It's dinner time. Papà will be home soon.'

She heard Luigi whistling from the bottom stair and started to slice the rest of the dry bread, sprinkling it with some water, dried oregano and a pinch of salt. As usual she drizzled it with olive oil, stopping too much oil coming out by covering the opening with her thumb. She licked her fingers, smacking her lips.

'*Ho una fame.*' She'd got hungrier as she'd got older.

She put the last of the mozzarella from lunch on the table. They ate what they bought that day as they had no icebox. She had heard that some people in Naples did. They had become selfish, saving their food for a few days and buying more than they needed. But Annunziata managed as she always had, sharing what food she had every day.

'Annunziata!' Luigi's whistle shrilled again.

'What's he whistling again for? I heard him.'

Vincenzo came in first.

'Mamma. *Attenzione.* We have a visitor.'

'*Che?*'

She heard another voice with Luigi. She looked at Vincenzo, who was looking a bit flustered.

Annunziata instinctively tidied her hair, trying to pull back into the comb the little stray piece that always fell over her eye. She smoothed her apron and faced the open door as Luigi came in with his guest.

The stranger she had seen parking his car at the quayside came into her room with her husband.

'Annunziata, we have a visitor from la Scozia. From Edimburgo.'

*

Vittorio Crolla had never enjoyed himself so much in his entire life as he did that evening *ngopp' 'a terra*. When he had arrived at the harbour in Pozzuoli the fisherman had directed him towards Carlo's father's wood yard in no time. Luigi had been taken aback by this stranger arriving unannounced so late in the day. He was amazed at his Italian, a dialect that reminded him of the shepherds who came down from the mountain villages above Monte Cassino in the spring to sell their pecorino.

When Luigi realised this was the brother of the girl Carlo had been writing to them about, he was overjoyed. From that moment it was as if the king's envoy had arrived and he was treated immediately as one of their family.

When word spread that there was a visitor from Edinburgh with news of Carlo, all the family arrived: the grandparents, Ninuccia and her husband and children, the boyfriends of Rosetta and Antonietta. Vincenzo and Ernesto sat at one side of Luigi, who was at the head of the table. To show respect Vittorio was given Carlo's chair on Luigi's left.

After the first astonishment of seeing a stranger, and then hearing who it was and why he had come, Annunziata was thrilled. He had come to meet them and introduce his sister to them. He had thoughtfully brought a photograph of his sister for them to see. They all loved her at first sight.

'*Olivia, che bel nome.* What a lovely name.'

'*Che bella ragazza.* What a beautiful girl.'

Vittorio had even stopped in Naples and bought a few flasks of wine and a tray of *pasticceria* and *rum babà* from the Caffè Gambrinus.

He ate with them, food that was so flavoursome, so delicious, so familiar yet so unusual. Better than anything he had ever tasted.

They drank the wine that was on the table and the Chianti that Vittorio had brought; then more wine that appeared from somewhere, no one really knew where.

They laughed; Vittorio spoke the dialect of the mountains with a Scottish accent. He told them about his family, their experiences and their love of food.

Carlo's family talked in their *Puteolano* dialect. Vittorio had to translate in his mind what they were saying. They told him about Carlo: his antics as a boy, his opportunism during the war, his generosity to his family, his triumph as a policeman.

He told them about his family, their Italian heritage, and about Olivia and her love for Carlo.

The sun had long since set behind the island of Ischia and the sky was dark with a glowing full moon and a dusting of stars before the meal ended. The window was still open, and the room was refreshed with the cool evening air.

Gradually, with the last *rum babà* gone, the sisters and their families and the cousins and their children went off to their own homes. The grandparents left and helped each other hobble back down to the port. Some birds chirped as they flew past the window, just checking all was well inside. A guitar sounded across the piazza, the beauty of the melody drifting into the room.

It caught their mood and they fell silent.

Vittorio, Annunziata and Luigi were left alone. Annunziata poured another coffee and Luigi passed the bottle of Anisetta.

'Vittorio, *fratello mio,* my brother, we need to explain something to you. There is only one thing Carlo didn't tell you, because he doesn't know himself.'

Then, with a grave voice, Annunziata told Vittorio what the

priest had written for them in the letter they had posted to Carlo that very morning.

Vittorio listened, but didn't say a word.

*

Vittorio stayed for three days, enjoying getting to know and understand Carlo's family. They tried to insist he stay in their home, but he preferred the small hotel on the seafront; he felt humbled by their hospitality and openness. He thought back to the conversation they had had that first evening. Annunziata had been quite overcome with grief at the thought of the letter she had sent to Carlo. Vittorio had given the news a lot of thought.

What fortitude they had. He came to respect them and to understand why it was that Carlo was such an impressive young man. When he told Annunziata about his own experience during the war, and losing his father, she wept with him.

While he was there, Vittorio became intrigued by the *mozzarella di bufala*. He had seen the buffalo in the fields along the road while he was driving through Campania towards Naples. They were striking beasts, slightly incongruous in the parched landscape. When Vincenzo offered him some fresh mozzarella to let him try he thought he had never tasted anything so very delightful. It was creamy and smooth, milky and light. It made his stomach feel coated with comfort.

'You'll see, we'll help you find suppliers for your shop. Wait till we can get *mozzarella di bufala* from Mondragone direct to Edimburgo! *Mannaggia!* That would be wonderful!' Vincenzo was enthusiastic.

'You know, Vincenzo, stranger things have happened.' Vittorio was particularly taken with Vincenzo. Here was a young man who radiated integrity.

When they stood at the quayside when he was leaving to return to Edinburgh to take their blessings to Carlo and his own family, the Citroën was filled with wine and pasta and pecorino. Annunziata gave him a battered old suitcase with green leaves sticking out from the sides. She stuck her chin out and looked at him to tell him he had no choice but to take it.

'It's *friarielli* and *carciofi*, Carlo's favourite. You can't grow those in Edimburgo!'

Vincenzo had gone all the way to Caffè Gambrinus in Naples early that morning and bought three trays of *rum babà*.

'Drive fast and they'll still be good ... you have five days to get home ... unless you eat them on the way!'

Vincenzo hugged Vittorio. He felt he was his new older uncle, but one who had lived and had an exciting life; the uncle he would always look up to, just as Carlo had looked up to Zi' Antonio.

'Vittorio, next time you come, I'll take you to see the new pasta factories they are building in Napoli. You and I will do some deals!'

As Vittorio drove off, he saw them all standing together at the bottom of Rione Terra. He had tears of joy in his eyes. His new family were very poor, hard-working, generous and God-fearing. They were full of the joy of life, not surprising in this glorious country.

He just made out Vincenzo's voice calling after him; 'Next time the pasta factory! *Non dimenticare!* Don't forget!'

Vittorio pumped his horn twice and shouted out of the window, '*Non ti preoccupare!* Don't worry! I'll be back!'

Chapter Twenty-one

Olivia was exhausted. She'd been working in the hospital since early morning. It had been a difficult shift. There had been a polio scare but thankfully the child had recovered. It hadn't been polio at all, just severe influenza.

She just wanted to lie down for a bit, but as soon as she opened the door of the house she heard Gloria calling her.

'Olivia, is that you?'

Gloria came through from the kitchen. She looked very anxious.

'Who's in the shop?' Olivia asked. They had been working extra shifts because Vittorio was away and Domenico was still unwell.

'It's OK, Phyllis and Mrs Glen are there. It's not busy today.'

It was unusual for Gloria not to be at the shop when she should be.

'Are you all right, Gloria? Is Mum not well?'

'No, it's not that. Everybody's fine. It's Carlo.'

Olivia felt her heart lurch.

'He has been looking for you. He looked very upset.'

'Why was he upset?'

'He wouldn't say. He just went out again.'

Olivia had always been afraid something was going to happen. The whole idea was too ridiculous. The whole thing was too fast. Maybe Carlo's great plan to apply to stay in the country had backfired. Maybe he had been called to return to Italy.

His time had run out and he had resigned from the police force officially already. They were just waiting for Vittorio to return. One way or another they had both agreed that they would marry, whatever news Vittorio brought back.

Once Vittorio had left to go to Pozzuoli it had been clearer to Olivia what she wanted. She had spoken to Carlo and they had agreed that whatever happened they were destined to be together. It might be that her family did not yet trust Carlo, but having opened her heart to her brother, she knew for sure that she did.

She took her coat and hat off and, laying them on the hall table, joined her sister in the kitchen.

'Sit down, Olivia, I'll make you a cup of tea. Mum's having a lie-down.'

Olivia sat. It was no good looking for Carlo. He could be anywhere. They were due to go out this evening so no doubt he would come back at some point.

She put her face in her hands. It was all so upsetting.

Gloria brought her the tea, sat down beside her and put her arms around her. She pushed some cake towards her.

'Olivia, you need to eat something.'

Olivia just looked at her. 'Did something happen? Did Carlo say something to you?'

'No, everything is all right. He just said he needed to talk to you.'

Olivia thought of their embrace last night when he left her to go home. She had been a bit off-hand, a bit cool. With Vittorio away in Italy she was still worried about what he would find when he was there.

'Oh Gloria. I feel so bad. I've been pushing Carlo away and being difficult. I am so wrapped up in myself. I forget he's the one away from home. He has no family here to support him. It's just all so fast and I feel so pressured to make decisions.'

'We're his family here, Olivia. We all love Carlo too, you know. If he's right for you we'll embrace him into the family.' Gloria didn't say so, but she had doubts about the whole romance. It was so hard to know what Olivia wanted. It did all feel so quick, but they had spent a lot of time together, nearly every evening in the shop for the last five weeks. They seemed very close, most of the time. She tried to think how she could ask Olivia what she was still worried about.

'What does Carlo feel about leaving Italy? Is he sure it's what he wants?'

Olivia didn't want another big discussion. She stood up.

'I'm going to lie down, Gloria. I'm tired.'

'What about your tea?'

Olivia just went to her room and closed the door.

Gloria was left holding the teacup. 'Romance! What a lot of fuss!'

She sat down and had the tea herself; and just a small slice of cake.

*

In her room, Olivia sat on the bed, feeling drained. It was so stuffy in the flat, she needed some air. She went across to the window and, pulling the curtains aside, opened it a little. The trees in the gardens were almost fully in leaf now, creating a glorious canopy of silver and lime green. It was a glorious sight. Olivia felt such relief that the dark of winter was well behind them.

Carlo would find the weather in Scotland difficult. How could he even think of giving up the sunshine of Italy to come to live here? The climate was so different. She had visited Italy when she was 15, at the Fascist *balilla* camp in Rome. It had been so exciting. She remembered the first time she had felt the heat of the Italian sun. Oh, it was so delicious, like sitting beside a roaring fire. It had been wonderful not to have her back braced against the Edinburgh wind; to take the heavy layers of clothes off and feel her body relax; to walk every day barefoot in the sand.

How could Carlo give that up? Maybe he didn't want to. Maybe he'd changed his mind.

She looked across at the gardens again. Something caught her eye: a man was sitting alone on the park bench opposite her window. His head was bent in his hands.

The man stood up and started to walk away, slowly, dejectedly.

She strained her eyes. Was that Carlo? It was.

She shouted from the window, 'Carlo!' He kept walking away.

She ran out of the door without her coat or even telling Gloria she was going out. She rushed down the stairs and, dashing between a tram and a few cars, ran across the road.

She looked around. She couldn't see him.

She ran along the path. The person she had seen was at the top of the gardens now, walking towards Regent Terrace. She wasn't even sure now if it was him. She called his name.

'Carlo! Carlo!'

The person kept walking away, but from his stride she knew it was Carlo.

'Oh my God. Carlo!'

She started to run and tripped over a branch, righted herself and called again. Her heart was pounding. The path was steep and winding. He was almost out of sight.

She'd never catch him if she had to run after him.

She stopped and shouted as loud as she could, 'CAARLO!!'

She tried again, 'CARLO!!!'

The figure stopped. He turned and saw her, and raised his hand.

'*Amore!*'

She waited as he walked towards her. As he came closer she saw he had been crying.

*

They didn't know where to go. It was getting dark, and although Carlo had put his coat around Olivia she was shivering. They had been walking for hours but still didn't want to go home. They still needed to be alone.

'Olivia, come on. We'll go into the cathedral.'

The church was very dark, and not that warm either, but the candles at the shrine of the Madonna were still flickering. They walked towards the altar. Carlo lit a candle. They just sat quietly, his arm around her, protecting her.

'Carlo, read me the letter.'

Olivia wanted to hear the words. Maybe they would sound better when they both got used to them.

Carlo had received the letter that morning. The words had been so devastating he couldn't read it again. He couldn't believe them. He surely must have misunderstood.

'I can't. I can't read it, Olivia. I can't understand it.'

'I'll read it. Oh, Carlo darling, I'll read it.'

Carlo took the letter from his pocket and handed it to her.

She bent towards the statue of the Madonna. The lights of the candles shone just brightly enough to let her see the words. The paper was parchment, creamy and textured. The writing was italic, in black ink, with a very clear, strong hand.

'It's not Papà's handwriting. It must be Monsignor Michele's.' Carlo squeezed her hand.

'*Figlio mio*, my son, you know Mamma and I love you with all our being and always will. You will always be our first and cherished son.

'Now you are a grown man and have told us you may have found your own way.'

Carlo pulled Olivia towards him.

'We have prayed to the Madonna and we know we need to let you go. We need to give you freedom to live your life the way you want to.

'Carlo, you know how hard it was at the start of your mother's and my life together. How the Good Lord took so many of our babies from us so soon in their short lives.'

Olivia had not known about this. She looked at Carlo, her brow furrowed.

He didn't say anything. He was looking at the letter, waiting for her to continue. She reached out and stroked his face. He looked so sad.

'Carlo, *figlio mio*, I can find no other way to tell you this. We cannot come to Scotland to tell you and you cannot come home to hear from us. Maybe this is the way it should be and God will give you time to understand.

'Carlo, when we lost yet another child, Mamma prayed to the Madonna. If she would bless her with children, she would go to the *Chiesa dell' Annunziata* and bring an abandoned infant into our home.'

Olivia's voice shook. She turned to Carlo and held him close, kissing him on his face, pulling his body towards her.

'Oh, Carlo,' she whispered.

'*Figlio mio*, there were so many infants in the hospital. The Madonna guided us and we chose to bring you, an infant of a few days, into our home. You were our gift from God.'

There were more words, more explanations, but Olivia couldn't read more. She just read the end of the letter.

'Carlo, *figlio mio*. We love you always.'

The letter was signed 'Papà' and a simple 'X' from his mother.

What could they say? They sat together silently, tears running down both their faces.

After a while, Olivia spoke. 'I'm sorry Carlo, so sorry.'

Carlo looked at her with a frown.

'Why are you sorry Olivia? Don't you understand? Don't be sorry for me. Don't be sorry. Look how fortunate I am! I can't explain, but you know, suddenly it makes sense to me, it all makes sense.' He shrugged his shoulders and pulled away so she could see his face, 'Olivia, it's as if I always knew.'

He shook his head, his hands in front of his chest. He put his hand to his mouth, as if to stop the words coming out. 'I can't explain.'

He put his arms around her, holding her close. He felt complete with her in his arms. This was what his life had been preparing him for.

'Olivia, with you here, my life is complete. What came before was to make me the best I could be for you. For us.'

They sat quietly, oblivious of the cold. Carlo felt at peace. This was what he wanted: a life with this darling girl.

He was brought from his thoughts by a deep, exhausted sob from Olivia.

'*Amore, carissima*, please don't cry. *Ho capito*. I understand. I realise now, I knew I was different. I have been searching for answers all the time. It all makes sense now. *Non piangere*. Don't cry.'

He took her face into his hands and kissed her mouth. She kissed him back fully for the first time. Their love together was sealed as if they had committed their vows, this very moment.

'Olivia, my mother is my mother. Either she gave birth to me or she chose me in an orphanage, she has always been my mother and always will be. I'll always look after her.'

After a long, quiet time together, Olivia gave a deep sigh.

'Be good to your mother or I won't come back.'

Carlo didn't understand. 'What do you mean? I *will* be good to my mother!'

Olivia said it again. 'Be good to your mother or I won't come back.'

'What do you mean?' Carlo pulled back again and looked at her. Tears were running down her face. She looked so beautiful, so vulnerable.

'*Carissima*, tell me.'

'When they took my father away, when they came and took him from the house in the middle of the night, he patted me on the head. He didn't hug me. He patted me on the head. That's what he said, "*Capa Nera*, be good to your mother or I won't come back."'

'Oh Carlo … it's the last thing he said to me.' She took a deep breath, her chest heaving with passion. 'Be good. Oh, Carlo, I've tried so hard to be good …' She sobbed again. 'I've tried so hard.'

After a while she stopped weeping. She fell quiet. Carlo didn't say anything. He waited till she was ready. He thought about his mother writing that letter. She had waited till he was ready to know the truth; so he waited now.

'Ever since that night, whenever the doorbell rang, I would run to the door, hoping it was my dad. Sometimes, on the tram, I'd see someone walking up London Road, I'd look round to see if it was him. I'd read the newspapers looking for news. Mum just told us all he had died but nobody talked about it, no one explained what had actually happened. We were very young when it happened. I didn't know until much later that he had drowned.

'Carlo, even now, sometimes when I go into Elm Row, I think I can smell his cologne and turn around to see if maybe, just maybe he didn't drown and he managed to find his way home.'

She fell silent again.

'I tried so hard to be good.'

'You are good, darling Olivia. You are so good.'

'He isn't going to come back is he, Carlo? Even though I tried to be good, he isn't coming home.'

Later, when Father Gallagher came through to lock up the church he found the Neapolitan and Olivia Crolla huddled together under the boy's coat, both sound asleep with exhaustion.

'So this is where they are. Everyone has been looking for them.'

He woke them gently and took them through to the sacristy. After a while he took them home.

Chapter Twenty-two

What a night that was, when Father Gallagher took Olivia and Carlo back to Brunton Place. Maria had been terrified something had happened; Olivia had been away for about six hours. Everyone had been looking for them.

When they came in and Carlo told them all about the letter from his mother, everyone was distraught. Maria thought about it a lot. The news went round and round in her head, and that night, when Carlo had eventually gone home and Olivia had gone to bed, Maria sat in Alfonso's chair and tried to say her rosary.

Who could make head or tail of this? Only the Holy Madonna.

In the morning, she had woken still sitting in the chair, and, as so often happens, the answer to her worries was as clear as day. Carlo's adoptive mother was the person Maria had wept for. How brave she must have been to cope with losing so many babies. How kind she had been to open her heart and her home to a stranger's child. How understanding and wise to protect him all his life by giving him the gift of living in her family without the burden of growing up feeling he was different.

Carlo's adoptive mother, Annunziata, was a woman to respect and admire. Maria accepted Carlo then as her daughter's future husband.

*

It was another week before Vittorio's Citroën drew up at Brunton Place. The journey back had been much slower than he had anticipated, and he was ashamed to admit Vincenzo's *rum babà* had one by one disappeared from their box.

The boot, however, was still full of jars of tomatoes and *melanzane sott' olio*, packets of strong coffee which had tempted Vittorio all the way home and two bottles of *mirtillo* liqueur which Vittorio had promised himself he would open as soon as he got back.

The *friarielli* in the suitcase had started to rot; the odour was not pleasant, but the pecorino, though sweaty and pungent, had given Vittorio a sense of comfort, reminding him of the shop in Elm Row.

There had been great excitement when he'd arrived, and he had been glad neither Olivia nor Carlo was around. While Gloria and Phyllis were unpacking the car, he had taken his mother into the living room.

'Mum, did a letter arrive for Carlo from Pozzuoli?'

'Yes, Vittorio. So you know all about it as well? Did Carlo's mother explain everything?'

'Yes, Luigi and Annunziata told me the night I arrived that they'd posted a letter to Carlo that same day to explain that he had been adopted. How did Carlo take it?'

'He was shocked at first. It's only to be expected. Olivia was. We all were.'

'So was I. I've thought so much about it on the way home. You know, Mum, it's not so unusual. If you think about it, it shows a wonderful, secure family and upbringing.'

'I know, I've spent a lot of time talking with Carlo while you've been away. You know, Vittorio, he is a good man.'

Later that night, after an unbelievably delicious *spaghetti al pomodoro* made with the tomatoes from Pozzuoli, and once Gloria had stopped teasing Vittorio about the missing *babà*, the young ones all went into the kitchen, leaving Vittorio with his mother.

'Vittorio, tell me, what was it like in Pozzuoli?'

Vittorio stretched across and held his mother's hand on the table.

'Mum, I can't describe it. The town they live in is like heaven on earth. The sea sparkles, the sun shines, there's life, music and laughter; people living their lives outdoors. The food for sale on carts along the seafront is like nothing I've ever seen: so many types of fish straight out of the sea, piles of colourful vegetables, varieties we've never even dreamed of. And the fruit is abundant, and so delicious. It's like the Garden of Eden compared to here. I never knew before how good Italian food tastes and how plentiful it is.'

Maria nodded; she had been brought up in Italy. She understood, but that was not what she needed to hear.

'And ...?'

'Mum, Carlo's family are wonderful. It took a bit of time for me to find my way from Naples to Pozzuoli, but from my first hand-shake, his father, Luigi, welcomed me like a son. They are a big family, just like us. They are all together, working hard, laughing and joking, and they think the world of Carlo.'

'And ...?'

'Mum, they are *so* good, but they are very poor. They have nothing. They live all together in a few rooms at the top of the ancient part of the town. They share beds, they have a table and a couple of electric lights, but the electricity keeps cutting out. The plumbing still hasn't been repaired since the war. They're not alone. The whole of the south of Italy is the same. It's as if they're a hundred years behind us.'

His mother listened, nodding.

'Vittorio, I know, I know.'

'How, Mum, how do you know?' Vittorio had been shocked at the poverty and squalor he had seen. 'I have never imagined anything like it. Maybe the slums in Glasgow are like that, but I didn't expect such harsh poverty in a land with such abundance.'

'I know, Vittorio, because that is why your father and I decided to come here to Scotland and make a new life. You leave everything that is wonderful – sunshine, food, family – but you also leave poverty, insecurity and corruption.'

Vittorio was pensive.

'Are you glad you and Dad came here, Mum? Would you ever want to go back to Italy?'

'It's too late. Once you leave, you can't go back ... and neither will Carlo.'

Carlo had already resigned from the Italian police while Vittorio was away and was now waiting anxiously for the letter with the official paperwork from the immigration authorities to allow him to stay in Scotland until he got married. He longed to go back to see his mother and tell her everything he was feeling. It had been very difficult for him, but the more he thought about the content of the letter, the more he loved her and Luigi, and was overwhelmed by all they had sacrificed for him.

He remembered how, at the start of the war, when he was 15 and had been posted to the factory in Genoa, Annunziata had given him half the family rations to ensure he would not go hungry. It was hard to believe, when she had had so many other mouths to feed.

Since Vittorio had returned he had told Carlo more details about the adoption. Unbelievably, Luigi's family's name was not even Contini. That was Carlo's own surname. Luigi's family name was actually Silni. By Italian law, a family had to take the name of the adopted child rather than the reverse. This news was a strange comfort to Carlo, it reaffirmed his identity.

'So I really am Carlo Contini. This is who I am.'

In the light of all this revelation, he was even more overcome with gratitude. He desperately wanted to speak to Annunziata and Luigi face to face, to thank them, to reassure them he would always be loyal to them as their oldest son.

As things stood, it was impossible for him to leave. If he returned to Italy he was in danger of being refused entry when he tried to come back to the UK. Here he was, in no-man's land again. He couldn't leave Olivia anyway. He would do nothing that would risk losing her.

Olivia's greater family were cautious about the step she was taking. To marry someone who, in effect, was a stranger, was still regarded as a high risk by the whole community. People were talking. When he heard about Carlo's past, Alfonso's brother, Giovanni, came to talk to Maria. Her relations too were voicing opinions, advising her against possible bad blood coming into the family.

'Maria, are you mad? What if the boy is from a family of

thieves? What if his mother was a bad woman? What if he is really a Sicilian?'

But when Carlo was with them, their fears were allayed. He was so charming and had such an infectious air of optimism and enthusiasm they found him impossible to dislike.

Carlo was aware of the pressures and concerns everyone had. He wasn't a rich man, and was all too aware that if he had been, his path would have been somewhat smoother. He had saved quite a bit of money; it would have been a larger sum if he had not sent so much home, but he would never forget his responsibilities. He made more ice cream carts and started making some pieces of furniture for Italians who had heard he was a good craftsman.

Olivia was worried. 'Carlo, you're working too hard. You'll make yourself ill.'

'Leave it to me, Olivia. I know what I have to do.'

*

Vittorio wanted to talk to Olivia and Carlo in private. They went into 19 Elm Row for the conversation; Olivia felt secure coming into the shop, the smells were all so intense and familiar and she felt the presence of her father here more than ever.

It was just before six. The men behind the counter were starting to tidy up, washing down the counters, sweeping the floor and taking the cheeses down to the cool of the cellar under the shop.

Vittorio had locked the door but a few Italians hung around, smoking cigarettes and chatting, waiting to get their orders completed. Vittorio had his pencil and paper and was finishing adding up a bill.

He led the couple up to the office, bringing a whisky bottle from beside the till. Vittorio was frank – there were a lot of risks and they needed to follow the law – but after long discussions they all agreed that the wedding should go ahead as soon as possible. They all understood that the war had devastated both their families and, given an opportunity for a better future, surely any chance of happiness should be embraced?

Vittorio had seen both scenarios in the Italian community:

217

marriages arranged by parents that had been complete failures, and marriages parents had resisted that had been great successes. Look at Anna Di Ciacca, no one had wanted her to marry Bill Brown, not least her mother and brother. And look at her now: expecting her first child and laughing and happy every time Vittorio saw her.

He too had been in love when he was younger, but the girl was already married and their lives were not to be together. He knew the pain that loneliness caused. Why would he inflict that on his sister? Surely his sisters had suffered enough. He had made up his mind to help as much as he could.

'Carlo you need to get a job before you can apply to have permanent UK residency. I think I have a solution.

'You know Mr Millar from Loanhead, who supplies the milk to Easter Road? He says he has a job on the farm. He can give you a letter to say he'll employ you full-time. It's until the harvest, so if we set the wedding date for the end of October that will give you the entitlement to stay here until you're married.'

So here was Carlo, taking another step in his career path from coffin polisher to security officer in the police service, to milking the cows on a farm in Scotland. Well, that was a turn-up for the books. Never mind. He had learned in life so far that every opportunity should be embraced. He was not sure what milking cows would do for his future prospects, but who knew what might happen?

*

It was agreed the wedding was to be in the North British Hotel on Princes Street, right beside Waverley Station; it was perfect for family coming from all over Scotland. Most of Olivia's family was in Edinburgh, but there were cousins in Glasgow, Ayr, Troon and beyond. In fact, as Vittorio was drawing up the guest list he realised that there was an Italian family connected to them in some way or another on practically every high street in the country.

Mr Aldridge, the banqueting manager at the NB, knew Vittorio Crolla well. Over the last few years Valvona & Crolla had become a good source of unusual continental produce, the type of product his clients asked for but his own suppliers couldn't get. They even had supplies of Cinzano, the new drink everyone was asking for.

In those remaining years of rationing, the black market was a vital source of goods that would spare fancy guests from the better addresses in the city any inconvenience. It had been interesting to observe, during the war years, how the most unexpected clients had become very much richer. Mr Aldridge was very careful to make sure he was available to advise them how to enjoy their good fortune.

He was very pleased Mr Crolla had approached him. It was a pleasure to be asked to host the wedding; even more so that they hadn't chosen the Caledonian Hotel, their arch rivals at the other end of Princes Street.

As expected, when Vittorio had come with Mrs Crolla to have the first meeting, they knew exactly what they were looking for. Unless they were members of the clergy, the Italians were all in the catering and food business one way or another and knew what they were talking about. The North British had already hosted four Italian weddings over the last two years, including Mrs Di Ciacca's daughter's in February, when Anna had married the fishmonger Bill Brown, another of Mr Aldridge's suppliers. It was a small world, the hospitality business.

The great advantage from the hotel's point of view was that each Italian family had to put on a better show than the previous one; there was plenty of opportunity to upsell. A very competitive bunch, the lot of them!

Mr Aldridge explained to his area manager, 'You see, as long as we do a good job for them, it's definite repeat business for years to come. They have very large families and they're all intermarried. You please one, you please them all. They are always having cele-brations and they are obliged to invite all of each other's families every time, even if they are not on speaking terms. The guest lists just get longer and longer.'

The area manager snorted in disdain. He was French, and not favourably inclined towards Italians.

'They like to throw a good wake as well!' Mr Aldridge tried to elaborate his point of view.

'I wouldn't be surprised if they wanted an ice cream cart at the door when people come in,' the area manager said sniffily, trying to justify his prejudice.

'Now, now, sir. Let's be European. It's all good for business.'

Mr Aldridge had seen this all before. The area managers came in unannounced, picked fault with his management decisions then swanned off to pick fault in the next place.

But it was he, Mr Aldridge, who was making all the money for the company. He just smiled and kept his lips sealed. When the generous gratuity came from Mr Crolla he would have the last laugh.

*

When Olivia came home from work the following evening she found Vittorio sitting in the kitchen with a large sheet of paper. He was counting the replies they had received so far from the invited guests, 170 so far. Maria was sitting opposite him, looking a little agitated.

'Oh good, Olivia. Here, sit down. I need to talk to you. The hotel's booked. I've spoken with Mr Aldridge. I must say he looked like he was dressed for a funeral, but nevertheless, he was very charming.'

'Thank you, Vittorio. How did you get on with the planning?' Olivia was so grateful to her brother for arranging everything for her.

'Well, we've to choose from these menus. See what you think.'

'What menus? We've already decided on the menu.' Maria was confused. They had spent weeks talking about the dinner they would serve. All her female acquaintances would judge the wedding on the food, not on the bridegroom or the bride or her own new black dress; it was all about the food.

Vittorio had learned over the years to be diplomatic. The meeting with the hotel manager had been interesting. It was a help that they already supplied the hotel with wine and spirits; in fact, the bar at the NB was now one of his best customers for Cinzano.

But the kitchens were a different department. The French chef frequently ordered Brie de Meaux, Heinz Russian salad and Dijon mustard from Vittorio, but it seemed impossible to supply him with their coffee. Hopefully, using the hotel for the wedding would bring some extra business in the long run.

'Mum, you have to remember, it's a French chef. He has his own menus.'

'I'm not interested in French menus. Are we getting antipasto? And macaroni? We can't have a wedding without macaroni! And roast beef. How long is it since we've all had a good piece of beef?'

Gloria came into the room.

'Are we having trifle? We have to have trifle and ice cream!'

Vittorio looked exasperated. What a bother it was with all these women to please all the time.

'Well, I've tried my best, Mum. There are still rationing restrictions. I can go up to the Highlands and rustle a cow myself if you want!'

'Why not? That's a good idea.'

Vittorio was exasperated. He ran his hands over his hair, which was not consoling at all as it just reminded him how little hair he had left.

He tried again.

'Right, let's read the menu together and see what you think. You have to remember it's a French kitchen.'

'*Hors d'oeuvres*,' Maria was not impressed. 'They had that at Anna's wedding. It was just a lot of creams and patés and pickles and Russian salad! If it's a French kitchen why do they serve Russian salad! Tell them we just want antipasto: salami, prosciutto, *salsiccie*, olives. What's so complicated about that?'

'OK. I'll speak to them.' Vittorio made a note on the menu. 'Right, are you all paying attention? Then we can have "Crème Marie Stuart".'

'What on earth is that?' Maria hadn't heard of Mary Stuart except when she had visited Holyrood Palace last Easter.

'I think it's soup, Mum.' Olivia was trying to keep calm. 'It sounds nice.'

'Nice? Soup? We don't want soup at a wedding; we want macaroni!' Maria was almost fainting with shock.

'Here, Mum, drink this,' Gloria gave her mother a glass of whisky with a drop of water – or was it a drop of water with a glass of whisky? Anything to calm her down.

'Mum, I don't think they'll know how to make macaroni.'

'Wait a minute, Mum,' Vittorio was trying to keep control. 'I'll read through the rest of the choices and then we can decide. The next course is "*Supreme de Turbot au Chablis*".'

'What's that?' Maria was starting to think of cancelling the venue, and cancelling the wedding.

'It sounds like fish in a white sauce.' Gloria quite liked the sound of that.

Maria looked aghast.

'*Che?* Why would you put fish in a white sauce? Can they not just fry the fish?'

At that moment Domenico came into the room with Phyllis. They had just locked up the shop at Easter Road. The questions started all over again.

'Can they do roast beef and Yorkshire pudding? Surely even they can do that!'

Vittorio decided the only thing to do with this comment was to ignore it.

'For the main course, on the menu is "*Faisan casserole aux celeris, pommes croquettes et petits pois fins*".' Even Vittorio thought this was funny.

'What's that?' Gloria knew Vittorio had studied languages when he was on the Isle of Man.

'Sounds like stew and peas,' Vittorio was teasing them now.

'*Che? Stew and peas? Stufato e piselli?*' Maria nearly had a fit. 'Gloria, pass me the whisky. I need another drink!'

Vittorio had already decided he would manage the rest of the menu without any of them. 'Gloria, I hope you're not intending to get married soon. I'm not going through this again!'

His mother had taken the menu but got completely confused with the language and terminology and handed it back, passing the buck back to him as usual. She went for another line of attack.

'Since you're reading the menu, Vittorio, what do they want to charge us for this French food we don't want and don't even like?'

Vittorio went for the big laugh.

'Twenty-one shillings a head!'

'What? That's robbery! Daylight robbery! French daylight

robbery!' Maria really lost her rag. 'Right, that's it! Cancel the venue. We'll do the catering ourselves. Vittorio, call Father Gallagher now. Tell him we'll hire the church hall. I'll make lasagne!'

'Oh, Mum.' Listening to it all, this was the last straw for Olivia. She ran crying out of the room.

*

In the end the hotel was booked, the menu decided and the church hall, though provisionally booked, was cancelled. A four-course lunch would be served at 1 p.m. for 210 guests.

It was all to be 'French muck', as Maria described it to Marietta when they met at church, but as a compromise they served mine-strone instead of 'Crème Marie Stuart', Vittorio declining the offer of calling it 'Potage de Rizzio'. Although there was no chance of securing a supply of roast beef for 210 guests, the French chef, who turned out to be an army chef from Govan with a fictitious French accent, agreed to serve fried lemon sole and chips at 5.30 p.m. as a compromise.

'Dinna worry, Vittorio, I'll get broon sauce and vinegar from the chippie. Once it's on the table Mr Aldridge won't be able to take it off. It would cause a riot!'

When Mr Aldridge heard about the menu, the number of guests and the price per head he was quietly thrilled. He couldn't wait to see his area manager's face when he reported that he had secured a high tea of fish and chips to be served at a further 7/6 per head.

Chapter Twenty-three

Maria and Gloria were waiting, perched precariously on a low sofa in the wedding salon in Jenners department store.

Miss MacDonald, the head sales manager, was displaying a beautiful couture wedding dress, fanning it out over the white Axminster carpet, gently stroking her hand down the duchess satin to indicate the luxuriousness of the fabric.

'Mrs Crolla, I'm sure this is exactly the style that will suit your daughter perfectly.'

'*Che dice*, Gloria? What is she saying?'

'She says this dress will suit Olivia. Mum, wait till you see it on.'

'There are a selection of co-ordinating bridesmaid's dresses, matching shoes and fur boleros as required.'

'*Che dice?*'

'She wants to sell us the dresses for the bridesmaids as well.' Gloria looked longingly at the fabric.

Miss MacDonald smiled as sweetly as she could at Mrs Crolla. Maria sat with her back as straight as possible, her black hat established firmly on her head and her long black coat with the mink fur collar equally firmly closed. She had an imperious-looking black handbag on her lap and an even blacker umbrella furled and planted resolutely in front of her, protecting the bag and its contents.

She was ready for action.

Miss MacDonald assessed her adversary. She looked extremely

warm in her winter coat ('1949, end of season sale,' she whispered to her assistant).

She cleared her throat.

'Mrs Crolla, may I take your coat for you? Can I offer you a glass of champagne?'

'*Che dice?*'

Gloria conveyed her mother's answer to Miss MacDonald. 'Just the champagne, if you don't mind.'

Miss MacDonald signalled to her assistant, who approached with a tray of Edinburgh Crystal glasses and a bottle of Moët & Chandon lodged in an elaborate silver ice bucket. Maria accepted her glass.

'Mrs Crolla, we can prepare a wedding list for your guests to choose gifts which we can deliver to your address directly.'

'*Che dice?*'

When Gloria translated for Maria, she laughed rudely out loud. '*Che* "wedding list"?'

Miss MacDonald looked a little startled.

Gloria nudged her mother, 'Shh, Mum!'

Mrs Crolla was well known in the Model Gown department at Jenners. This exclusive room was at the end of the grand balcony, behind imposing brown leather doors. It had been managed by Miss MacDonald for the last 15 years. She was an immaculately dressed, tall, elaborately coiffed lady, a practised sales manager; authoritative in her assessment of her clients. With her personal team of top sales girls she showcased the new couture lines from the Paris and London fashion houses, made even more desirable every season by the impact of the beautiful young princesses, Elizabeth and Margaret, and the glamorous film stars on screen. Now that clothes rationing was ending, the department store was anticipating a boom in sales. The continual challenge for Miss MacDonald was to use every trick she could to prevent any clients walking along to the rival stores in town, R.W. Forsyth's or Patrick Thomson's. This had to be avoided at all costs.

For this reason she was astute enough to pay particular attention to the Italian women in Edinburgh and Glasgow, who were potentially good clients. She was well aware that the younger generation liked to dress well and impress each other. And, over the last few years, they had developed a habit of holding big parties: baptisms, first Communions, engagements. They kept themselves to themselves, but there seemed to be a fair enough number.

Mrs Crolla visited the department regularly, at least once a month, ostensibly to see the new fashions arriving. She was of a size and age that firmly put her 'model' looks behind her, but she looked to buy well-made black garments in a size for the larger woman. She was a shrewd purchaser and invariably bought only during the final days of the annual end-of-season sale and, notably, paid in cash.

Mrs Crolla's daughters were more promising clients. Young Miss Olivia Crolla came in often with the new Mrs Brown, a much valued customer who embraced the new fashions with great enthusiasm.

An Italian wedding would be a great opportunity to attract the young socialites from Glasgow. They were far easier to encourage to spend money, and definitely had plenty to spend. They frequented Fraser's in Buchanan Street, which was serious competition. Miss MacDonald was aware she had to maintain a good level of service and competitiveness at all times.

Maria drank the champagne; Miss MacDonald was clever enough to keep her glass topped up. Maria couldn't really understand all this fuss for a wedding. It was a major outlay. Each one of their relations had to be invited, including those in the main Italian families in Glasgow and other cities. They had to think about their customers, keep them happy; and the church as well. There would be at least six priests at the wedding. You had to cover all angles. In all, looking at the list so far, they had over 200 guests to feed and entertain. And that wasn't counting the children and the cousins. That looked to be an additional 100 guests for the evening reception.

Maria could not help but reflect on her own wedding, all those years ago. Growing up in Italy in the tiny mountain hamlet of Fontitune, she had known Alfonso all her life. She was betrothed to him for as long as she could remember but, because he was always away, they didn't marry till she was 24.

It seemed unimaginable now, but Alfonso had fought in Abyssinia, had brought her to Scotland and then fought again in another war in the north of Italy in 1914. It was tragic that he had died so young, but he had packed a lot of life into his 52 years.

The tiny hamlet they came from, the highest in the Apennine Mountains, was so far away from the church that it took her and her father and mother an hour to process down the hill to get married, with every person from their village, 37 in all, parading behind them. She'd worn an embroidered black skirt with a green-patterned apron and a white blouse. Her hair back then had been luxurious jet-black and had hung down abundantly as far as her waist. For the ceremony, it had been piled up on her head and fixed with ebony hair combs, a white lace mantilla modestly covering her face.

Alfonso had been so handsome: tall and strong with his thick dark hair and his thin moustache just lining his beautiful lips. It was his eyes that she'd loved the best. They were dark, sleepy and wise. She blushed at the thought of their wedding night. He had been so gentle. He'd stroked her hair and touched her face, tracing the shape of her eyes, and her nose and her lips, whispering such sweet words to her.

'Oh, *carissimo* Alfonso, I feel so lonely without you.' Her eyes filled with tears. Turning away so the saleswoman would not see her, she caught sight of herself in the large gilt mirror. '*Oddio*, I'm just an old woman!'

She was well over 60 now. Her body had thickened, her legs were swollen, her once-beautiful hair was wiry and grey.

'Oh, Alfonso, what would you think of your bride now,' she thought, and unconsciously mumbled out loud, '*Ah, la vecchia!*'

Gloria saw her mother looking at herself in the mirror. She put her arm around her and kissed her cheek.

'You're not old Mum. You'll always be beautiful to me.'

'Ah, Gloria,' Gloria was her mother's favourite and they had been inseparable since they had lost Alfonso. 'Will you look after me when I *am* old?'

Gloria hugged her mother again.

'Well, Mum, it'll depend if I'm not too busy,' she teased, making her mother laugh.

Gloria left with the salesgirl to help her sister. Maria was left unheeded, lost in her thoughts, sipping her champagne with her right hand firmly on her black handbag.

'Oh, Alfonso, if only you were still alive. You would know if Olivia was doing the right thing. Aren't you so proud of her, your *capa nera*? Look how beautiful she is now! You would get the measure of Carlo. She's had so many suitors to choose from. And what does she do? She chooses a Neapolitan! A Neapolitan of all things!'

'I even tried to match her with Johnny Di Ciacca. He's a nice boy. She missed her chance; she could have had a nice shop in Cockenzie and lived above it. From what I hear he's courting an Irish girl from Glasgow.

'Can you believe it Alfonso? One's taking a Neapolitan and the other an Irish? What is the world coming to?'

It was just as well Maria had Vittorio.

She was relieved Vittorio had gone to Pozzuoli to visit Carlo's family. If he hadn't been and seen Carlo's background with his own eyes and got to know the family, she would never be allowing Olivia to take this step. The last few months had been such a drama.

Why did life have to be so complicated?

Miss MacDonald noticed Mrs Crolla looking distracted. She rushed across with the champagne and topped up her glass.

'She won't be long now, Mrs Crolla. We are just getting the right shoes. Your daughter has a large foot.'

Maria looked up. She hadn't understood a word of what the lady had said. Miss MacDonald was concerned at the unhappy look on her client's face.

'Oh no, that's it. I've blown it! She's insulted that I mentioned her daughter had big feet!'

Oblivious to the concerns of Miss MacDonald, Maria drank the champagne, getting even hotter in her mink-collared coat.

Gloria popped out of the changing room. Her mother was quite flushed now.

'Mum, are you all right? We won't be long now.'

Maria nodded.

As young brides usually do, Olivia had lost a lot of weight and her figure was very slight. Miss MacDonald had measured her height, back, bust and waist and declared her 22-inch waist Paris model standard. She went to the changing room to check how things were progressing and opened the door with a flourish.

'She's nearly ready, Mum. Wake up.' Gloria nudged her mother. Maria had dropped off to sleep, lost in her thoughts.

Miss MacDonald held open the door of the changing room to allow Olivia to come out. Even she was impressed.

'Miss Crolla has the perfect figure; she could be on the front cover of any magazine.'

Olivia stood in front of her mother. The dress was full-length ivory duchess satin with a three-foot train. It had a Queen Anne neckline with a high collar behind her slender neck and a modest lace sleeve, narrowed elegantly to her wrist.

The ivory satin shoes gave her just enough height to carry off the gown. Olivia had longed to be married in an ivory duchess satin gown ever since she had seen the Princess Elizabeth walking down the aisle to marry Prince Philip. Standing here in front of her mother she felt as beautiful as a princess herself. When it was her turn she would walk down the aisle to marry her own Carlo, who would look even more handsome than the prince.

She looked at her reflection and twisted to see how long the train looked at the back of the dress. It extended at least halfway along the floor. The tiny white buttons down her back were each covered with lace and the edge of the train was embroidered with lace and small luminous pearls. She couldn't believe it was herself looking back from the mirror.

'Oh Mum. Isn't it just lovely? Gloria, what do you think?'

'Mrs Crolla, congratulations. It's the perfect gown for her. Just perfect.'

Miss MacDonald couldn't have selected a better gown. The ivory satin complimented Olivia's complexion, the high neckline framed her face and her dark, thick hair was an exotic mysterious contrast to the satin. Miss MacDonald was thrilled.

'These Italian girls are real beauties,' she thought, slightly envious. Then she glanced at Mrs Crolla and consoled herself. 'But their looks don't last that long!'

Maria saw Miss MacDonald look at her and knew exactly what had crossed her mind.

'*È bella,*' she admitted. '*Ma quanto costa?* It *is* lovely. But how much is it?'

When the reply came, Maria answered with an outraged '*Che dice?!*'

*

Carrying a parcel of seven yards of ivory duchess satin, four bobbins of thread and a paper pattern from Patrick Thomson's, Olivia cried all the way home. Gloria felt so sorry for her sister. It had been very embarrassing when her mother, on hearing the price of the dress, had stood up, shouted something rude at Miss MacDonald and stormed out of Jenners, leaving poor Olivia in floods of tears, trying to get untangled from the dress.

'Olivia, it'll be fine, you really didn't want to look all fancy like Anna did you?'

Olivia looked at her in amazement! Was she mad? That was exactly what she wanted to look like!

Chapter Twenty-four

No one from Carlo's family was able to attend his wedding. Vittorio had talked to his mother about sending money to bring Annunziata and Luigi across to Scotland but Maria was sensitive enough to appreciate the expense of coming was not what would cause them concern. She was all too aware that Carlo's family did not have the means at all to participate in the kind of affair that was being organised.

'Vittorio, if I were Annunziata I would feel very anxious about coming to the wedding. From what you've told me, it would be too difficult for her. You have to understand our family is two generations ahead of Carlo's. I remember too well the kind of poverty we came from. It would have been impossible for my father and mother even to consider coming so far.'

'It must have been very hard for you, Mum.'

'Vittorio, never forget the sacrifices your father made for us all. Alfonso was so proud and had such great plans. If you think about it, it's the same sacrifice Carlo is making now for Olivia. He is almost surely setting poverty behind him, but he is also sacrificing his connections with his family and his country to marry Olivia. He must love her a great deal.'

'Please God, let's hope so.'

*

To make Carlo feel welcome and to prevent any unfortunate

gossip about his itinerant status, it was decided the groom would stay in the North British Hotel the night before the wedding. Carlo's last night as a free man was to be spent in the lap of luxury.

When he was shown to his room by the young porter, who absolutely insisted on carrying his bag, he could not believe his good fortune. It was sumptuously decorated in cream and gold, with brocade curtains, fitted carpets and a bed that looked bigger than his whole home had been in Pozzuoli. On the wall a beautiful picture of the Forth Rail Bridge at night showcased its stunning silhouette reflecting on the water.

The porter showed Carlo the wardrobe in which his (hired) wedding suit was already hanging. Going through a door, he explained the workings of the bathroom, with its elaborate shower, gleaming white bath tub, sink and toilet. Carlo tried to pay attention, but he was distracted: he had never seen so many pieces of equipment in a bathroom! He laughed to himself. 'If signor Bruno Cacasotto saw this, he would never leave!'

After showing Carlo the view of Edinburgh Castle from the side window, the porter finally went to the door, his hand behind his back, smiling. 'Is there anything else you would like, sir?'

'No, thank you. Everything is very nice.'

The young man didn't move.

It took three requests before Carlo realised he was waiting for a tip.

Carlo took some change out of his pocket and selected a farthing to give to the boy, patting him on the back as he told him he had done a great job.

The porter left, smiling. 'What a nice chap.'

It wasn't till later he realised he'd only been given a farthing; never mind, he was still a nice chap, after all!

After a wash, Carlo went downstairs to have a look around. He wandered into the bar and ordered a beer. He could hardly believe the way events had overtaken him. It was barely six months since he had arrived in Scotland and here he was: on the eve of his marriage to the most beautiful girl he had ever seen and on a path to start a whole new life.

Everything had come together at the last minute, but there had been a lot of anxious waiting to make sure all the licences and paperwork were in place. To be allowed to stay in Scotland he had had to register as an 'alien', and he would have to report to the police station every month.

'Huh! I was a policeman and now I have to report to the police! Madonna, this time I really am an immigrant!' He could hardly believe it. 'I wonder what Olivia is doing now,' he thought to himself.

As if the barman had read his mind he answered, 'She'll be doing exactly the same as you, sir. Wondering just what you are doing.' The barman had seen many a bridegroom the night before his wedding, excited but anxious, the enormity of the decision they were making slowly dawning. He knew the routine. Not too many drinks but just enough to calm the nerves.

'Are you all ready for tomorrow, sir?'

Carlo had to concentrate to understand. He had stopped his English lessons, and having spent so much time recently among Olivia's family he had been speaking mostly Italian.

'You've got the best of the bunch there. All the lads admire Miss Crolla. She's a great catch.'

'She is, isn't she?' Carlo was happy to chat and take his mind off his nerves.

'Where are you from?'

'Napoli, Italy.'

'I thought so. I was there during the war. Landed in Salerno, we did.'

Carlo was amazed. What a small world it was.

'I was in the Royal Scots Greys. We had a hell of a time but we made it. I was there when we liberated Naples.'

Carlo put his hand out to shake the barman's hand. 'I can't believe it! I'm Carlo Contini. Pleased to meet you.'

The barman shook his hand. 'Sandy, Sandy Thomson: 3rd Division, Royal Scots Greys. Oh, we saw some terrible things. Terrible.' the barman fell silent for a moment. 'I'm a piper. I'll never forget it. We piped from the outskirts of the city right into the centre. Oh, what a welcome we got, I can tell you.'

Carlo was overwhelmed. '*Grazie*. Thank you. You boys saved our lives you know, and our country.'

Sandy told Carlo about the landings and the ferocity of the

233

retreating German army. They had fought for ten days before they finally withdrew. It was carnage. He lost so many friends.

'You know, Carlo, after the battle our commanding officer told us if it hadn't been for the Greys, the Allied beachhead might have been destroyed and the landings would have failed. It's something I'll never forget. After the breakout we made our way to Naples. What a beautiful country you have. The heat of the sun, the sea so blue and warm. We had some fun swimming in it, I can tell you.

'It broke our hearts to see the senseless destruction: villages bombed, fields burning. The poor peasants, so bedraggled and desperate, lined the road clapping and cheering us. When we came to the outskirts of the city it was already liberated, the citizens had done it themselves.'

'My Aunt Francesca was there, Sandy. She told us it was the *scugnizzi,* the street urchins, the women and the Italian partisans that had overcome the enemy. They were so desperate they had nothing left to lose.'

'We saw that. Eventually, when we were ordered to advance, we started our bagpipes and marched into the city.' Sandy's eyes filled with tears. 'I'll never forget when we fired up our pipes and started to march forward. Oh, the relief on the faces of those poor starving people: women, barefoot children. What a welcome. They cheered and ran after us, the kids ran beside us banging sticks on pot lids to join the parade. They climbed up on the tanks, and waved and cheered.

'Carlo, I've never had so many good kisses in one day. Those Neapolitan girls know how to kiss, I'll tell you that!'

He laughed and patted Carlo on the shoulder. 'You're going to have your fill tomorrow, you'll see!'

'Did you not get a lovely Neapolitan *ragazza* for yourself?'

'I had a few offers! They were very friendly.' Sandy laughed, remembering the fun they had had and the relief they had felt having survived the fight they'd just experienced.

'I am sure they were if you were in your kilt.'

'That's what they loved. There were so many toothless grandmothers dancing with us.'

Carlo thought of his own two toothless grandmothers. He

knew only too well grandmothers had memories of their own. They'd had passions and loves and kisses in their time.

'Carlo, we couldn't believe our luck. We were actually billeted in the opera house. Can you imagine? I just remember the singing and music all over the city.'

'Well I never. I've never been in the opera house. Maybe I'll go one day as well.'

'Oh, it's beautiful, Carlo. You'll have to go. Take your bride! I've never seen anything like it. It's like a chocolate box, with fabulous gold and red booths all the way up the sides. It's the most stunning place I've ever been.'

An hour or so later, on hearing a commotion in the bar, Mr Johnston, the concierge, went to see what was going on. He didn't want any fracas before the big Crolla wedding tomorrow. He entered to find the groom himself swaying behind the bar with the barman, singing '*Addio, mia bella Napoli*', the customers clapping and singing along with them, Mr Aldridge, the banqueting manager, standing at the far end of the bar surveying the scene and smiling. He had fought in Sicily and he understood perfectly.

As Mr Johnston tried to separate them to take the bridegroom safely up to his room, Carlo embraced his new friend. 'When we get settled I'll invite you to our house for lunch. My Olivia is the best cook you can imagine, apart from my own mother of course. She'll make egg pasta and Italian sausage *sugo*. You'll think you're right back in Napoli!'

'Carlo, you know what I'll do? I'll ask Mr Aldridge if I can get some time off. I'll come to the church tomorrow and play for you and your bride. What do you think? Would your Olivia like that?'

'Would she like that? She'd love it. Just you come after I'm married though. I don't want her running off with a Scottish soldier before I've got her hitched myself!'

*

The next day was perfect: blue skies, crisp and still air. Coming out of the cathedral after their wedding, Carlo and Olivia stood at the top steps, smiling and happy. They made a very handsome couple.

The bride's dress was as close to the one she had tried on in

Jenners as the Italian seamstress in Broughton Street could manage: white duchess satin and a modest neckline with a long sweeping train. Miss MacDonald had come along herself to see what the bride had ended up wearing. So, they had got it made! She had to take her hat off to Mrs Crolla. It was a fly move and it had paid off. Olivia looked stunning. She just hoped all the Italians wouldn't follow suit; it would ruin her business.

Carlo felt on top of the world. He looked around at the fancy cars, the wedding guests dressed in the height of fashion, the crowds watching and smiling.

'*Madonna mia, grazie, Madonna.*'

He bent over and whispered to his bride. '*Lilla, ti voglio tanto bene, ti voglio.*' He pulled her towards him and kissed her. All the male guests cheered and encouraged them, clapping and shouting.

'*Baci! Baci!*'

Catching the mood, the large crowd of onlookers joined in. What an exciting spectacle, seeing all the Italians enjoying themselves instead of in their shops working.

'*Baci! Baci!*' the crowd didn't know what 'bachee' meant, but it sounded fun to shout.

Carlo pulled Olivia into his arms and kissed her full on the lips, passionately. He'd show these '*paesani*' from the mountains how a Neapolitan can love!

A whole crowd had gathered to watch: Italians, Scots, priests and altar boys, nuns and nurses, policemen and road sweepers, tramps and passers-by. Nannies from Regent Terrace with navy-blue Silver Cross prams stood uniformed in twos and gossiped, and young mothers congregated with their children as the wedding group moved from the church stairs towards the car.

When Carlo saw the cream and black Bentley Vittorio had chosen to bring his sister up to the church in he laughed. Look at that! The cream at the front and black trim and upper were the exact same colours as the dancing shoes of Zi' Antonio which he had so coveted as a child.

Gloria settled her mother and Marietta comfortably in the back seat ready to take them up to the hotel. Maria was relieved that the Mass had gone well and that the groom had turned up. It was always a relief to get a daughter off your hands. Given the precarious status of Carlo's earning potential she couldn't be sure Olivia was categorically 'off her hands', but Maria was not too disappointed by that. The more her family depended on her, the better.

Seeing Anna supported between Bill and Margaret slowly coming down the steps of the cathedral, Gloria called them over. Anna was in the family way but was still dressed to the nines, with her favourite peep-toe high heels on.

Maria looked at Anna. She congratulated Marietta. '*Auguri! Ha una bella pagnotta nel forno!* She looks ready. When did she get married? End of January?' She counted the months on her fingers. 'End of October now – nine months. It might come today!'

'Well, let's hope not, Maria. Not until the dancing is over at least,' Marietta laughed.

It was not uncommon for the first child to be born exactly nine months after the wedding. You really didn't want it born any sooner than that. All the women would check, she knew. Anna didn't know what was ahead of her, and a good dance might just get her started.

'Better safe than sorry,' Gloria thought. She called over to them. 'Anna, Bill, come with us. We'll take you up to the hotel in the car. It's such a lovely day, the wedding guests are all going to walk.'

Anna came across and greeted her Zia Maria. 'Are Olivia and Carlo going to walk?'

'Yes. We can watch from the car.'

Anna was particularly content with her husband. Bill was six years older than her and either he wanted to do everything she asked, or she managed to persuade him; either way she got her own way, which made for a very happy couple.

Tall and handsome, with his wide, happy smile Bill looked very impressive in his full RAF uniform, although he wasn't in the RAF any more; he was a fishmonger in Goldenacre. But Anna preferred him dressed in uniform; her baby was due any day now and she was hoping for a romantic evening. Why should the new bride have all the fun?

'Zia Maria, if you don't mind, I'm going to walk with Bill and Margaret. With a bit of luck it'll start the baby! Mum, you go up in the car with Zia Maria. We'll all go together up to the hotel.' Despite what she'd just said, she hoped the baby wouldn't come;

not till tomorrow morning anyway. At the thought her laugh rang out, attracting her brothers Johnny and Alex. Gertrude Hilley, Johnny's new fiancée, was at his side. She was nine years his junior and quite a catch. Her father was a famous Celtic footballer and she had a taste for the high life.

'What a cracker!' Bill thought. 'Trust Johnny to strike it lucky.' If Anna could have read his mind he would have had a black eye!

Bill bent over to kiss his mother-in-law. Gradually he was working on Marietta to get her to accept him into her family. When he had converted to Catholicism in order to marry Anna, he may have made Marietta happy but he had not pleased his own mother one bit. True to his word, he made sure he followed his adopted faith, and though he wouldn't admit it to his mother, he was beginning to find it quite refreshing after the dourness of the Church of Scotland.

'Bill, tell Maria how well you are getting on with Anna,' Marietta wanted to show that her daughter's marriage was successful even though the community had been against it.

'Oh, very well indeed, Zia, we get on like a house on fire.'

Anna chipped in, 'Zia Maria, Bill and I have a lot in common. He's very interested in me and so am I.'

'*Che dice?*' Maria didn't understand a word.

Marietta gave Anna a withering look. Vittorio heard and burst out laughing! This was going to be a great day.

He spoke to the driver, 'Go slowly, pal. They'll want to see everything.'

He gave the driver a half crown and handed his mother a linen bag filled with pennies and halfpennies.

'Mum, here's the money for the "poor-oot". Throw it on the pavement side to get the kids away from the car.'

True to his word Sandy the barman from the NB had come down. He was dressed in his full regimental uniform complete with his kilt, busby and bagpipes. Mr Aldridge had been happy to let him off work.

'Good idea,' he thought to himself. 'Two hundred Italians all marching up the hill dressed in their finest and coming into the North British Hotel for their wedding luncheon: what a great advertising opportunity. Wait till I tell my snooty area manager.'

He had taken the liberty of calling the *Evening News*. It was going to be some shindig, he was sure of that.

As the piper started to play his pipes everyone became very excited. He stamped his feet three times as he set off up the road, playing the wedding march for 'Mairi's Wedding'.

The wedding party started to follow, arm in arm, laughing and clapping. Passers-by stopped to line the streets and cheer them on, applauding and encouraging them as they started to dance to the music. The bride and groom led the procession, the little bridesmaids danced around them, beaming and waving to everyone. Bill and Margaret walked with Anna between them, singing the words to the Scottish wedding song, changing the last line to honour the bride:

Step we gaily, on we go,
Heel for heel and toe for toe,
Arm in arm and row on row,
All for 'Livia's wedding.

Johnny walked with his arm around Gertrude, happy as well, looking forward to his own wedding in the spring. Alex took Gloria and Phyllis, one on each arm, laughing and joking at Anna's slow pace and the size of her bump.

The clergy were waiting to help people on their way. They couldn't be seen in public to be joining the celebrations but Vittorio had arranged for the car to come back and whisk them up in time for the drinks reception.

The Bentley waited till the guests had all passed then slowly started to drive behind them. Looking from the back of the car, Maria and Marietta watched, both still dressed in widow's black. Neither looked at each other, both lost in their own thoughts.

Marietta turned to Maria. '*Auguri, commar*'. Congratulations. You've done a great job, and I'm sure Carlo will make a wonderful husband for Olivia.'

'*Grazie, commar*'. Please God your new grandchild arrives soon and well. I am just so grateful that life for the young ones is starting to look normal again.'

The women fell quiet again. Looking at their daughters both

now happily married to good-looking, caring young men reminded them even more painfully of their own widowhood. Without intending to, they were gradually becoming a little embittered by their misfortune.

Maria thought it was scandalous that Marietta had allowed Anna to marry a Scotsman, and a Protestant at that. Marietta thought it was scandalous that Maria was allowing Olivia to marry a Neapolitan with no money.

Maria tried to be brave. What could they do? They had to cope the best they could.

'Do you remember the last time we all processed up this hill, when we followed Alfonso and Cesidio and the other Italian soldiers up to the war memorial at the top of the Mound? Do you remember, they were laying a wreath for the Unknown Soldier?'

'It's not so long ago. Maybe fifteen years?'

'The pipers of the Scots Greys were following them.' Maria held Marietta's hand. 'Do you think it's true they were side by side when the ship went down? I really hope so. Do you think they are watching us now?'

'Yes, they are. I'm sure they are.'

They embraced, not weeping, just trying hard to be content that their daughters were getting a better future.

The local children were running round the car, jumping up to see the plush, cream leather seats. A young girl laughed to her mother, 'Look at the two grannies in the car!'

'They're torn-faced. They look bloomin' miserable!'

One brazen young lad jumped up at the open window. 'When's the "poor-oot", missus?'

Glad of the distraction, Maria took the bag of money and laughing to Marietta, threw a scatter of coins out of the window. The kids all cheered and with a few tramps who had been watching and waiting as well, scrabbled to gather as many coins as they could.

Maria kept throwing the coins out, a few at a time. There was still a substantial amount at the bottom of the bag when she closed it over and slipped it back into her handbag.

What a stupid Scottish custom, to throw money into the street!

In her experience, you never knew when you would need some extra pennies yourself.

As the procession approached the top of the hill it started to slow; Anna was struggling to keep up with the crowd. Carlo shouted something to the piper and he started to play a tune he had heard often in Naples.

Jamme, jamme, 'ngoppa jamme ja,
Funiculi, funicula! Funiculi, funicula!
Jamme, jamme ja, funiculi, funicula!

All the wedding guests burst out laughing and joined in. Carlo laughed too, and turned to Olivia, singing along, 'That's us, Olivia. You and me, we're on our way to the top!'

*

By the time the priests arrived at the hotel, Carlo and Olivia were just preparing to cut the cake. It had taken the best part of an hour for all the guests to arrive, line up, kiss all the members of the wedding party and congratulate the bride and groom.

Gloria was strategically on hand to keep the envelopes that were being flamboyantly pushed into Olivia's hands as she was kissed and congratulated.

When the last person had handed over their gift, Patrick, a charming Irishman and the hotel's resident Master of Ceremonies, stood at the door to the dining room. He was much shorter than the towering Italians but his voice was bigger than the lot of them put together.

He banged a gavel three times.

'Monsignor, Father, Bride and Groom, Laaaydeees and Gentlemen, I invite you all to proceed to the dining room. The wedding lunch is served.'

The crowd erupted with a loud cheer: '*A mangiare!*'

As expected, the wedding party ran well over schedule. Between continuous toasts, speeches and general rumbustious behaviour, the fine timing and silver service of the hotel was discarded, completely out of control.

Mr Aldridge came across to speak to Vittorio.

'Mr Crolla, I am afraid we are an hour behind schedule. The orchestra are getting ready to play. The chefs are waiting to serve the high tea, what shall we do?'

'We can eat and listen to music … tell the orchestra to start playing and let the chefs bring on the fish and chips!'

Carlo had been waiting for his moment. He had planned a surprise with the band leader and Patrick, who had come up beside him.

The band played three rolls of the drums.

Startled, the guests actually stopped talking and shouting and looked expectantly at the stage. Patrick took the microphone and announced, 'Laaydees and gentlemen. I give you the groom: Mr Carlo Contini!'

And as everyone stood and cheered and clapped Carlo, with the help of the microphone, sang a message to his mother and family. With tears rolling down his face he sang goodbye to his beautiful Napoli. His life would never be the same again.

Addio mia bella Napoli,
Addio, addio.
La tua soave immagine,
Chi mai, chi mai scordar potrà?

Goodbye my beautiful Napoli, goodbye, goodbye!

As they started to serve the fried lemon sole and chips, to more cheers from the guests, Margaret slipped out of the dining hall and headed to the front door. She looked very pale and a bit unwell.

'Margaret, are you all right?'

'I'm fine Mr Johnston. It's just a bit noisy in there. I'll just go out for a wee bit fresh air.'

'It's pouring rain, Margaret. They were lucky. It started five minutes after everyone arrived.'

He went behind the desk. 'Here, take my Mackintosh. It'll keep you dry. Just stand at the door.'

It was dark now and the cold autumn air made her feel dizzy. Princes Street was busy and she thought she'd take a walk away from the fumes of the cars. She crossed the road and went behind Woolworths, up to the lane behind the Café Royal, just to steady herself.

Two bobbies on the beat came round the corner from St Andrew Square. They looked at Margaret in her blue dress, small high heels and oversized navy mac.

'Aye, aye, what's all this here?'

'Hello, Miss. What are you doing out here on your own?'

'Oh, it's OK, officer. I was at a wedding in the NB. I've just come out for some air.'

'The Crolla wedding?'

'Yes.' Everybody knew the Crolla wedding was on today.

'What are you doing out here, then?'

Margaret put her hand against the wall. She felt really queasy now.

'Officer, they've been eating solid since one o'clock. They've had about eight dinners already and now they've started on fish and chips.'

At the thought of fish and chips she put her hand to her mouth and turned, steadying herself at the wall.

'That sounds like it's a great wedding, miss.'

'Oh it is, officer, it's just that I need to be ...'

'Take your time, lass.'

One of the policemen stood at the corner and diverted any pedestrians to another route until she felt better. The other one got her a glass of water from the Café Royal.

'Here you are, lass. Are you feeling better now? If there's any extra fish and chips when you go back in you can send some out for us!'

'If you're feeling better we'll take you back.'

When Margaret went back in she met Anna and Bill leaving.

'Oh, there you are! We wondered where you had got to. Can you go home later with Johnny and Alex? I'm off to the hospital. I think the baby's coming now after all.'

As it turned out, Anna didn't give birth for another six weeks. By the time Olivia saw her friend again she had a lovely baby girl.

Chapter Twenty-five

Once she was married, Olivia gave up her nursing career. She would have preferred to keep working, but Carlo insisted: 'You can't be a wife *and* a nurse, darling.'

The newlyweds set up home in Wellington Street. As a wedding gift from her mother, they had managed to put down a deposit and buy a small flat halfway between her mother's house and her brother's business. It was perfect.

In all, the money in the wedding envelopes had grossed upwards of £493.10s; not all that far short of the £576 Vittorio and his mother had estimated on the back of the invitation list. The invoice from the North British Hotel for the hire of rooms, the wedding meal, high tea and corkage (the wine was of course supplied by Valvona & Crolla) was £502. Vittorio was quite pleased. In all, it was a break-even event.

Considering this was more money than Carlo had ever seen in his life, he was wise enough not to comment, or to request control of any of the funds. He felt at a disadvantage, but he made up his mind to do all he could to contribute equally to the fortunes of his new family, and as always looked for any alternative opportunities.

His work at the farm in Liberton with Mr Miller was good, and his position had been extended for another six months. He enjoyed being out of the city and away from everyone. It gave him time to think. He left the house at 4 a.m. and managed to complete his tasks and be home in time for lunch.

Olivia spent her mornings cleaning the house, washing Carlo's clothes, ironing and preparing his lunch. She did all she could to make food for him that he liked, but with very limited supplies it was difficult. Her afternoons were spent shopping, queuing at the butcher, the fishmonger, the greengrocer, the dairy. The list was endless. Sometimes she had to go to two or three different shops to find what she needed.

Carlo had been helpful in explaining what he liked. 'Olivia, I need to eat every day at one o'clock. I can eat anything; but no Scottish food, it is a bit, how do you say, *sciapo*?'

'I think you mean bland.'

'Yes, bland … and definitely no polenta, my darling. That's bland as well.'

Olivia tried her best, sticking to the recipes she had cooked with her mother. At least Vittorio was managing to get more Italian supplies through Soho. Her cooking was simple and tasty. One Sunday, when Maria had inadvertently served him polenta in the form of *'tirdiglione'* – polenta with bitter greens and garlic – he had refused to eat it. Olivia had to quickly make him a separate plate of spaghetti, *aglio e olio*.

Maria was slightly put out. It was the first time Carlo had let her down. In the kitchen she raised it with her daughter, 'Olivia, is Carlo a little bit fussy? Why does he not like my *tirdiglione?*'

'I don't know. He just said he doesn't want to eat polenta. He said it was *sciapo*.'

Maria looked doubtful. Her *tirdiglione* was anything but *sciapo*. It had been Alfonso's favourite. She tried to hide her disappointment.

'Olivia, it's your duty to feed Carlo what he likes to eat. You need to keep his strength up!' Maria was joking, but she and Olivia had no idea of the memories of hunger and hardship Carlo would always associate with surviving on polenta during the war. In his memory it was all they'd had to eat for months on end. He didn't dwell on or talk about it. Why remind them of what he had come from?

After his lunch and a short siesta Carlo got into the habit of walking along to 19 Elm Row. He would stand at the corner of Windsor Street and light a cigarette, breathing in deeply. By the time he reached the door of the shop, the evocative smell of roasting coffee would invigorate him and, flinging his cigarette butt into the gutter, would, without being asked, lift a couple of the boxes that would typically be stacked outside into the shop, and take them down to the basement.

It wasn't long before Carlo was serving in the shop every afternoon. Here at least he was surrounded by things Italian: the smells, the chatter, the laughter and the music that was always playing. Somehow it was a tonic after the homesickness he was starting to suffer.

Yet he was happy, deliriously so. He loved Olivia, she was truly the girl for him, he had no doubts. He prayed to the Madonna and thanked her every day for his parents, who he realised now had saved his life. Olivia and he had their whole life ahead of them and hopefully soon he would have a son of his own.

But sometimes, when he was alone, he felt a longing for Pozzuoli. He missed the sun. He missed the warmth. He missed the light. He found the dark winter days insufferable. In the mornings when he went out it was dark; when he finally left the shop at night it was dark again.

He was getting used to Olivia's food; it was good. But he missed his mother's *zuppa di pesce* and the flavour of her pasta and chick-peas.

He asked Olivia to buy some fruit. She bought apples and pears. He dreamed of sweet yellow peaches and juicy black grapes, of voluptuous ripe figs and juicy watermelon that dripped down your chin when you took a bite.

But mostly he missed his mother. He still wrote to her, always enclosing some money. He had sent her photographs of the wedding. She had sent a letter back and a gift for Olivia: a set of six teaspoons with black coffee beans at the end, the same as the set her mother had given her. This was nothing compared to the extravagant gifts of money they had received from others, but Carlo knew it was a far greater effort for his mother to send this small token from the little she had. Olivia loved them; she understood more than Carlo realised.

The revelation about his adoption that had come in the letter from his mother was frequently on his mind, nagging him. He didn't even want to think of who his birth mother might have been, but when he was least expecting it, the thought would cross his mind. Who was she that she would abandon a child? What terrible events had driven her to do such a thing?

Carlo knew about the '*ruota dei bambini abbandonati*' in the Istituto dell' Annunziata in Naples, where desperate women would secretly abandon their babies to the care of the nuns, and slink away unobserved.

When he thought of this he found himself involuntarily pushing at the air, physically shoving his hands away from himself. Would his birth mother have done that? What would that feel like, pushing away your offspring?

He knew in Naples hundreds of unwanted babies were left on the doorsteps of churches, in hospitals, even abandoned in the streets. They were unwanted, but perhaps not unloved. He realised now he had been one of those babies.

Carlo had a recurring nightmare. A ball was rotating in a drum, like a lottery ball, round and round, never stopping. He would wake up in a cold sweat and then, as he came to, the harsh reality would sweep over him again. His nightmare was true.

He had always been so proud of his achievements as a youngster; his diligence and ingenuity; his ability to think ahead and take advantage of a situation; his ability to survive. He always said he was a *scugnizzo*, a street urchin.

It dawned on him that somewhere, deep in his earliest memory, he had always known he had been abandoned.

*

Vittorio had sensed Carlo's nostalgia and anxiety. He was part of his family now and they needed to do all they could to support him. Vittorio would never admit it to his brother-in-law, but Carlo knew far more about Italian food than Vittorio ever could.

One Saturday evening, Vittorio took Carlo aside and gave him some folded notes. 'Carlo, here are your wages for the work you have done so far. Best not tell Olivia. She'll spend it in Jenners before you know it. From now, we'll register you as an employee and I'll add up your hours and pay you weekly.'

With rationing gradually coming to an end, Vittorio was trying to anticipate the growing market. He was aware of so many people of different nationalities settling down in Edinburgh. Not just his own compatriots from Lazio but immigrants from all over Italy. And also ex-prisoners of war: Poles, Russians and Germans were staying in Scotland rather than returning to their own countries. Vittorio was excited; so many people from the Continent, so many potential customers. What would they be looking for? Food and drink from their native countries!

The following week Vittorio fixed a sheet of paper beside the till. He called Domenico and Carlo across.

'Now, lads, this is the new "Goods Required" list. Anything that a customer asks for that we don't have in stock, write it down on this list.'

As he spoke, reflecting on Mr Sklar and the Cinzano episode, he had another idea.

'Not only that, when you are writing it down, call the item out to everyone in the shop. It's no use us buying a case of Hero Polish cherry jam, for example, if only one person wants a jar. It's our job to create a market. Repeat the call! That's it. Repeat the call!'

'What do you mean, Vittorio? What does it mean, "Repeat the call?"' Domenico didn't know what his brother was talking about. Vittorio did this all the time, had an idea and by the time he'd told them about it, it had changed into a whole different thing. It was sometimes hard to keep up with him.

'Watch, I'll show you. It's like being in the army. You are given an instruction and you repeat it to acknowledge you have understood.'

This didn't help. Domenico was more confused than before. 'But Vittorio, we're not in the army!'

'Ah, but we are! We're in the battle of commerce and we need an army! Watch. Carlo, you call out for something you miss from home that we don't stock.'

Carlo thought for a moment. The list was endless.

'*Babà*! I miss *rum babà*!'

Vittorio laughed. Carlo had never forgiven him for eating all the *babà* that Vincenzo had sent him from Gambrinus.

'Good. Now pay attention, Domenico. When I call out the goods required you repeat the call.'

Vittorio called out in a loud voice so everyone in the shop could hear.

'Goods required! *Babà, rum babà*!' and proceeded to write it down on the list by the till. Domenico followed suit, getting into the swing of it.

'Goods required. *Babà, rum babà*!'

Pasquale from the chip shop at the bottom of Leith Street had been standing at the back of the queue waiting to be served.

'Who said *babà*? I haven't had *babà* since I was at my nonna's knee in Napoli. Vittorio if you have *babà*, I'll take six!'

Pasquale didn't understand what he had said that was so funny when Vittorio, Carlo and Domenico all burst out laughing.

'They'll be arriving next week, Pasquale. I'll put you down for six.'

'Well done, Carlo. You're our secret weapon. You've got the desires of an immigrant. We're going to channel that! We're going to serve your desires!'

Domenico was lost again. He was busy looking for a girl to marry and his desires were far from satisfied!

'Vittorio, I remember what it was like to be in Genoa the first time. The smells were different and there was plenty of food, but I still searched out what I missed from home.'

'Exactly! When I went to Pozzuoli to visit your wonderful mother I was overwhelmed with the richness of the flavours. Carlo, we can get some basic Italian food from London, but nothing like the flavours I tasted there. The *mozzarella di bufala*! Annunziata's *melanzane sott'olio*! The *gelato*! We have to find a supply direct to Elm Row!'

Vittorio was enjoying getting to know Carlo. Having been born in Edinburgh, his understanding of Italy was only what he had learned from his immediate family. His only personal experience of Italy so far had been his visit to Pozzuoli. Italy itself was a whole new world to learn about … and Carlo was the key.

He took Carlo with him round Edinburgh, checking out the competition. They visited T.G. Willis in George Street: 'Too posh'! Forsyth's food hall in Princes Street: 'Too expensive'! Shops in

Morningside: 'Too pretentious'. The Co-op in Leith: 'Vittorio, no. Too Scottish!'

They visited the wine merchants: no one sold Italian wine at all! All you could buy was expensive French chablis and claret.

'Vittorio, the wine merchants are so exclusive. Don't people have a glass of wine with their lunch?'

'Yes, but only the lawyers and accountants who drink in the New Club.'

'What do you think? Should we buy some to see what it tastes like?'

Vittorio burst out laughing. 'French wine, Carlo! Do you see what they are charging? *Non toccare* with a bargepole!'

Carlo had no clue what Vittorio meant but he laughed with him just the same.

'You know, Carlo. You've given me an idea. We've been buying wine through the bonds down in Leith. We should think about bottling some to sell under our own brand. What do you think?'

Carlo laughed.

'You'll never believe when I last bottled wine!' He proceeded to tell his brother-in-law about the time he and Tullio sold wine to the South Africans in Mondragone.

'I'm joking, but you know, Vittorio, I can help you. It's a great idea. We could even sell the wine in bulk and let people bring their own bottles to be filled. That's what we did at home.'

'Perfect. Fill-your-own-bottle sherry! We could sell sherry by the pint!' Vittorio was listening to every idea Carlo had.

'That lovely lady that comes in would come more often!' Carlo had already served the 'signorina' from Morningside and now, much to Vittorio and Domenico's irritation, she waited in the queue until Carlo was available to serve her. The last time, Vittorio had been left with old Mrs Gasparini, who had come in again to get a refund for her mortadella because it was sliced too thick. Last week she had asked for a refund because it was sliced too thin!

Vittorio had been to London twice since the start of the year. As items were added to the 'goods required list' Vittorio sourced them. The shop was filling up with items on the shelves that people had not seen in years. His aim was to be the place people could get everything they needed, and things they didn't need at all. Before they knew it, the shop was full of pickles, sardines, sauces, onions from France, garlic from Brittany, fresh sausages, dried sausages, Italian olive oil, Greek olive oil, nasi goreng, lemon grass, *dolcelatte*!

Domenico thought they had both gone mad.

'It's all very well buying everything you see, Vittorio, but who's going to sell it all?'

'We are, Domenico! We are!'

*

'Carlo, Olivia! Quick! The shop's on fire! Vittorio says to come now; hurry!'

Phyllis came running round to Wellington Street to get Carlo and Olivia. They all ran back to Elm Row.

Outside, Vittorio, Domenico, Gloria as well as about 20 customers were standing at the far end of the street. The firemen were in the shop with their hoses and water was pouring out of the front door. Another fireman was up a ladder spraying water down the side of the building to put out the flames.

'What happened, Vittorio?'

'It's the coffee roaster. It's nothing. We just had a small fire.'

'A small fire, Vittorio? We just about burned the shop down!' Domenico was visibly shaking.

'Don't worry,' Vittorio was unperturbed. 'It won't happen again. I've got a plan.'

The firemen told them they had been lucky, again. This was the third time the coffee roaster had caused a fire.

'You really need to put an extraction tube in, Mr Crolla.'

'Aye, Vittorio. I'd prefer it if you don't burn my house down as well as your daft shop!' Their Italian neighbour, a cousin, Josephine, lived in a flat above the shop, on the same landing as their office. All the smells of the food and coffee roasting seeped up through her floorboards. It was not unpleasant; it reminded her of Italy.

Driving back down to the station the firemen felt rather lucky themselves; they were each clutching another couple of bottles of that nice Chianti. Good chap, Mr Crolla, but he really needed to put an extraction tube in.

The next time the coffee roaster went on fire, a few weeks later, they didn't need to call the fire brigade.

Vittorio's plan had worked. He had constructed a home-made extraction tube under the floor of the shop, stretching from the basement to the back shop. Every three feet, he had arranged a complicated series of fire buckets filled with sand and in each an empty plastic soap bottle filled with water. They had had their fire training after work when the shop was closed.

'Right, *ragazzi*! When we smell the coffee starting to burn I will shout "*FUOCO! FUOCO!*" When you hear the call go immediately to your stations. Carlo, you go to the roaster and turn it off and put the fire blanket on it to douse the flames. Domenico, you go to the basement by the front ladder. Get your water bottle and wet the pipes, squirt water into the holes that the smoke escapes from. The other staff will go down to the basement by the back stair with me. We'll take our positions and between us all we'll extinguish the fire.'

Carlo could hardly believe what he was hearing. It made him think of his mother when she used to say: '*Fai come fosse in tempo di guerra*; just behave as if it were wartime.' Only the war had been over for almost ten years!

Vittorio's plan, though well thought through, was not a consistent success as the fire brigade were soon back.

'Vittorio, they'll close us down if we keep setting the shop on fire,' Domenico was getting worried.

Carlo sensed an opportunity. 'Boys, why don't you give me the job of looking after the coffee? I'll make sure the pipes are cleaned so the oil doesn't build up and I'll keep an eye on the roasting so we don't burn the beans.'

'Good plan, Carlo. Good plan.'

When Carlo went home for lunch that day he thought he had landed in a mad house. Vittorio was a great businessman and an exceptional brother-in-law, but he was very eccentric. And they say Neapolitans are excitable! They had never come across the Crollas. One thing was sure, he never had a chance to be bored.

He was excited to tell Olivia about his conversation with

Vittorio. He was going to have a real responsibility in the shop. He knew he could do a good job with the coffee. He would mix a different blend of Robusta and Arabica beans and keep testing it until he could get the coffee tasting exactly like it did at home: rich and smooth, full of aroma and definitely not burnt. He had already been testing the coffee every day, keeping notes to get the taste he was looking for. Every afternoon after his shift on the farm he would head to the shop to create his new blend of his coffee.

Life was starting to take shape.

He was in effect doing two full-time jobs but he felt better being busy, and the sacrifices he was making were starting to have results: his savings were building up. The sun was even starting to shine a bit more, but there was little warmth in it.

The following day he arrived home for lunch, ready to start his new job in the afternoon. Best get started as soon as possible, just in case Vittorio changed his mind.

'*Ho fame!* I'm hungry!' As usual he whistled to alert Olivia he was nearly home so she could put the pasta on as he arrived.

'I wonder what she's made for lunch today?'

He was surprised when he got home that the door was locked. Olivia always had the door ajar ready for him to come in. He shrugged his shoulders and got his key out.

He whistled again.

'Lilla? Olivia?'

He went into the kitchen. On the table was a covered plate with a small note on top of it. He opened the note.

'Carlo, darling. I've gone out for lunch with some friends. I'll see you tonight. I love you, Olivia x.'

Gone out for lunch? He shook his head. He couldn't understand it.

'Some friends? Friends? She's my wife. She can't have friends!'

He lifted the cover to see what she had left him to eat. That couldn't be right. Under the cover was a sandwich! There must be some mistake. He looked on the cooker and in the refrigerator.

A sandwich? He'd have to speak to Olivia tonight. This was not good enough!

What would his mother say if she found out?

Chapter Twenty-six

Olivia and Anna hadn't met since Olivia's wedding. They chose Fuller's, their favourite tearoom.

'Let's have high tea: fried haddock and chips! What do you think?'

Olivia was looking forward to having lunch out. She had to admit she was finding it a challenge to cook for Carlo. She was used to cooking with her mother for all the family, not just for two. Carlo was always very appreciative, but if he hadn't enjoyed something or when she gave him the same meal two days running he delicately let her know. She really missed going home every day and her mother having a meal ready for her. At least on Sundays they always went to Brunton Place for lunch. She loved getting her mother's home cooking. She noticed Carlo never complained to her mother!

Anna was looking a bit tired. She had been unwell since the baby had arrived and was trying to build up her strength.

'Anna, look at us. We're like two old married women. Happy to get a break! It seems like only yesterday we were kneeling in front of the Madonna in Lourdes praying for a husband.'

'Our prayers were well and truly answered. Now we know the consequences of taking on a man.'

'Is Margaret well? She's so kind to take the baby round the park, Anna. You're very lucky.'

'Betty's with her too. They're having fun. The gardens are lovely for pushing a pram.'

'It's nice to be alone, anyway. There are different things to talk about now we're married.' Olivia was so glad Anna had married first. She could talk about things. Her mother was not one for discussing anything even vaguely personal and Gloria and Phyllis weren't married so they didn't have a clue.

'Anna, I thought you would have warned me a little about married life.'

'What's wrong? Are you getting on all right with Carlo?'

'Oh, yes, we're getting on fine. It's just his attitudes are so different from ours; it's like he's from another age, even another planet!'

Anna had suspected there might be some friction. Bill was different. He was much more free and easy about everything and was no bother to look after. He did lots of things to help Anna, was happy to make her something to eat and help around the house. He even pushed the pram for her. His time on the fishing boats as a youngster had made him very self-sufficient. Carlo was from the south of Italy. The rules for married women there were very different.

'What is it? Tell me.'

'Well, first he doesn't want me to work any more. I thought that would be all right, but to be honest I get bored in the house all day. I miss my nursing. I even miss going to the shop.'

'Oh, Olivia, don't worry. He needs to get used to our modern life. It'll take time. I'll get Bill to talk to him.'

'Oh no, he would be furious if he knew I'd spoken to you. He's very proud.'

'I know, I know. Listen, I know Carlo likes going down to Leith to look at the fishing boats. I'll get Bill to take him fishing. He goes up to Loch Lomond on a Sunday. He could take Carlo.'

'That's a good idea, Anna. Thank you. I'll ask Mum if she won't mind if Carlo misses Sunday lunch one day.'

'Oops,' Anna thought to herself. 'Sounds like Carlo's not getting much freedom either.'

Olivia felt relieved. Carlo would love to go fishing. They must take a trip down the coast to Cockenzie as well, he'd love that.

Anna wanted to hear more gossip. 'Well, tell me. How was London? Did you enjoy your honeymoon!'

Olivia blushed.

255

'Oh, you did then.'

'Anna I'll tell you a secret, but promise never to tell anyone.'

Anna moved across the table conspiratorially so Olivia could lower her voice.

'Well, our first night was …' Olivia hesitated.

'Yes?' Anna encouraged her.

'Well, put it like this, I didn't know what to expect,' Olivia continued, now pink all over her face. 'I went to Confession the next day, you know, in Farm Street, the Jesuits.'

Anna burst out laughing.

The people on the table next looked across at them.

'Shh, Anna!' Olivia looked round, embarrassed.

'What were you doing going to Confession on your honeymoon? And to the Jesuits!'

Olivia moved forward.

'Sshhh … Well, I didn't know!' she started to giggle.

'Didn't know what?'

'I didn't know anything.'

Anna looked confused.

'Put it like this, when I told the priest what had happened, he asked me who I had been with. When I told him it was my husband, he burst out laughing as well. Anna, I've never heard a priest laugh in the confessional.'

Anna's laugh was so loud the whole restaurant looked across at the pretty Italian girls in the window. What on earth could be so very funny?

Oliva laughed as well. When they stopped giggling Anna pressed Olivia again.

'Well, has it worked? You look a bit pale. Do you think you're expecting?'

'I don't know. I think maybe yes. What will I do?'

'Take a sample to the doctor. They'll test it and see if the rabbit dies.'

Olivia looked shocked. 'What are you talking about? What rabbit?'

'I don't know, that's what happened when I thought I was expecting. They test your sample of urine with a rabbit and if it dies it means you're going to have a baby.'

Olivia had never heard anything like it.

'So, Anna how are you managing with the baby? You look a little tired.'

'I am. To be honest the birth was quite difficult. I'm still a bit under the weather. The doctor says I've to try not to have another baby for a year or so.'

Olivia was confused. How could you do that? As far as she saw with her mother and her aunts, you just had babies when they came, surely? Annunziata, from what Carlo had told her, had had a baby every year.

'Anna, how will you manage that?' Then she thought and realised how it could happen. 'Oh, I know. Do you and Bill sleep in separate rooms now?'

Anna roared with laughter. 'No, darling! I just tell him to get off at Haymarket.'

It was not till many years later that Olivia worked out what she meant! She didn't dare to ask Anna there in the middle of the tea room.

They chatted and laughed all through their lunch, married now but just as if they were the young girls who had grown up together.

'You know, Olivia, we really do need to thank the Madonna. Look at all the blessings she has sent us.'

Looking out of the window, Anna saw Betty waving from across Princes Street.

'Oh, there's Betty. The baby must be crying. We need to go. Be good to Carlo now. You know what I mean. It's the easiest way to keep him sweet.'

As they pushed the pram, Anna chatted to Betty and Margaret about all the gossip she'd heard, but nothing personal. She didn't want to shock the girls. She was uncommonly chirpy. She was looking forward to telling Bill everything.

'Olivia was worried Carlo would be like one of those Italians that end up going back to Italy.'

Margaret laughed, 'No, Olivia, you'll be OK. Carlo will be too well fed in your family!'

They enjoyed a lovely afternoon walking in the park. Olivia and Anna walked along happily arm in arm as Margaret and Betty pushed the pram. Even though it was cold, the gardens were full of happy families and children running around. There were young office girls, hanging onto each other's arms and chatting and giggling along the road. There was such a difference now the war was over. Life looked like it was going to be a lot of fun. The windows of all the shops were full of spring fashions, bright new clothes with shorter skirts and cute hats.

Margaret and Betty been very busy in the last week and needed a break. Sweet rationing had been lifted on 5 February. There had been queues all along the High Street in Cockenzie, with children waiting patiently to buy their fill of all the treats that had been on ration for over ten years. Margaret and Betty had been working with Johnny and Alex in the shop. Margaret had never had such a happy week. They had sold out of gobstoppers, pineapple chunks and Spangles. It seemed as if the kids had been waiting all their lives to get to the sweetie shop to buy anything they wanted.

'It's the old men who buy all the barley sugars. Olivia, you should have seen all the kiddies. They were all standing at the corner like old men themselves smoking their sweet cigarettes.'

Eventually Anna caught the tram home with the baby, while Margaret and Betty went off to the pictures together; *Gone with the Wind* was on and they both had a fancy for Clark Gable. Olivia made her way home, checking the time on the NB clock. It was nearly five o'clock and it was starting to get dark. She was so light-hearted now she'd shared her concerns with her friend. Maybe she *was* expecting, and that was why she had been feeling a bit unsettled. She'd go to the doctor tomorrow. She'd just get home now in time before Carlo got back from the shop.

'I'll go in to Mr Sanderson's and buy him some pork sausages. He'll enjoy that after just having a sandwich for his lunch.' Anna had kindly paid for her lunch before she left so she had a little extra money left from her budget.

It was quite dark by the time she got back to Wellington Street. She saw the lights were already on in the hall. She checked her watch. It wasn't six o'clock yet. Carlo was home early.

When she opened the gate, she stopped to look for her key in her bag. She didn't want to ring the bell in case Carlo was having a rest.

Just as she put her key into the door it opened. Carlo was standing in the doorway. She took a step back, alarmed.

He looked very angry.

She put her face up to receive his kiss and he stepped back and signalled for her to come into the house. She went past him and into the kitchen.

'Carlo. What's wrong? Has something happened?'

He turned towards her.

'What's wrong with *me*? My wife has been out all day, I don't know where she is and she doesn't come back till late!'

'But Carlo, I left a note.'

'You left a note and a sandwich. A sandwich! Thank you very much. I had a sandwich for my lunch! I don't understand, Olivia. How could you do that to me?'

Olivia was taken aback. Surely he wasn't angry because she hadn't been at home to make his lunch? She'd left lunch for him! He hadn't even had to make the sandwich, she had made it for him.

She tried to salvage the situation.

'I've been to Sanderson's. I have some lovely pork sausages for your supper. I'll grill them now with some tomatoes. You'll enjoy them.'

He didn't say a word.

'Mr Sanderson says they might get some beef next week so I ordered some. It's Angus ... beef.' She said as a last feeble attempt to change his mood.

She was just about to tell him she thought she might be expecting a baby but before she could he lost his temper.

'Olivia, I've had a terrible day. I was at the farm this morning and the shop almost went on fire again this afternoon. That coffee roaster is so dangerous. We've had to clear everything out and clean it all. The firemen were threatening to close us down. And what thanks do I get? A sandwich!

'And not only that, I come home and you're out, in the dark, walking down Leith Walk. What kind of woman are you to go out for lunch, stay out all day and then walk down the road in the dark alone? I am so disappointed.'

That was the last straw for Olivia.

She took the sausages she was still holding and threw them in his face as hard as she could, turned round, pulled her hat over her head and walked out, slamming the door behind her, and, bursting into tears, ran up the road and into the London Road gardens.

She wandered for a while until, realising it was cold and dark, she sat under a light on the bench opposite her mother's house.

What on earth had she done? She'd thrown her life away to a Neapolitan who had no respect for women. He wanted her chained to the kitchen sink!

She wasn't allowed to work, she wasn't allowed to go out with her friends. They were from different cultures. Carlo just didn't understand her.

She put her hands to her face and started weeping again, overcome with grief.

'What have I done?'

*

After a half an hour Olivia shivered. She looked around. It was now pitch dark and well after seven.

She thought of going to her mother but she knew she would get no support there. She had complained once about Carlo's old-fashioned expectations, but her mother was having none of it: 'You've made your bed. You lie in it!'

Olivia got up, waited for a tram to pass and crossed London Road. She started towards Wellington Street, but instead of going towards home she turned left towards Elm Row. She walked past Pierce's Bar, trying to keep her head down so none of the men going in and out saw her. She stood outside the shop and looked up at the grey shutters.

She was still crying.

She looked up at the Crolla flat above the shop; the light was still on behind the shutters. Vittorio must still be in. She rang the intercom of the stair door. Vittorio didn't answer so she rang Josephine.

'It's me, Josephine, Olivia. Can you let me in please?'

The stair door buzzed open.

Olivia went up the stairs and, using her key for the flat, let herself in. The rooms at the back were all dark. The smell of spices and coffee hit her. Each of the rooms in the flat was piled high with stock: boxes and crates, sacks of rice and beans, pepper and chillies.

She went into the next room and had to take a step back. Her stomach turned. Vittorio had bought ten sacks of *baccalà*, salt cod, ready for Lent. He had run out last year so he had bought double this time. The smell was overpowering.

She coughed.

Going through into the small cash room she smelled the familiar aroma of Vittorio's cigar and felt comforted. Just as she was about to open the door she heard him click his record player and the familiar sounds of opera start to fill the space. She stood quietly. Maria Callas's voice rang out like an angel from heaven, soaring into the atmosphere.

Not wanting to startle him, she gently pushed his door open.

In the office only the light over his desk was on and the room was dim. She could just make out the green and cream wallpaper of trellises of grapes and shepherdesses with headscarves climbing to harvest them. The wallpaper had been there as long as she could remember.

Callas was singing Vittorio's favourite aria, from *Norma*.

With tears running down her face she slowly went over to her brother. His face was away from her, his shoulders bent over his desk. He was quiet. He moved to take a drink of his whisky. She whispered his name. He didn't start, just turned towards her; he must have heard her.

'Olivia, darling, come in, come in.'

Olivia looked into his face and saw the tears rolling down his cheeks as well. They had a good talk that evening.

'Olivia, you were young when we lost our father so you don't remember him and our mother as a couple. I saw him with her, sometimes they were happy and laughing, sometimes quarrelling and shouting at each other. You never saw it but, you know, it's what happens in a marriage.'

'But Vittorio, Carlo was so angry with me. I didn't do anything wrong but he was so upset.'

'Well, you have to look at it from his point of view.'

'What do you mean?'

'You think you've given up your freedom to marry Carlo? What has he given up to marry you?'

Olivia was quiet. Vittorio was right.

'He's given up his family, his mother, his father, his brothers and sisters. He's given up the sunshine ... no matter how we kid ourselves, the sun shines far more in Naples than in Leith.'

Olivia smiled a little at that.

'But Olivia, more than everything, he's given up his country, his *bella Italia*. It's what we long for the most, we immigrants. Whether we are born here or born there, our blood and soul is Italian and it is a hard thing to give it up. A great sacrifice.'

He looked at the picture of Alfonso that sat on his desk.

'Sometimes a sacrifice that's too great.'

*

When they had locked up the flat Vittorio walked with Olivia along London Road as far as her street. As they approached Wellington Street they saw Carlo, distraught, calling up the road. She called to him to alert him and turned to kiss her brother good-night.

'*Buona notte*, Vittorio. *Grazie.*'

Carlo came towards her.

'Olivia, Lilla, *vieni ca.*'

Olivia turned and ran into his arms.

Chapter Twenty-seven

EDINBURGH, VALVONA & CROLLA,

CHRISTMAS EVE 1955

At 6.45 a.m. there was already a queue of about three dozen customers stretching up Elm Row. Vittorio and all the staff had been in since five, getting the shop ready for the day.

'Christmas Eve on a Friday: couldn't be better!' Vittorio was fired up for a bumper day's trade.

'*Attenzione! Ragazzi!* Do we all know what we are doing? You've all got your positions. Stay there and the sales team will call the orders up and down the shop so we can get the customers served as quickly as we can.

'Let's check. Slicing! Toni!'

'Rossini!' Toni answered.

'*Formaggio!* Lui!'

'Rossini!' shouted Lui.

Toni and Lui were sons of relations in Italy. Vittorio had helped to get them to Edinburgh. He was talking to the Italian consul to help them get the necessary visas to emigrate. They were about 17 years old and just like his father and his Uncle Cesidio had been when they had first come to Scotland; they were just young shepherd boys who had never left their village before. They could only speak the dialect from their village, not a word of English. They couldn't even read and write.

Vittorio had given them strict instructions.

'Stand at the counter and prepare all the orders that are called up to you. Remember to repeat the call so there are no mistakes.'

The advantage of having these boys was they both understood

the product they were handling and knew instinctively how to slice and cut it perfectly. Just the way they liked to eat it!

Carlo winked at Lui.

He was helping him compose love letters to try to woo a pretty Sicilian girl he had met at a dance. Carlo felt he had good experience in this field; not only was he adept at writing love letters, he had proved very successful in wooing girls met at dances!

Vittorio noticed minds wandering.

'*Attenzione!* Focus, please! Pizza and La Meta lasagne. Franca, are you ready?'

'Rossini!' Franca giggled nervously.

She was a young girl from a small village near Mondragone, not far from where Carlo and his family had been at the end of the war. When it was all over her family had been left impoverished. To try to survive, Franca, aged only 13, had been sent over to Scotland by her parents to work in an Italian household to earn some money. When she used to come into the shop to get goods for her employers, and Carlo discovered her background, he asked Vittorio to give her a job.

'Carlo, I remember the American soldiers. They were really kind to us. They gave us shoes and coffee, and chocolates. It was the Moroccans we were afraid of. After the battle at Monte Cassino they went on a rampage. My mother hid me and my sisters under the ground so we couldn't be attacked or abducted.'

Carlo had heard these stories and worse, of the savagery of the Moroccan soldiers, who had fought with the Allied forces during the war.

It turned out Franca was a very good cook. With the help of Maria she had been making trays of lasagne with the off-cuts from the counter, ends of salami and the edges of cheese. It was a good way to use the whole product. After the food shortages they had all experienced no one would dream of wasting anything.

Vittorio had proudly named this product 'La Meta' in honour of the highest mountain near his home village. 'La Meta; the highest-quality lasagne available in Edinburgh!' It was fast becoming a feature on dinner tables in posh Morningside.

To help over Christmas Vittorio had taken on four young local boys: two Scots lads and two turbaned Sikh boys from an Indian family who lived next door. They were useful for bringing boxes up and down from the cellar, filling the shelves during the day and carrying customers' shopping out to their cars or to the bus stop. They were classed as *tenenti*, lieutenants. As Vittorio said 'Why start anyone at the bottom rung of a ladder?'

Their task was to answer the calls and support the sales staff, leaving the sales team free to keep entertaining and selling to the customers. 'Boys, remember what I told you. Don't say "Yes, Mr Crolla", just answer "Rossini!".'

The boys had no clue what he was talking about but had learned the best way to keep out of trouble was to follow Mr Crolla's instructions as best they could.

'Now, are we all ready to go? Remember to repeat the call!'

'Repeat the call!' All ten of them shouted out together, laughing at Vittorio's latest idea.

'And don't leave the counter. Apart from a *gabinetto* visit, stay where you are. If you need something for a customer call "*Tenente!*" and one of the young lads will go to the stockroom to get it.'

Nobody answered.

Vittorio got annoyed.

'Excuse me, gentlemen. What have you to call if you require something?'

'*Tenente!*' nine of them answered correctly.

Domenico had lost interest. He answered 'Repeat the call' in error, making them all burst out laughing again. That did not go down well.

'What's wrong with you, man? Have you not woken up yet?'

'No need to shout, Vittorio. We're just opening a shop, you know. It's not the start of the Battle of Bannockburn.' Domenico was a laid-back, easy-going chap of a less entrepreneurial nature than his brother.

'That's OK, Domenico. You're right. In this life you're either a doctor or a patient. And in this situation, I'm the doctor.'

Carlo looked at them sideways and shook his head. It was going to be a long day.

He was a bit anxious himself as they were not closing for lunch as usual. He had never worked through his lunch break in his life. Even in the factory in Genoa, they had stopped for an hour for lunch.

'Vittorio, just so you are aware. My *gabinetto* break will be at 10.45. I need to keep regular.'

'As I said, Carlo: I'm the doctor!'

Last night before they had gone to sleep, Carlo had shared his concerns with Olivia about not being able to come home for lunch. She had looked at him, slightly amused.

'There's always a first for everything, Carlo. You'll be fine. I'll make sure I bring you plenty of food.'

He trusted her but he was still a bit concerned. He had already been roasting coffee all morning and there were six sacks piled at the door, ready for grinding. The shop was full of caffeine-filled fumes and oils, creating an intoxicating atmosphere even before the doors had opened.

'Are we ready, boys?'

'Rossini!'

Vittorio was counting down to signal to open the doors. He knew once they were opened there would not be a minute's respite! He had his bottle of Muirhead's ready ... just in case.

In the fridge, hams, sausages and salamis were piled high, all ready for slicing. Toni and Lui had already skinned ten *prosciutto*. Now they were precariously balanced in a pink, soft, gleaming pile, just like the Leaning Tower of Pisa. Vittorio's idea to serve three cuts at different prices was working well; best slices, knuckle and skin, *la cotica*.

Carlo thought about his mother. He knew which cut she would choose: the cheapest and the tastiest. She'd be using this to add delicious flavour to her *zuppa di lenticchie*, which he was sure she would be cooking on New Year's Eve.

It was wonderful to think that next week everyone across the whole of Italy would be eating the same meal on New Year's Eve: the small brown lentils are a sign of good luck for the following year.

It was a thought. Garibaldi had tried to unite Italy but the differences he himself had experienced between the wealth of the north and the incapacitating poverty of the south showed there wasn't a lot of unity at all. Only once a year, when the whole country eats a humble plate of lentils on New Year's Eve, is the whole country, from Sicily to Milan, united.

Carlo allowed himself a moment of nostalgia. What he would give to be eating his mother's *zuppa di lenticchie* this New Year's Eve!

He had already agreed with Vittorio that he and Olivia would go back to Pozzuoli for Easter next year. It was nearly three years since he had seen his mother: he had to go home.

A few weeks before they had all been invited by the Italian Cultural Institute to St Cecilia's Hall for a musical evening. There were performances by a military quartet composed of Italian bagpipe players and players of percussion instruments from the Scottish Highlands. The combination of Italian and Scottish music had been delightful. To someone far away from his home country at Christmas time, it had been overwhelming. The very next day he had spoken to Vittorio to tell him it was time he needed to go home for a visit.

Vittorio called him out of his daydreaming.

'Carlo, are you ready?'

'Rossini!'

He looked around.

Every inch of space in the shop was festooned with food; bulbous, creamy *caccio di cavallo* cheeses dripped like teardrops from the ceiling. A whole hundred-pound *provolone* hung above the counter among sides of salted *baccalà*, like the drying salt cod that was hung on the fishwives' washing lines at the harbour in Cockenzie.

Every available style of fresh and dried sausage nestled beside a selection of beautiful, brightly coloured ornate boxes and packages of *panettone*. This was not ideal, but they had run out of space by the time all the stock had arrived from all over the Continent.

Carlo had realised you had to be careful to wipe the drips from the sausages off the *panettone* before you gave it to the customers. It was unfortunate that, in the warmth of the shop, all the salamis and cheeses sweated and dripped a little.

Vittorio also thought it was unfortunate. As they dripped they lost weight and so the company lost profit!

'We really need to think about getting more refrigeration,' he said every Christmas Eve when the tills were stuffed with cash. But the time January came and the bills from suppliers had built up and impending tax returns were looming, the notion usually left him.

Never short of ambition, Vittorio had ordered three whole wheels of Gruyère which had finally been delivered from Switzerland late the night before. He and Carlo had wrapped them in jute coffee sacks and rolled them through the shop to stack them up against the back wall. Already one had been opened and cut into huge triangular slabs ready to sell.

'Build the counter like the Alps.' Vittorio was focused: large soaring cuts of cheese at the back and smaller *burrino, ricotta salata* and soft, fresh, wet, *ricotta* making the valleys at the front.

'Now, Toni will cut the *parmigiano* into smaller triangles and these can go further down the counter at the east side of the Alps.'

The boys screwed up their faces, confused and hoping Domenico had a clue what Vittorio was talking about.

'Aye, aye, Vittorio.'

'Right, you, Tosto, come with me.'

Vittorio had rechristened all the local *tenenti* with an Italian name and had named all the rooms in the shop and all the shelves in the rooms after Italian composers and writers.

'Vittorio, why do you have to make everything so complicated all the time?'

'It adds mystery, Domenico. You need a bit of intrigue and mystery. A bit of theatre!'

He turned to 'Tosto' again. 'Come over here and work for Carlo. Carlo, do you have the wine ready?'

'Yes, Vittorio. Ten cases of each.'

'Good, show Tosto here how to fill the shelves. The ladder is here and we can use the pincers for the shelves that are too awkward to reach.'

On his travels in London, Vittorio had come back with long extended bottle grips which were very useful for getting bottles from the high shelves.

'I have the new sweet Orvieto *abboccato* ready here Vittorio. I thought it best to let the customers taste it before they buy it, just to make sure they like it. I've piled them here near the sherry casks, in the right spot to catch the customers who like a sweet drink.

'Good idea, Carlo. You go for it.'

Vittorio was ever so slightly envious of his brother-in-law's ingenuity. He seemed to be able to be just a step ahead of Vittorio most of the time, and this was not quite to his liking. Since the start of the year Carlo had been working full time in the shop. Apart from managing the coffee roasting and ordering, his main responsibility had been managing the bottling of the wine. It gave him a great source of satisfaction to have a job that he could develop on his own.

Carlo and Vittorio had created a range of wines that they were bottling and labelling in the old ice cream equipment display room in Montgomery Street Lane. The wine was imported in bulk from Spain and Yugoslavia. Carlo's job was to check the flavours and blend them to create their range. This Christmas they were already selling Spanish Sauterne, Spanish Beaujolais and Spanish Burgundy.

The French wine growers refused to export their wine in bulk, which left a good opportunity to create a French-style wine that could be sold a lot cheaper than the French Cru wines they had seen in the fancy groceries and wine merchants elsewhere in town.

The blending had been tricky at first. Carlo had had to learn how to use sulphur to stop the wine turning to vinegar, a problem he had had at the start of the year.

Rather than waste it, remembering his antics with signora Richeta in Mondragone he had created a new line of Valvona & Crolla red wine vinegar. With its small amount of residual alcohol, it had proved very popular.

'That's good vinegar Carlo. How did you make that? I'll put the recipe into our files.'

'It's easy, Vittorio. Take wine that has fermented and leave it to its own devices.'

Vittorio was suitably impressed. Carlo hadn't told Vittorio but this problem had happened again, to another two hogsheads of wine that had started to ferment. He was reluctant to reveal this to his brother-in-law, now also his boss, especially as he had asked for a holiday. Vinegar was good to sell, but not as a loss leader! He would have to find a solution himself.

As always, when he was anxious or worried he liked to wander down to the docks at Leith. Being beside the sea calmed him and helped clarify his thoughts. This time, though, he was beginning to panic. If Vittorio found out he'd ruined two whole casks of wine, his efforts to prove he could be an asset to the business would be seriously compromised. Walking home, almost giving up hope, he passed the courtyard of one of the port blenders Vittorio bought from.

'Hello, Carlo, what are you doing down here?'

Davy Dods, the blender's delivery driver, recognised the tall Italian. He was always very helpful when he was unloading a lot of cases of port. Funny they bought so much, it was such a small shop.

When Carlo explained his problem Davy took him into the bond.

'Come with me, I know the man who might just be able to help you.'

So today Carlo had ten cases of bottles of his new line of 'Spanish Orvieto *abboccato*' to sell to his customers.

Vittorio had tasted it and thought it was actually very pleasant.

It was years before Carlo would admit that he had used a powder from the port blender and a bag of sugar to create his new blend. It was not bad at all, not unlike the *rooi* he and Tullio had sold to the South African soldiers all those years ago.

*

Vittorio had been right.

From the minute the door opened there was a queue all morning: people shouting for orders; customers skipping the queue; Domenico getting lost in conversation and forgetting to call for his customer's order and then quarrelling with Toni because it wasn't ready. They had closed the Easter Road shop today so that Domenico and Phyllis could help here and Olivia and Gloria were free to help their mother to prepare the Christmas lunch at home.

By 11.15, when Carlo had come back from his break, Vittorio had already had his second nip of Muirhead's.

With perfect timing as always, Anna Brown chose the moment it was all going to flare up into a big argument to make her grand entrance. Standing at the door in a figure-hugging black lace dress with a short, brown mink jacket, one low length of pearls resting in just the right position she declared her intentions: '*Buon Natale, ragazzi!*'

The shop was completely jammed full so she had to squeeze her way in between the customers.

Vittorio came across to kiss her, 'Anna, come behind the counter beside us; it'll keep the customers focused. They like to have something beautiful to distract them.'

Anna's laugh could be heard at the end of the queue up Elm Row, and encouraged another handful of people to join. Something exciting was going on behind those grey shutters and it was worth hanging around to find out.

Chapter Twenty-eight

Philip dragged the chair over to the table to see what Nonna was doing. Struggling to reach, with the help of Gloria, he pulled himself up.

He was a fine-looking child, with enchanting deep brown eyes in a healthy round face framed with a mop of blond hair. He had an engaging, inquisitive smile.

'I help you, Nonna.'

Maria took his face between her hands and squeezed it, smudging his cheeks with flour.

'*Amore mio! Bello di Nonna!*'

Maria had long since given up even attempting to speak English and as Carlo insisted on talking to his son in *Puteolano*, and Olivia spoke Scots, the boy was blessed with exposure to all three languages.

'You help Nonna break the eggs; here, I'll show you.'

She broke the egg into his hand and he squealed with delight as the white slipped through his fingers into a bowl beside a large mound of flour on the table.

The golden orange ball trembling in his hand reminded him of the Cadbury's chocolate egg his Auntie Gloria had given him at Easter.

'No!'

Anticipating his actions, Gloria rushed forward.

'Philip!'

Too late.

Excited, he stuffed the yolk into his open mouth. Shocked and severely disillusioned that it didn't taste of the sweet goo he remembered, he spat it out and, wiping his hand over his face to try to get rid of the taste, started to cry.

'*Ah, non piangere.* Don't cry. *Guarda*, look!'

Maria separated another egg and dropped the yellow yolk into the mound of flour, 'Come and help Nonna make the pasta.'

Gloria scooped him up and took him to the sink, splashing his face and mouth with handfuls of freezing cold water.

The poor boy shivered with shock.

'Come to Auntie Gloria. I've got real chocolate.'

Olivia looked across exasperated. Philip's clean jumper was all wet and stained with egg yolk and now his face was covered with chocolate.

'Oh, for heaven's sake, I can't leave him with you for a minute!'

By now the boy was running round the table squealing with delight as Gloria tried to catch him to change his jumper.

'I thought it would be mad in the shop today, I didn't think it would be worse in here. Gloria, get him cleaned up and we'll take the food round to the shop. He'll fall asleep in the pram. Mum, we've got thirty eggs of macaroni to make. It'll take all day.'

Maria judged one egg yolk per person and worked out by the feel of the dough how much flour she needed. It was a ritual she enjoyed.

'Oh, it's nothing. Leave it to me. You go and help Vittorio.'

Olivia had been up since six with Carlo. She had already made a pot of chicken broth for this evening. She was busy making the *sugo* now. She had bashed the slices of steak as thin as possible and studded them with finely chopped garlic and parsley. Once she had seasoned them she rolled them up and tied them with some thin string ready to brown in the *soffritto*.

'Mum, how many tins of tomato will I use?'

'I think eight, we'll be twenty-eight tomorrow now that Tony and Margaret are coming from Glasgow. Young Angela and Joe will have a lovely time playing with Philip.'

His Glasgow cousins were already excited to play with their little cousin. They hadn't seen him since Easter.

'Remember to make enough pasta for leftovers on Boxing Day.'

'*Certo!* That goes without saying. *Non ti preoccupare.* Don't worry, there's plenty of food. We won't starve.'

They all loved reheated pasta the day after a big party. It wasn't that it tasted better, it was just a delicious anticipation that the whole feast could be repeated again the next day. Vittorio would say the most delightful thing about a good meal was looking forward to the next one.

Olivia sieved the tomatoes and added them to the pot; before long the whole kitchen was filled with the evocative, comforting aroma of tomato *sugo* simmering.

Maria had already prepared the *baccalà con patate* and a tray of *pizza scarola*.

They had been on fast and abstinence for all of Advent, and after Midnight Mass tonight they would enjoy the first feast of their Christmas celebrations. The shop would be closed for three days, so they were all looking forward to a good rest and a happy time together.

A good rest for the women meant the men would need three meals a day. Maria was thrilled. She was at her happiest when all her family was around her table and she was preparing all their favourite foods; it was the same food her mother had made for her, and her mother's mother before her.

'Mum, is Phyllis in the shop already?' Olivia asked.

'Yes, she went early this morning. She's hoping Armando will come in.'

'No doubt he will. Poor Vittorio, it looks like he's going to have to pay for another wedding soon.'

Armando Margiotta was a young man with big ideas. Sensing the opportunity of an unsatisfied market for sugar after the austerity of rationing, he had opened a fudge shop in St Mary's Street off the Royal Mile, halfway between Holyrood Palace and Edinburgh Castle.

'One day, Vittorio, you'll see, every visitor who comes to Edinburgh will pass my door exhausted and will not be able to resist coming into my shop to purchase a sugar treat.' He was spot on. The shop was a huge success.

Gloria came in with Philip all cleaned and wrapped up ready to go out. His knitted blue and cream Aran jumper looked very cosy and his little hat with the white pompom on top made him look just like the young prince.

'Vittorio says Phyllis's wedding will be in the Caledonian Hotel. He has to keep all his customers happy.'

'Let's wait till Armando asks her.' Gloria would be left alone with her mother and her two brothers once Phyllis got married. She was reluctant to let her sister go.

'Well, after the noise we made at mine I think Mr Aldridge will be relieved.' Olivia had been embarrassed that Mr Aldridge had had to ask the band to turn the volume down as her wedding guests had become marginally too rowdy for the North British Hotel.

'Gloria, this afternoon are you going to start on the *creustella* and the *crespelle*? What will we do? Make the *crespelle* with potatoes or *baccalà*?'

'Both! Here's the *tirdiglione* and *sciadun*. Will we take them both to the shop? Mum, can I bring some pizza for Carlo? He won't be happy if I give him polenta.'

Hearing his mother talk about his father, Philip toddled across to the door, ready to leave.

'I go! I go, Mummy!'

Since he had been a baby, Philip had been fascinated with the shop at 19 Elm Row. It was an Aladdin's cave for him, a mystical space. The smells were powerful and intoxicating, and from his perspective the shelves went as high as the heavens themselves.

More to the point, this was where he was given morsels of the tastiest food, where there were plenty of people to hug and squeeze him, where Uncle Vittorio stood him on the counter and let him serve the customers and Uncle Domenico gave him continual slices of salami to chew.

This was where he would be given a soft, sugared *bombolone* which he would eat round the edges till the hole in the middle had disappeared.

Best of all, this was where he could sit on the counter and watch, fascinated, while his *papà* laughed and joked and sang songs to all the lovely ladies.

Olivia was ready to go.

'Oh, the *sugo* smells good already! OK. I'll take the lunch

275

along to the boys. Are you coming, Gloria? If we're late for Carlo's lunch he'll create a riot.'

Carlo's need for regular food was now a standing joke in the family. What could she do? It was how he was and Olivia had long since accepted it. She hoped Carlo would enjoy the *baccalà*. Since Gloria had given her the Elizabeth David book *Italian Food,* her life in the kitchen had been transformed. Rather than being a drudge she had started to really enjoy cooking and sharing her new knowledge of Italian food. She hadn't understood that so far her experience of Italian food had been limited to recipes from her own village. Reading about different regions and their food traditions had started a whole new interest.

Carlo still kept her on her toes. When she had made *spaghetti con cozze* for him with juicy mussels from Musselburgh he had kissed her as usual and said thank you. Leaving the kitchen for his *mezz'oretta* he had casually called back, 'When we go to visit my mother, Olivia, then you'll learn how to cook real Neapolitan food!'

She laughed. At the start of her marriage she would have been upset but now she knew that Carlo never wanted to be seen to be dependent on anyone, not even her. She still didn't understand him, but she was learning how to keep him happy.

*

The smell of the roasting coffee hit her nostrils as she turned the corner into Elm Row. As she made her way down the street she could see a queue of customers waiting.

'OK, Gloria, wait while I get Carlo. He'll want to see his son.' Olivia looked through the window to see if Carlo was at the coffee machine as usual.

She took a step back, laughing. Anna was behind the counter looking like Gina Lollobrigida, helping Carlo entertain the customers.

'Gloria, look at that. Anna's causing a riot.'

She gave the pram to Gloria, 'Go on, can you take him round the gardens? You'll probably see Bill pushing his pram! I'll go in and help. Come later if there is anything else we need for tomorrow.'

Gloria went off happily with the pram; she preferred helping behind the scenes.

The shop was pandemonium, packed with what looked like every single customer who had shopped there during the year. Having enjoyed the experience of exotic flavours once, they had an irresistible desire to indulge again in the non-Calvinistic hedonism of thinly sliced *prosciutto di Parma*, the savour of *Parmigiano-Reggiano* or the addictive habit of freshly roasted coffee.

Carlo had positioned himself right at the door to catch every customer coming in. As he saw Olivia enter he winked at her, his smile broadening.

He turned to the next lady in the queue, '*Signorina, bella*, can I tempt you with a sip of my sweet wine? It's not as sweet as you, of course, but have a taste. What do you think?'

He had already shifted a quarter of his stock and was determined to sell out. Nobody was likely to notice what they were drinking once the Christmas celebrations had got underway, especially this year when, at last, all food rationing was over.

Ten cases of half-pints of olive oil were stacked at the front door beside the boxes of pasta and the sacks of dried lentils and beans. The publication of Elizabeth David's book had generated an impressive increase in sales. No one else was selling olive oil in Edinburgh except Mr Lyndsey the chemist, so Vittorio had a monopoly on the market. In fact, Elizabeth David's writing had done a great deal to open the treasures that they sold in the shop to the local customer.

Reading about a whole new world of flavours and exotic foods, the new young wives of the lawyers and bankers of Edinburgh had time on their hands and money in their pockets to experiment with new recipes. The result that they came up with was probably very far from the original that David had experienced herself in her travels in Italy, but no one knew what they were comparing it to.

Looking round, Vittorio noticed this was the first Christmas that at least a third of his customers were not Italians.

The 'Goods Required' system was working well. The stock listing was growing all the time: spices, herbs, porcini, even balsamic vinegar.

Olivia was asking for more ingredients as well. He didn't tell her, but it was very useful that she was interested and keeping him informed of what was being talked about in the food shops she went to for her meat and milk.

'Vittorio, can you get extra virgin olive oil?'

'What on earth is that?'

'Elizabeth David says it's the new season's oil, when it's harvested and immediately pressed and bottled. It's better than the manufactured and processed oil we sell.'

Vittorio was doubtful. Olivia was not going to be put off.

'I spoke to Carlo. He says it's just like the local oil they use in Pozzuoli when the farmers take their olives directly to the *frantoio*, and they're pressed there and then between stone wheels. The oil is bottled and they keep it in a dark cellar. It's the year's supply.'

Vittorio remembered the intense, fruity flavour of the oil Annunziata had drizzled on the first piece of dried bread she had offered him in Pozzuoli. When he thought about it, the rich, aromatic sensation came back into his consciousness. It had made such an impression he could almost taste it now.

'That's it!' he thought. 'That's the key to the wonderful flavour Annunziata's food had. Even that simple piece of dried bread tasted like nectar.'

'OK, I'll ask Giordano and Matta in London. They'll know.' Vittorio was intrigued. He made enquiries in London, and when the quotes came in for the new season oil he nearly choked on his Muirhead's whisky.

He discussed it with Carlo. 'No one will pay five times the price for a bottle of extra virgin olive oil when they are just getting used to using olive oil. I've been thinking. What if we blend them? We'll create a house blend of 20 per cent extra virgin olive oil and 80 per cent olive oil. We'll offer extra flavour at a fraction of the cost!'

Carlo looked doubtful. He was getting used to Vittorio's hare-brained schemes. This one was worse than usual. He tried to put him off.

'OK, Vittorio; but how will our customers know we are blending this? There'll be nothing for them to see to make a differ-ence. Maybe the colour will be a little darker, that's all.'

'Don't worry. I've thought of that! We'll label it. I've thought of a new name as well.'

'Oh?' Carlo just looked, waiting to hear what Vittorio would come up with next.

'We'll call it "semi-virgin olive oil". No one else will think of that.'

Carlo burst out laughing, 'This time, Vittorio, I have to agree with you. You're absolutely right. No one else would think of that!'

Valvona & Crolla's house blend of 'semi-virgin olive oil' out-sold the standard olive oil six to one.

*

On the way to the back shop with the plates of food, Olivia saw Marietta and Johnny. Domenico was serving them. They already had a mountain of goods in front of them. Olivia greeted them, asking after Gertrude, who was expecting another baby. She already had a boy, Cesidio, called after his grandfather.

'She's very well, thank you. She says she wants to have eight children.'

'Really?'

Olivia was surprised. Anna had told her that all Gertrude liked to do was visit Jenners designer room and look for designer clothes.

Johnny burst out laughing. 'Actually, Olivia, that would be her worst nightmare!'

Olivia asked after Alex.

'He's helping Betty and Margaret in the shop. We can't keep up with the sales of sweets and chocolates. The whole country has become addicted to sugar! Great for business.'

It looked like everyone was doing well.

The lady next to Marietta in the queue was paying attention to everything this Italian woman was buying. Domenico was careful to let everybody in the queue taste everything that was being sold.

'I'll have some of that *prosciutto* ham, please. It's very flavour-some.' The lady had always wanted to try the ham but had been shy to ask.

279

'Absolutely, signorina, for you, anything.'

Olivia pulled her apron over her head and joined the row of family selling next to her husband.

'Carlo, lunch is at one.'

Vittorio was trying to make a pretty girl blush by suggesting she purchase some semi-virgin olive oil.

Olivia looked at her brother, frowning. 'Vittorio, *stai bravo*, be good.'

'Why? My life is too good to *be* good!'

Olivia looked at the shop packed full of good food and happy customers, full of laughter and happiness.

'You're absolutely right, Vittorio, your life is good. Well done. You're doing a wonderful job. Dad would be really proud of you.'

Vittorio looked around at his extended family: his customers, his staff and his relations. He looked at his tiny space that he had filled with everything he loved from Italy and Scotland – cheeses, pasta, coffee and wine; smoked salmon and oatcakes and whisky.

He overheard Domenico sell two bottles of Cinzano to a minister of the cloth and Carlo shift a dozen bottles of his new-style Spanish Orvieto *abboccato* to Mr Aldridge from the North British Hotel, and he smiled at his sister.

'Thank you, darling. You're absolutely right. Dad would be very proud.'

Dear Alfonso,

Standing here, looking across my beloved Bay of Pozzuoli, I feel like I've never been away.

Look at the sea, it's glorious, bluer and more dazzling than I can remember.

The waves are gently lapping at the edge of the shore. I am tempted to dive right in, swim once more in the cool, refreshing water.

It is such a relief to feel the sun warming my back again; how it makes me relax, throw my worries to the wind. Apart from my mother and my family, it is the glorious sunshine I miss the most.

My heart is trembling with emotion.

To think I have given up all of this to make a life in Scotland? Only for one person: to spend it with your beautiful daughter, my darling Olivia.

Your dear wife Maria extended such a warm welcome to me, embracing me into your family. I am going to make my life's work alongside your sons, Vittorio and Domenico, making your vision for Valvona & Crolla reach fruition. What an experience that is going to be!

My mother is well. She hasn't changed at all and is still happy and excited by every small joy in her life.

As always, my friend, there are still more mouths to feed; everyone is married, with children of their own. At least now there is plenty of food around, though still never enough cash. Some things will never change.

Your first grandson, Philip – they call him Filippo – has been helping his Nonno Luigi in the yard. Seeing him learn to handle the wood and breathe in the shavings, see the value of work from his grandfather, has reminded me of my own happy times spent here as a young boy myself, and all the adventures I had.

How we regret he will not be able to stand with you and learn from you as well.

Here they all love him. He is already talking to them in *Puteolano* dialect. We're staying here for a few months; by the end of it, you'll see, he'll be a real *scugnizzo*, a true Neapolitan.

You know, Alfonso, when I look at my son here, running around Rione Terra, at home with my Neapolitan family, I realise I haven't given anything up at all. With the inspiration of the sacrifices you made for your family I realise now I am able to give my family more than I could ever have hoped for, the richest heritage of two cultures.

So, Alfonso, *con la faccia per terra*, with all humility, I'll thank God and live my life to the full. My children will have all the benefits of this rich tradition of Italy and the culture and opportunities of Scotland. They will have the best of both worlds.

*

The church bell sounded and interrupted Carlo's thoughts.

Twelve thirty.

Lunch would be at one.

He looked up at *ngopp' 'a terra*, his spiritual home, still broken and damaged from the war.

There, standing at the window looking down, was his darling Olivia. His mother was beside her, hand stretched out, beckoning him to come up. A diminutive figure, greyed and wrinkled, more beautiful than ever before.

'*Carlo!*' she called to him, her hand cupped at her mouth, her voice clear in the still air. '*Carlo, figlio mio, a mangiare!*'

He looked up, raised his hand and whistled.

He turned to his son and beckoned him, '*Filippo, vieni a mangiare*', and, started to climb the 178 steps to his home. The sound of a guitar and a lone voice drifted from a window.

As he climbed, the familiar smells he loved made his mouth water: sweet, juicy tomatoes slowly simmering with green olive oil and basil; charcoal-blackened fish grilling with wild fennel and lemon; a whiff of bitter greens sautéing in olive oil and garlic.

282

He stopped to inhale, savouring the thought of his meal to come. *'Madonna, ho fame.'*

'Papà! Papà! Aspett'!'

Filippo's voice expressed a slight hint of distress. Carlo glanced back to see where he was. He caught sight of him far below, with the parcel, wrapped in newspapers, tightly grasped to his chest as he lifted his short legs to climb each step. His blond curls were dripping with sweat. He called again louder.

'Papà!'

'Filippo, forza!' Carlo couldn't wait. He was too hungry.

Two women scrubbing clothes at the water fountain watched the scene unfold. They reproached him, laughing.

'Carlo! Wait for him, he's only three. *Poverino!'*

Carlo flashed an amiable smile and ran on up the steps.

Filippo would just have to catch up.

Previous page: Philip Contini, Pozzuoli, aged three.

Part Five

Annunziata's recipes

Overleaf: Annunziata Conturso in Silni.

'If you don't have it, you don't need it'

Annunziata Conturso in Silni

I first met Carlo's mother, Annunziata, in September 1979, on the first week of my honeymoon. I was a naïve 24-year-old who had visited Italy only twice before and, although I had been brought up in an immigrant Italian household in Scotland, I had little knowledge or understanding of Italy or its culture.

Over an enchanting week in Pozzuoli I experienced the revelation of Annunziata's cooking, fresh, seasonal food prepared with the most modest of ingredients. From a tiny scullery, she managed to feed all her family, up to 20 people twice a day, and with a magical enthusiasm and alchemy she introduced me to the most flavoursome, exquisite and mouth-watering food I had ever tasted.

I hope you enjoy this celebration of Annunziata's cooking. She had no concept of 'food waste.' Every morsel of food was shared among too many mouths. The cheapest cuts of food were skilfully converted into delicious meals, bolstered by use of bread, pulses and pasta. Seasonal abundance was preserved and stored.

Insalata di Pane
Bread salad

In Pozzuoli bread was still bought from the baker by the kilo and lasted up to a week wrapped in a cloth in the kitchen, dark crusty chewy bread that was satisfyingly full of flavour. As the bread dried Annunziata enjoyed it more. When she was over ninety and had only one tooth left she dipped the hard bread in her wine and sucked on it all day, giggling with delight.

3–4 handfuls of dried sourdough bread cubes
Sea salt
5 or 6 ripe tomatoes
1 red pepper
Half a red onion
4–5 tablespoons extra virgin olive oil
1 tablespoon red wine vinegar
4–5 anchovies in oil (to taste)
Fresh herbs: chopped: mint, oregano, basil, flat-leaf parsley
Stoned black olives preserved in olive oil (optional)
Caper berries (optional)

Drizzle the dried sourdough bread cubes with some cold water and some sea salt, and leave to soak.

Chop the tomatoes into quarters, deseed and slice the red pepper and thinly slice the half red onion.

Mix everything in a bowl with the bread and dress with the olive oil, vinegar, the chopped anchovies and the fresh herbs. Add some black olives or capers if you have them. Mix everything with your hands so the flavours all blend together. Season to taste, but the anchovy should supply enough salt.

Spaghetti al Sugo di Pesce
Spaghetti with Fish-head Sugo

Annunziata often made a good flavoured *sugo* with a few fish heads. The flavour in the head is sweet tasting and moist, especially the cheeks and the juicy meat near the bones; the eyes the most prized. A friendly fishmonger will give you a few fresh fish heads for next to nothing. Choose sea bass or bream, red snapper or even a few langoustine heads for a delicate flavour.

3–4 tablespoons extra virgin olive oil
2 cloves garlic, peeled and finely chopped
1–2 small dried pepperoncino crushed
3 handfuls finely chopped flat-leaf parsley
100 ml dry white wine
2 fresh fish heads
Half of 400g tin San Marzano or good tomatoes, roughly chopped
Sea salt and black pepper
300g spaghettini or linguini

Rinse the fish heads well in cold water, making sure any spines are removed. Pat dry to remove any stale water which will spoil the flavour.

Warm the oil in a wide shallow saucepan and sauté the garlic and chilli to release the flavours. Add half the chopped parsley, turning it in the oil, then add the fish heads, turning them in the oil to start to cook.

Raise the heat and add the white wine and allow it to boil for 4–5 minutes allowing the alcohol to evaporate. Add the chopped tomatoes and their juice and turn the heat down to medium. Add a good pinch of sea salt and simmer the *sugo* with the lid half on the saucepan for 20–30 minutes. Remove the heads and keep warm.

Boil the pasta until al dente and serve in the thickened sauce, adding a little of the cooking water if the sauce is too dry. Sprinkle with the rest of the chopped parsley and serve with the fish heads in the middle of the table to share out and enjoy.

For a more intense flavour, liquidise them and add the strained juices to the sauce.

Zuppa Di Pesce con Bruschetta all'Aglio
Fish soup with garlic bruschetta

A variety of fresh fish, about 5–6 pieces per person, plus some crustacea
Extra virgin olive oil
2 garlic cloves, finely chopped
1–2 pieces of dried chilli pepper or peperoncino, crushed
3 handfuls flat-leaf parsley, finely chopped
125ml dry white wine
Several ripe tomatoes, chopped, or half a tin of San Marzano plum
    tomatoes
Sea salt

For the *Bruschetta All' Aglio*
2 slices dry sourdough bread per person
1 garlic clove
Sea salt
Extra virgin olive oil

Select a variety of fresh fish fillets from a fishmonger, such as coley, hake, catfish, cod, monkfish. If you see some, get some fresh squid and crustacea, like mussels, shrimps and scampi.

Prepare and clean the fish, washing it in plenty of cold water and cutting it into good bite-sized pieces: remember that fish shrinks as it cooks.

Select a deep sauté pan. Warm the olive oil and add the garlic and dried chilli pepper or peperoncino.

As the aromas are released and the garlic starts to colour, add 2 handfuls of the finely chopped flat-leaf parsley.

Add the wine and boil fast for a few minutes to allow the alcohol to evaporate.

Turn the heat down and add the fish pieces, one at a time, the larger pieces first. Turn them in the oil for a few minutes.

Add two to three large tablespoons of very fresh ripe tomatoes, peeled and chopped, or half a tin of San Marzano tomatoes and, if required, a few tablespoons of water to loosen the sauce.

Add a good pinch of sea salt and cover, simmering gently for 20 minutes.

If you have shellfish or prawns, clean them and de-vein the prawns and lay them on the soup for the last 5 minutes, steaming them with the lid on till they open or the shells of the prawns change colour.

Add more water if required, check seasoning and add a final handful of finely chopped flat-leaf parsley to finish.

Note that if you are using a lot of mussels or clams it is better to sauté them separately and add the strained juices and cooked shells at the end of the cooking in case there is a lot of grit in the shells.

For the bruschetta, rub the slices of dried bread on one side with a clove of garlic and sprinkle with sea salt and olive oil. Toast on a hot griddle until crunchy, turning so both sides get lovely blackened stripes from the griddle.

Riso Con La Mozzarella
Rice with Mozzarella

Annunziata always treated an upset stomach with a starvation diet of plain boiled rice seasoned only with a little salt. With plenty of boiled water and hot camomile tea, speedy recovery was assured.

She seldom made risotto, but on occasion boiled rice with mozzarella and basil, a delicious easy meal.

1 cup Arborio rice
Sea salt
Bufala mozzarella
Extra virgin olive oil
Fresh basil
Black pepper
Lemon zest and juice (optional)
Pecorino

Simmer the rice with 4 cups of boiling salted water until cooked, about 20–25 minutes.

Drain the rice and while it is still warm, tear up a *mozzarella di bufala* and stir it through with a fork to make long stretchy strands. Drizzle with some of the extra virgin olive oil and add some torn basil leaves and black pepper. You can add a squeeze of lemon juice and a grating of the rind to lift the flavour.

Finish with some grated pecorino fresco and if you want to cheat, a blob of unsalted butter. Don't tell Annunziata!

Melanzane Sott' Olio
Preserved aubergines

Vincenzo always had a jar of *melanzane sott' olio* on the table to share round everyone. He refused to take no for an answer, encouraging his guests, '*Mangiando, mangiando, vieni l'appetito*. Eat and your appetite will come.' Once tasted, no one needed much more encouragement.

1 kilo aubergines, organic if possible
Sea salt
Half a litre white wine vinegar
1.5 litres water
Dried oregano
2–3 garlic cloves
2–3 dried chillies
Sunflower oil or olive oil

Wash and peel the black skin off the aubergines. Cut them in slices, lengthwise, and cut them again into thin strips, not too long otherwise they will split in half. (Always cut aubergines lengthwise against the grain so the oil and flavours can penetrate the flesh.)

Mix them with some sea salt and cover with cling film and a cloth. Use a plastic colander or pierce a plastic container. Put a weight on top of the cloth, balancing the receptacle on a dish that can collect all the liquids that will be released. Store in a refrigerator for 24 hours.

Drain off the liquid and add the aubergines to a pot with the white wine vinegar diluted with a litre and a half of water. Simmer gently for ten minutes.

Once they have cooled down, drain the aubergines and, using your hands, squeeze out as much of the acidic water as possible. They are quite tough so don't be afraid to give them a good squeeze.

Arrange the aubergine strips in layers in a sterilised glass kilner or jam jar, adding a good pinch of dried oregano and some cloves of garlic, and a few dried chillies. Knock down the aubergines to get rid of any air pockets and gradually cover with sunflower oil or olive oil.

Make sure that there is enough oil on the top to completely cover the aubergines. Check again that there are no air pockets.

Seal and leave refrigerated for a couple of weeks to mature. This will make about 2 × 450g jars. They will last refrigerated up to six months.

Pomodoro Conservato
Preserved tomatoes

At the end of the summer in Napoli there is always a glut of juicy, ripe, garnet-red tomatoes. Annunziata would buy them at the keenest price, and preserve them to use for the coming winter. Her granddaughters still complete the same ritual today.

Ripe Italian tomatoes (if possible, or grow your own)
Basil leaves

Boil the ripe tomatoes in a large pot of water for about ten minutes. (They will only be about half cooked.) Drain them into a colander and while they are still warm remove the skins, seeds and stalks. Add the pulp to a blender to make a puree.

Fill up clean sterilised glass kilner or jam jars with the tomato puree and add a few basil leaves into each one. Alternatively, you can add a few cloves of garlic, or parsley instead of basil.

Knock down the tomatoes to make sure there are no air bubbles. Seal the jars.

Place the sealed jars in a large pot, cover with water, and bring to the boil. Keep at a brisk simmer for half an hour.

Allow to cool in the pot and once cooled store in a cool room or the fridge, where they will remain good for up to one year. Use in recipes instead of tinned tomatoes.

Scarola Farcito
Stuffed Endive

Escarole or Belgian endive
2 cloves garlic, chopped
2 handfuls toasted pine nuts
1 tablespoon salted caper berries, rinsed and soaked in cold water
1 tablespoon black olives in oil
3–4 anchovies in oil
3 tablespoons flat-leaf parsley
3–4 handfuls dried breadcrumbs
Extra virgin olive oil
Dried peperoncino or chilli plus a further clove of garlic

If you can't find escarole or Belgian endives, use small, tight heads of lettuce like Little Gems

Finely chop the garlic, pine nuts, rinsed capers, black olives, anchovies and parsley.

Mix all these stuffing ingredients together and add 3–4 tablespoons of extra virgin olive oil.

Hold open the escarole leaves and push the stuffing in between them. Tie the escarole with kitchen string to hold the stuffing inside.

Warm 2–3 tablespoons extra virgin olive oil in a flat saucepan and add a whole clove of garlic and 1 or 2 dried chillies. Gently sauté the escarole heads until they are lightly browned on each side. Add a good splash of water and steam for about 20 minutes or so with the lid on until the leaves are wilted and softened.

Serve at room temperature; do not refrigerate.

Sarde o Sgombri Alla Griglia
Grilled Sardines or Mackerel with Lemon Herb Insalata

Oily fish like fresh mackerel or sardines have attitude. They benefit from grilling to enable the skin to crisp deliciously while keeping the flesh juicy and moist. Buy oily fish as fresh as possible to get the best flavour. Serve with a pungent, feisty salad with plenty of lemons to augment the flavour.

4–6 medium sized sardine or mackerel fillets
Sea salt and black pepper
Extra virgin olive oil
Some lemon juice

For the salad
4 handfuls ripe tomatoes
1 red onion
2 tablespoons caper berries
2 tablespoons flat-leaf parsley
Oregano
Fennel fronds
1 lemon

Remove the pin bones from the mackerel or sardine fillets. Wash them in cold water and pat dry. Use a sharp knife to slit the skin across in 3 or 4 diagonals, being careful not to cut through the flesh. This stops the fish curling up as it griddles.

Rub with olive oil and sea salt and grind some black pepper on them. Leave to marinade for 15 minutes or so.

Pre-heat a griddle to high or better still, like Annunziata, keep a small grill outside on a balcony so the smells don't permeate the whole house.

Lay the fish skin-side down on the hot griddle. Cook until the skin crisps up and chars and the flesh cooks through, about 5–6 minutes depending on size. Resist overcooking, or the fish will become dry. The flesh will change colour from pink to soft brown as it cooks. It should not be necessary to turn the fish over as it will cook from the skin up.

Lay the grilled fish on a warm plate, skin-side up, and drizzle with some extra virgin olive oil and a squeeze of lemon juice.

Prepare the herb *insalata* by combining the ripe tomatoes chopped into eighths, the lemon zested and juiced, the red onion finely chopped and the coarsely chopped caper berries. Add the finely chopped flat-leaf parsley, oregano and fennel fronds and season to taste.

Spaghettini Sciuè Sciuè

In Neapolitan, *sciuè sciuè* means quickly, in a hurry. Fast food for Annunziata was having something ready when Carlo came home late from a visit to the cinema or taking a girl to a dance.

Serves 2
180g spaghettini
Sea salt
Extra virgin olive oil
2 garlic cloves
Ripe plum tomatoes
Basil leaves

Add a large handful of *spaghettini* to a pot of boiling salted water. Stir to make sure they are well loosened in the water.

In a wide frying pan warm 4–5 tablespoons extra virgin olive oil and add the garlic cloves cut into slivers.

Wash 4–5 very ripe plum tomatoes and, using your hands, squeeze them into the frying pan, discarding the skins and the seeds left in your hands.

Cook on a brisk heat and season well with sea salt. Tear in plenty of fresh basil leaves and before the pasta is cooked use a fork or tongs to transfer the pasta dripping with the cooking water into the frying pan to finish cooking.

Ready by the time Carlo has climbed up the 178 steps home. *Sciuè, sciuè!*

Pesto Alla Genovese

Annunziata made *trofie* pasta, small cigar-shaped rolls of home-made pasta and served them with a type of pesto, invented from descriptions of the green sauce Carlo described to her when he returned from Genoa. Use the freshest small basil leaves for most intense flavour. Always use freshly grated pecorino. Leave the final pesto coarsely textured to enhance its flavour.

100g fresh basil leaves, no stalks
1 tablespoon pine nuts
6–8 tablespoons Ligurian or a light extra virgin olive oil
2 cloves new season garlic
2 tablespoons fresh grated pecorino Romano
Sea salt to taste.

Put the basil leaves, pine nuts and a pinch of salt on a wooden board. Use a mezzaluna or a heavy knife to gradually chop the leaves and nuts together, adding small amounts of leaves at a time.

Put the resulting paste into a bowl and add the grated cheese, and after mixing everything, incorporate the oil to create a textured pesto. Taste and add some salt as necessary. So what if it takes a bit longer?

Sautéed *Friarielle* or Greens

500g leafy green vegetables
Extra virgin olive oil
2 cloves garlic
1–2 dried peperoncino
A handful of pieces dry sourdough bread and lemon wedges (optional)

Wash the green vegetables (such as *cima di rapa*, long-stem broccoli, spinach or chard). Add to boiling salted water and simmer for 5–10 minutes.

Drain and allow to cool, squeezing out the liquid from the leaves.

Warm 4–5 tablespoons of olive oil in a large frying pan, adding the garlic and dried chilli and allowing them to warm through, flavouring the oil.

Add the drained greens and toss in the oil. Warm through and cook for 5–10 minutes, adding the dried bread to pick up the juices.

Serve at room temperature in the middle of the table with some lemon juice to add just before eating.

Left-over Pasta Fritatta

Annunziata made pasta every day, often different dishes, to please those who wanted penne and those who wanted spaghetti. She ran her kitchen like a busy cafe, cooking for anyone as soon as they arrived, day in, day out. Any pasta left over was kept in the fridge, and after a couple of days she mixed it together and made a large frittata with the mixture of pasta.

8 large free-range eggs
300–400g left-over pasta
A handful of fresh mint
A handful of fresh basil
4 handfuls grated fresh pecorino.
Extra virgin olive oil
Seasoning

Beat the eggs in a large bowl. Add the left-over pasta, mint, basil and grated pecorino and season well. Stir everything together. Warm a tablespoon of olive oil in a non-stick frying pan. Add the egg mixture and cook slowly over a medium heat until the eggs are set and a crust has formed on the bottom.

Slide the frittata onto a plate and then turning the frying pan upside down, slide the frittata back into the frying pan. Cook for a further 10–15 minutes.

Eat at room temperature, don't refrigerate.

Lenticchie Con le Cotiche
Italian Lentils with *Cotiche*

Cotiche is the leathery skin of the *prosciutto di Parma* removed from the ham before it can be thinly sliced. It usually has a generous layer of white creamy fat attached. Often discarded, Annunziata knew it as a great cheap ingredient that adds bags of flavour to simple dishes.

150g cotiche or smoked lardons
Extra virgin olive oil
1 onion
1 carrot
1 stick celery
2–3 tomatoes
250g lentils, rinsed in cold water
Parmigiano Reggiano or pecorino rind
Sea salt
Black pepper
150g broken pasta

Sauté the chopped *cotiche* or lardons in 3–4 tablespoons extra virgin olive oil until it browns and the fat dissolves.

Finely chop an onion, carrot and stick of celery and cook these until softened to make a *soffrito*.

Add the chopped tomatoes and after 5 minutes or so add the small brown Italian *lenticchie*.

Cover with about a litre of hot water. Add a piece of rind of Parmigiano or pecorino if you have it (never throw this out, it is packed with flavour and goodness), and simmer for 30 minutes or so until the lentils are cooked and have absorbed most of the liquid, adding more water as necessary.

Season with sea salt and ground black pepper.

When ready to eat add the pasta and some more water and simmer until the pasta is cooked.

Annunziata's flavour secret …

In a small saucepan warm 3–4 tablespoons extra virgin olive

oil; add a clove or two of finely chopped garlic and a crushed dried peperoncino. Warm through to release the flavours.

When the pasta is cooked, check the seasoning and add in the hot flavoured oil and a couple of handfuls of finely chopped flat-leaf parsley.

Serve with freshly grated *Parmigiano Reggiano* and some warm crostini or pieces of dried sourdough bread.

Costs a little... tastes a lot!

Zabaglione

Carlo stayed in Pozzuoli with Annunziata and his Neapolitan family for extended holidays every year. He often stayed longer alone, enjoying spending time with his Neapolitan family. Annunziata lived until she was well over 90, and would make him a breakfast treat with eggs that she had collected fresh from the chickens she kept in the back yard.

3 large free-range egg yolks
6 tablespoons caster sugar
3 tablespoons Marsala dessert wine

Combine the egg yolks and caster sugar in a bowl and whisk them together with a fork.

Arrange the bowl on a pot of simmering water, making sure the water doesn't touch the bottom of the bowl.

Use a balloon or electric whisk to beat the mixture over the heat until it gets thick, pale white and creamy.

Take the mixture off the heat, add the Marsala and whisk it in. Serve while still warm with Pavesini biscuits.

Macaroni Con Ragù Alla Napoletana

After the war, once meat was available, Annunziata and most of the mothers in Naples made this Neapolitan *ragù* nearly every Sunday. It is best prepared the day before you need it.

8 thin slices of beef
Sea salt
Black pepper
Flat-leaf parsley
3 garlic cloves
Toasted pine nuts
8 thin slices smoked pancetta
Extra virgin olive oil
1–2 dried chillies
1 large onion
125ml dry white wine
3 × 450g tins San Marzano plum tomatoes
Bay leaf
Fresh basil
Parmigiano Reggiano

Take the slices of beef, *braciole*, and lay them on a chopping board. Flatten them with a rolling pin. Season well with sea salt and freshly ground black pepper.

Add some chopped flat-leaf parsley, some finely chopped garlic and a sprinkling of toasted pine nuts. Cover with a thin slice of smoked pancetta.

Roll each into a cigar shape and secure with some string, or a toothpick.

Warm about 4 tablespoons extra virgin olive oil in a wide saucepan and add the *braciole,* browning them on all sides. Set them aside.

Make a *soffrito:* in the same saucepan add enough extra virgin oil to cover the bottom. Sauté 2 chopped garlic cloves and 1 or 2 dried peperoncini, crushed to flavour the oil. Add the onion, finely chopped, and allow to cook slowly until it is soft and translucent.

Raise the heat and add a glass of dry white wine, boiling until the alcohol evaporates.

Add the tins of San Marzano tomatoes, liquidised. Add a fresh bay leaf and the *braciole* and any juices that have collected.

Bring to a simmer and slowly cook on a gentle heat with the lid half off for 2–3 hours.

Season with sea salt and black pepper and add a bunch of fresh basil to lift the flavour of the *ragu*.

Serve with macaroni such as *mezzi rigatoni* or *penne rigate*. Add plenty of grated Parmigiano Reggiano. Serve the meat in the middle of the table with a large dressed salad and a plate of sautéed *friarelle* or greens.

Limonata
Home-made Lemonade

1 litre cold water
175g granulated sugar
2–3 Amalfi unwaxed lemons
Fresh mint or basil

Make a sugar syrup by adding half of the cold water to the granulated sugar. Bring to a simmer and once the sugar has dissolved, boil for 10 minutes to make a syrup.

Add the rest of the water.

Wash and zest the lemons and then, after warming them in your hands, squeeze them to collect about 100ml of juice and pulp.

Add this to the syrup and check the flavour, diluting as required.

Refrigerate for about 4 hours to chill.

Serve with some cubes of ice and some fresh mint or basil leaves.

Caffè Freddo and Granita di Caffè
Chilled Coffee and Coffee Granita

Annunziata always poured any dregs from the coffee pot, sweetened with some sugar, into a bottle in the refrigerator, to serve later as iced coffee with a few cubes of ice.

In the summer she would also put it into the freezer, using a fork to break it up every fifteen minutes or so, to make *Granita di Caffè*. She also made *Granita di Limone* the same way.

Annunziata never owned a refrigerator or freezer till she was well over 60 years old. She always said that it was a dangerous invention. Instead of shopping every day for food and sharing with everyone what they had, she observed that people started to shop less often, buy too much and start to hoard food in the refrigerator and the freezer.

The consequence of this was people began to buy too much food and the modern curse of food waste became the norm. Makes you think.

Rum Babà

Annunziata never made cakes. As is common all over of Italy, patisserie and gelato are bought as treats in specialist bakery and ice cream shops.

Try these *babà*, but it may be better fun to take a flight to Naples and go straight to the Piazza Trieste e Trento: take a table in the Gran Caffè Gambrinus, sit in the historic painted tea room and enjoy with a glass of Cinzano on ice.

If they don't stock Cinzano tell them to contact Valvona & Crolla!

Makes 12 babà

250g strong bread flour
100g unsalted butter
10g fresh yeast or 5g dry yeast
5g salt
4 eggs
15g sugar

For the syrup
Juice of ½ lemon and ½ orange
500ml water
250g sugar
½ cinnamon stick
1 vanilla pod
1 tablespoon of orange and lemon zest, grated.
Dark rum for drizzling

For this recipe, you will need 12 *babà* moulds, 40mm in diameter. Grease the moulds with softened butter before using.

You will also need a mixer with a dough hook, as the dough is too soft to be handled, and a pastry bag with a plain nozzle for piping the dough into the moulds.

Measure the flour, yeast, salt and sugar into the mixer bowl, then break in the eggs and start mixing at low speed. Once all the flour has been incorporated, increase the speed to medium.

Cut the butter, which should be at room temperature, into small pieces, and start adding it slowly to the dough, without stopping the mixer. Keep mixing until all the butter is well incorporated into the dough, which should be smooth and shiny. Stop the mixer and transfer the dough into a greased bowl. Cover with cling film and let it rise in a warm place for about 1½ hours, or until doubled in size. In the meanwhile, butter the moulds and turn the oven to 165°C.

Gently deflate the dough with a spatula by folding it over itself several times, then transfer it into the pastry bag and pipe about 25g of the mixture into each mould, or about half full.

Let the *babà* rise until they reach the rim of the moulds, about 25 minutes, then place them on an oven tray and bake for about 15 minutes, until golden.

While the *babà* cool down, make the syrup, placing all the ingredients, except the rum, into a pan and letting them come to a boil. Let simmer for 15 minutes and then cool down.

When the *babà* are cold, place them in a container that can be sealed and pour the syrup over them. Let them soak up the syrup for about 30 minutes, turning the container every 10 minutes or so, until they are soaked through. Take them out of the syrup and drizzle with rum to taste.

Further reading

Balestracci, Maria Serena: *'Arandora Star': From Oblivion to Memory* (Parma, MUP, 2008)

Calvino, Italo: *Into the War*, trans. Martin McLaughlin (London, Penguin Modern Classics, 2011)

Colpi, Terri: *Italians' Count in Scotland* (London, St James Press, 2015)

Contini, Mary: *Dear Francesca* (London, Ebury Press, 2002)

Contini, Mary: *Dear Olivia* (Edinburgh, Canongate Books, 2006)

Contini, Carlo: 'This is how I was born' (unpublished private manuscript)

David, Elizabeth: *Italian Food* (London, Penguin, 1998)

Dunnage, Jonathan: *Twentieth Century Italy: A Social History* (London, Routledge, 2002)

Lewis, Norman: *Naples '44* (London, Collins, 1978)

mi misi vicino alla

la funzione dell'apert

lasciare l'idea di s

Vetro Non avendo

stavo andando inc

era di legno, fa~~Con~~

sfilare, che, erano

poco tempo, in me

poi lo infilo di n

avevo calcolato il

scalino, si feret

erano tre scalini;

stavo andando ince